IMAGES
of America

SERBS IN CHICAGOLAND

I0806198

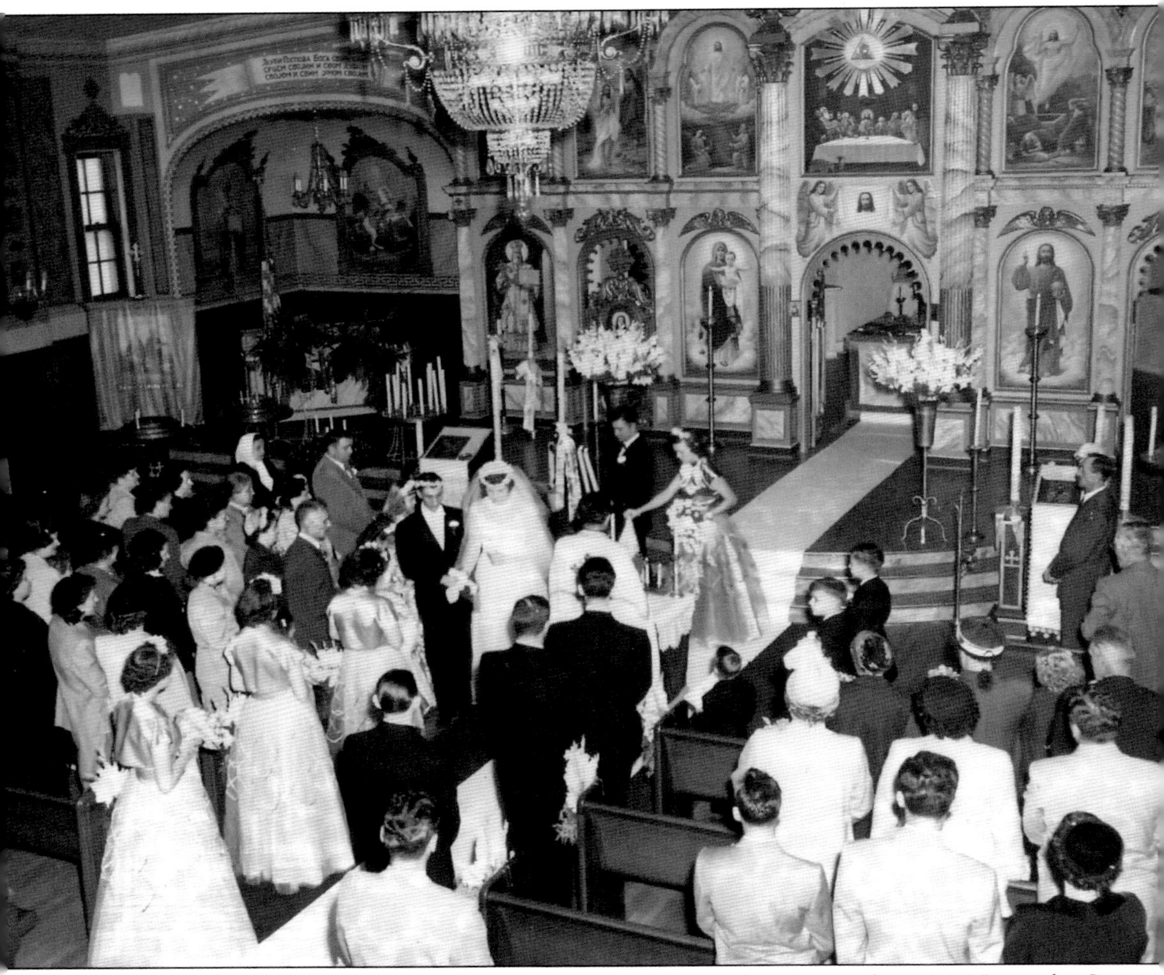

On the Cover: Milan Skrivan and Anne Bires get married on September 22, 1951, at the St. Sava Serbian Orthodox Church when it was located in Gary, Indiana. Their wedding included several traditional elements that are still part of Serbian Orthodox weddings today. (Courtesy of St. Sava Serbian Orthodox Church, Merrillville, Indiana.)

IMAGES
of America

SERBS IN CHICAGOLAND

Marina Marich

ARCADIA
PUBLISHING

Copyright © 2015 by Marina Marich
ISBN 978-1-4671-1230-7

Published by Arcadia Publishing
Charleston, South Carolina

Printed in the United States of America

Library of Congress Control Number:

For all general information, please contact Arcadia Publishing:
Telephone 843-853-2070
Fax 843-853-0044
E-mail sales@arcadiapublishing.com
For customer service and orders:
Toll-Free 1-888-313-2665

Visit us on the Internet at www.arcadiapublishing.com

To the Serbs of Chicagoland, especially Rajko and Ilija

Contents

ACKNOWLEDGMENTS

The contributions of many people made this book possible. First, I want to thank several individuals. Dorothy Paunovich, you are one in a million. St. Sava Serbian Orthodox Church is lucky to have you, and I can't thank you enough. Your herculean effort to collect thousands of photographs and artifacts that preserve Serbian history and culture is beyond words. A number of people also shared their personal photographs, and I especially want to thank Ljubi Ostoich Hayden and Dorothy Lalich—who shared family photos that date back to the turn of the century, when their families first settled in the area.

Second, I want to acknowledge the other contributors without whom I couldn't have completed this project. St. George Serbian Orthodox Church in East Chicago, Indiana, is a treasure that is worth a visit. The Serb National Federation's contributions brought back memories of my own basketball playing days for the Serbian Eagles. Thank you to Holy Resurrection Serbian Orthodox Cathedral for your help and for hosting the *zabavas* I attended in my younger years. I also want to acknowledge my late father-in-law, Milan Marich, and cousins Marija Mihajlović, Nena Vukanić, and Milena Radjenovich whose photographs helped round out the book.

Finally, and most importantly, I want to recognize my immediate family. I want to thank my husband, Mark, for encouraging me to take on this project and for supporting me unconditionally and with love. I thank my parents, Nikola and Ljiljana Dobrosavljević, *every day* for being brave enough to immigrate to the United States to make a better life for themselves, myself, and my brother, Milan, while instilling in us a sense of pride of our Serbian heritage and reminding us to never forget from where we came. To Rajko and Ilija, my incredible boys, you bring endless joy to me and your tata, and I am honored to be your mama. I hope this book shines a brighter light on how proud I am to be Serbian and how much it means to me that you love visiting Serbia as much as I do.

Niko nema što Srbin imade!

Introduction

The city of Chicago is synonymous with Serbs. With the largest Serbian community in the United States, Chicago teems with more than a century of Serbian history.

The earliest immigrants to the Chicagoland area date back to the end of the 19th century. They arrived from regions such as Lika, Dalmatia, and Herzegovina. These Serbian settlers viewed their new country as one with unlimited possibility. The very first Serbian immigrants to the United States went west, with hopes of benefiting from the gold rush, but those who chose Chicago traded the lure of gold for the promise of steel. The men worked hard in the steel mills along Lake Michigan, making a good living for themselves and their families.

Some settlers stayed only a short amount of time before heading back to their homeland. Others may have envisioned returning, but the start of World War I prevented that. Many more, however, chose to stay and build a life for themselves and their families—never returning to their villages. Those who remained established communities, relying on one another and keeping the Serbian traditions alive, and fraternal organizations and Serbian Orthodox parishes were founded throughout the Chicago and Northwest Indiana region.

After World War II, a second wave of immigrants looked to Chicago as a place to call home. These Serbs included people who opposed the new communist government and were seeking political freedom. This group of settlers also included those who saw the United States as many immigrants do—as the land of economic opportunity. Many of these immigrants maintained close ties with family in then-Yugoslavia, and would send money and care packages to loved ones in the old country.

Regardless of when Serbs immigrated to the Chicagoland area, all of them had one thing in common: A desire to embrace traditions and pass them down to future generations so they, too, can continue to honor and uphold those customs.

Without doubt, language is a critical element of Serbian culture. Serbs speak Serbian, a Slavic language that uses the Cyrillic alphabet. Vuk Karadžić devised the Serbian Cyrillic alphabet in 1814 on phonetic principles. When immigrants first arrived in the Chicagoland area, they spoke Serbian at home and within their communities. As more and more Serbs assimilated, they spoke less and less Serbian. Even though many immigrants with ancestral ties that date back more than a century do not speak Serbian—and some have never visited Serbia—they remain determined to uphold Serbian traditions and observe their Serbian Orthodox faith. Church services are held in Serbian and English, and Sunday schools teach the language to children with the hope of instilling a baseline of linguistic understanding.

Religiously, Serbs practice the Eastern Orthodox faith, and much of Serbian culture is identified by its religion. Conversions to Christianity began as early as the 7th century, hundreds of years before the Great Schism split between the Greek Orthodox and Roman Catholic Churches. The Serbian Orthodox Church uses the Julian calendar, which means that Christmas falls on January 7. For Serbian children in the United States, this meant celebrating "American" Christmas on

December 25 and enjoying a second Christmas—albeit one with fewer gifts—on January 7. Most prominent among these religious traditions is the uniquely Serbian celebration of Slava, a patron saint holiday that each family celebrates as the time that it converted from paganism to Christianity.

The biggest religious challenge to Serbs in the Chicagoland area came in 1963, when the "American Schism" occurred. Throughout the region, the once-unified Serbian Orthodox church split into two groups—primarily along the lines of churches that sided with the Serbian Orthodox church in Belgrade and those that formed another diocese in America and Canada. This was a deeply personal and painful time. The split lasted until 1992, when the church finally reunited.

The reunification reflects the family-oriented nature of Serbs, but one specific example demonstrates their kinship terminology. There isn't a word for "cousin" in Serbian. Instead, a cousin's terminology is tied directly to the blood relation between people. For instance, Serbs would say "*brat od tetke*" or "*sestra od ujaka*," which literally translate as, "brother from my father's sister" and "sister from my mother's brother." This makes it easy to classify the relationship between two people. Another easy way to identify Serbs is by their last names. Most surnames end with "*-ić*," which is pronounced "eech," and originally acted as a way to identify a person's father or ancestor. In some Serbian regions, names ended with "*-ov*" or "*-in*," which were combined with "*-ić*" to form surnames such as "Marković" or "Jovanović." When Serbs immigrated to the United States, an "h" was added to the surnames so that the "ch" sound was more obvious.

Serbs who live in Chicagoland display symbols that make it easy to identify someone of Serbian descent. At churches and functions, the Serbian flag is flown with its red, blue, and white horizontal colors. Some flags also carry a Serbian coat of arms, from the Nemanjić dynasty, which includes a white two-headed eagle. A Serbian cross is also more easily identified, due to its intricate look based on the Byzantine cross. These symbols have been incorporated into various Serbian fraternal and cultural organizations throughout the Chicagoland region.

As with many nationalities, food and drink form the cornerstone of tradition for Serbs here and abroad. Several foods are common among people of Serbian descent and are served at Serbian events at people's homes or at churches and restaurants in the region. *Ćevapčići*, a ground meat sausage, is considered a national dish. Other traditional foods include stuffed cabbage (*sarma*), spit-roasted meat (*pečenje*), roasted red pepper spread (*ajvar*), and homemade bread (*pogača*). Popular desserts include many that are made with fried dough, including *uštipci*, *krofne*, and *palačinke*. Fruit brandy (*rakija*) is omnipresent in Serbian homes and at Serbian celebrations.

Among the earliest immigrants, celebrations consisted of men and women wearing traditional folk costumes, or *nošnje*. These costumes consist of a cap for men, who also wear a loose shirt tucked into trousers that balloon around the thighs and tighten from the knee to the ankle. Women wear shirts tucked into heavy wool skirts, or a long white dress with embroidered velvet aprons. Men and women usually wear embroidered vests and special leather shoes, called *opanke*, that have a distinctive tip at the front. While *nošnje* aren't as common today, Serbs in the area do still wear them for cultural events and as part of folk dancing (*kolo*), *tambura*, and choir groups.

More than 100 years after Serbs first started settling in the area, the devastating wars in the Balkans of the 1990s drove a third wave of immigrants to the Chicagoland area. Their desire to come to Chicago demonstrates that this Midwestern city remains a welcoming place for Serbs. It also ensures that vital customs and traditions will continue to be passed down to future generations.

This book is not meant to be an exhaustive history of the Serbian people who call the Chicagoland area home. Rather, it is intended to provide a glimpse into the families, organizations, churches, and traditions that make a Serb a Serb.

Živela Srbija!

One

Our Culture

Serbs are proud of their heritage and have strong bonds to their cultural identity and traditions. Serbian culture dates back centuries, to the south Slav people who lived in the Balkans. For those who settled in the Chicagoland area, some of the same traditions Serbs followed in the past—in the villages, towns, and cities throughout Serbia and southeastern Europe—are observed today and help to strengthen Serbian culture. Among the most visible customs are music, dance, and the performing arts.

Starting with the earliest immigrants, Serbian settlers formed folk dancing (kolo) groups at local Serbian churches. The groups performed for parishioners but also traveled internationally to teach others about Serbian culture. The kolo is a traditional dance, done in a circle with dancers wearing folk costumes called nošnje. Nošnje vary from region to region but typically include detailed embroidery on vests, aprons, and shirts. One element that is common across regions is a shoe called an opanka. The shoe has a distinctive tip at the front, which varies to reflect the different regions of the country.

Kolo dancers perform to quick-paced music, played on accordions and *tamburas*—a basic, traditional stringed instrument—by small groups of musicians. Serbs have a rich musical tradition and have played their music all around the world. Among the most recognized and popular Serbian musicians were the Popovich Brothers, who played tambura concerts as early as 1926.

The performing arts have also been important in maintaining Serbian culture in the Chicagoland area. At the turn of the 20th century, lodges were formed under the Serb National Federation to help maintain camaraderie and community. These clubs held cultural plays presented at weekend programs. These performances retold historic events through original productions and played a key role in passing down stories from one generation to the next. This became a critical way to share the culture as more and more generations of Serbs settled in the Chicagoland area.

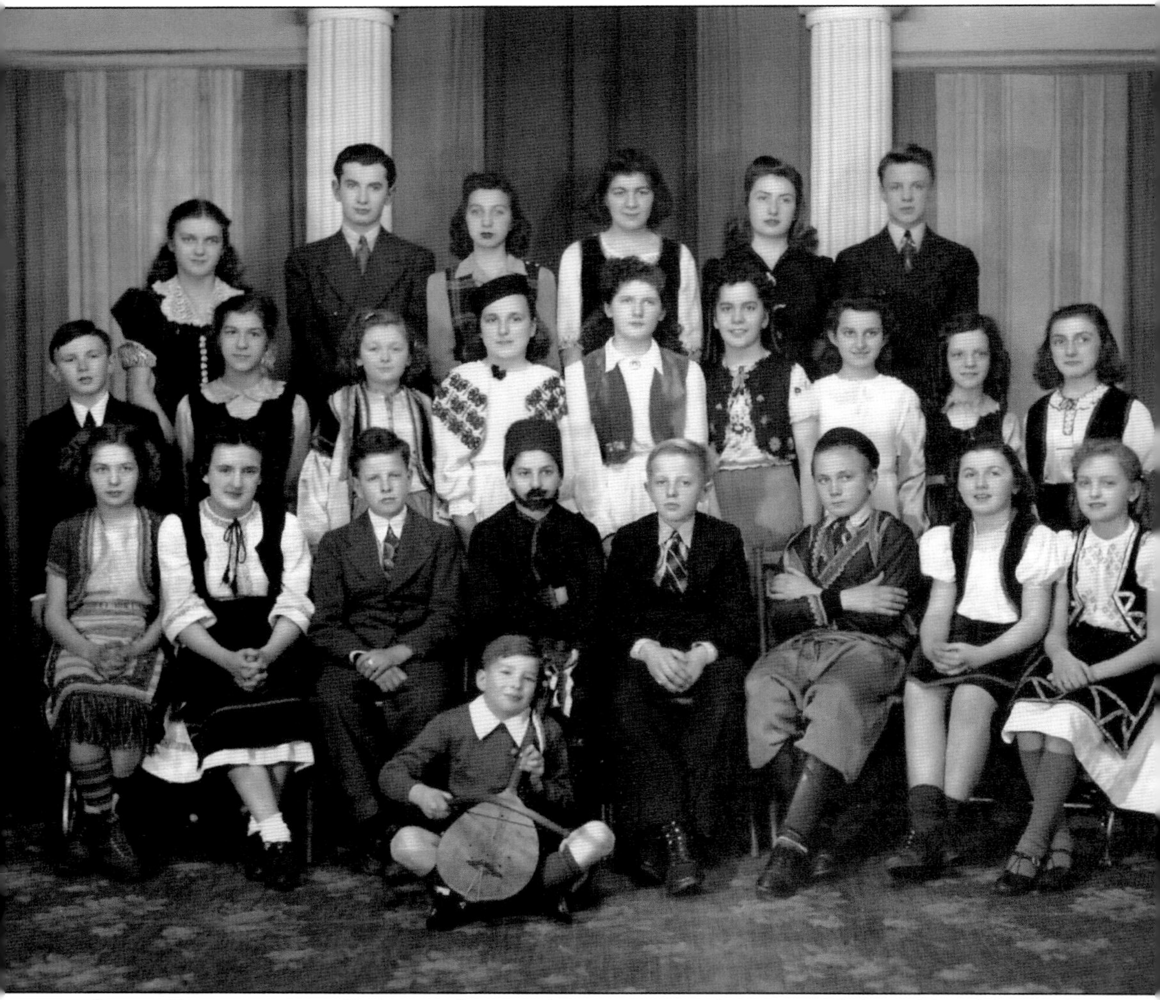

In an effort to preserve Serbian culture and entertain parishioners and the public alike, Serbian Orthodox churches hosted plays and musicals that featured Serbian music, songs, and stories. This play, called *Naša Slava* (*Our Patron Saint Holiday*), was held at the St. Archangel Michael Serbian Orthodox Church in South Chicago in 1941 and was directed by Ljubica (Lalich) Popovich. Pictured from left to right are (first row) "Junior" Lalich; (second row) Vera (Zorich) Vlamis, Rose (Ciganovich) Tadich, Joe Babich, Dan Zorich, Steve Zakula, Danny Boskovich, Ann (Dopudja) Vukobratovich, and Dorothy (Babich) Lalich; (third row) Radomir Vukobratovich, Mary (Lalich) Dietrich, Nada (Nikcevich) Carich, Mileva (Dopudja) Solaya, Mary (Vukobratovich) Zidnovich, Melvina (Dopudja) Solaya, Virginia (Sheemon) Milyasevich, Jelka (Lalich) Plesha, and Mary (Popovich) Stampar; and (fourth row) Violet (Panayotovich) Bundalo, Milan Solaya, Helene (Krainovich) Duffy, Sophie (Vukobratovich) Zatezalo, Sophie (Popovich) Ostoich, and Nick Babich. (Courtesy of Ljubi Ostoich Hayden.)

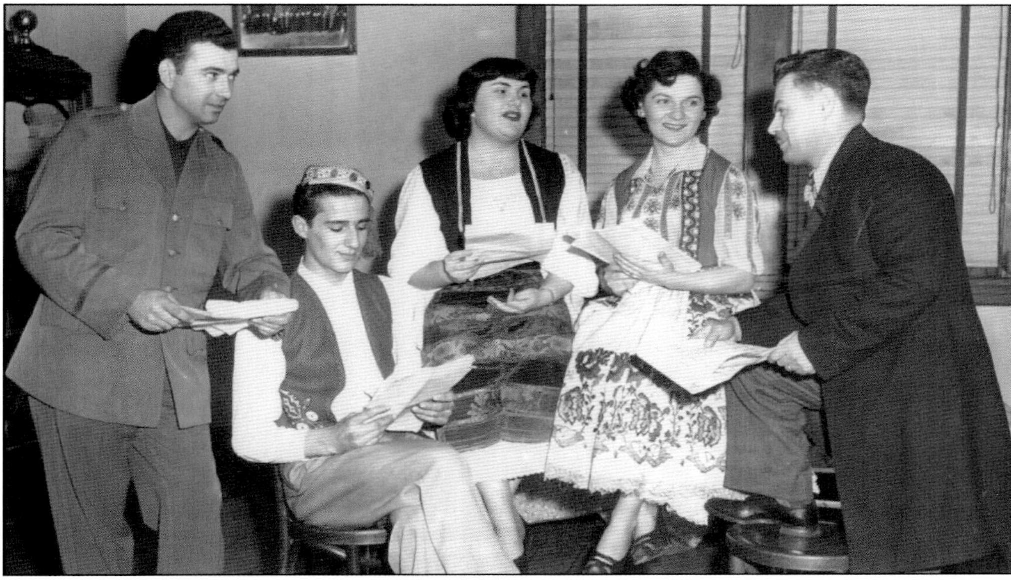

Members of the Srbadija Lodge at the St. Sava Serbian Orthodox Church practice ahead of a performance in 1938. Pictured from left to right are Milan Bundalo, Steve Majstorovich, Donna (Tarailo) Mace, Ann (Milovanovich) Versal, and director Emil Manyin. The plays were presented at weekend programs at the church. (Courtesy of St. Sava Serbian Orthodox Church, Merrillville, Indiana.)

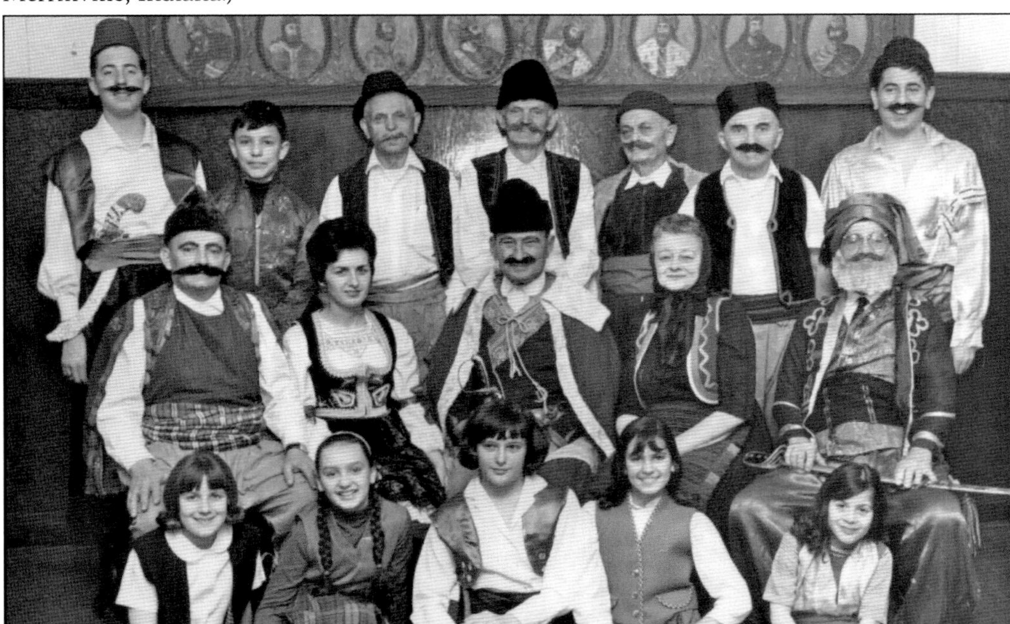

Srbadija Lodge—a club formed under the Serb National Federation to maintain camaraderie and community—prepares for a performance at the St. Sava Serbian Orthodox Church in 1965. George "Glisho" Rapaich, longtime president of Srbadija and a church founder, is at center. Kralj Petar (King Peter) Lodge was the other lodge at the church and is the only one that is still active. (Courtesy of St. Sava Serbian Orthodox Church, Merrillville, Indiana.)

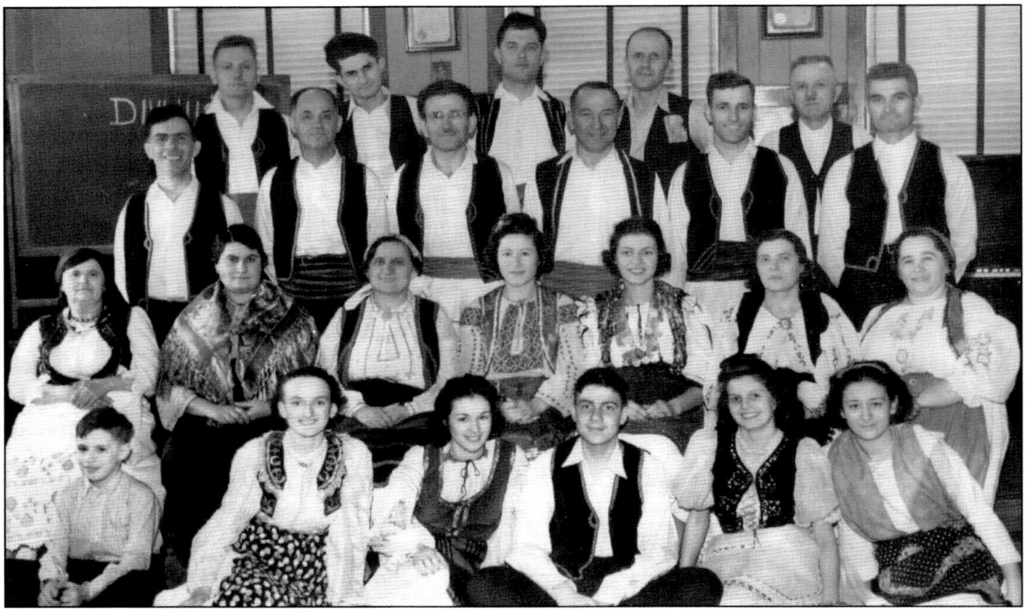

In the early 1940s, the Srbadija Lodge cultural organization—at the St. Sava Serbian Orthodox Church—included a famous parishioner: Peter Sekulovich (third row, second from left), father of Karl Malden (Mladen Sekulovich). The elder Sekulovich wrote, produced, directed, and acted in many of the plays at the church. Also pictured is Malden's brother, Dan Sekulovich (first row, fourth from left). (Courtesy of St. Sava Serbian Orthodox Church, Merrillville, Indiana.)

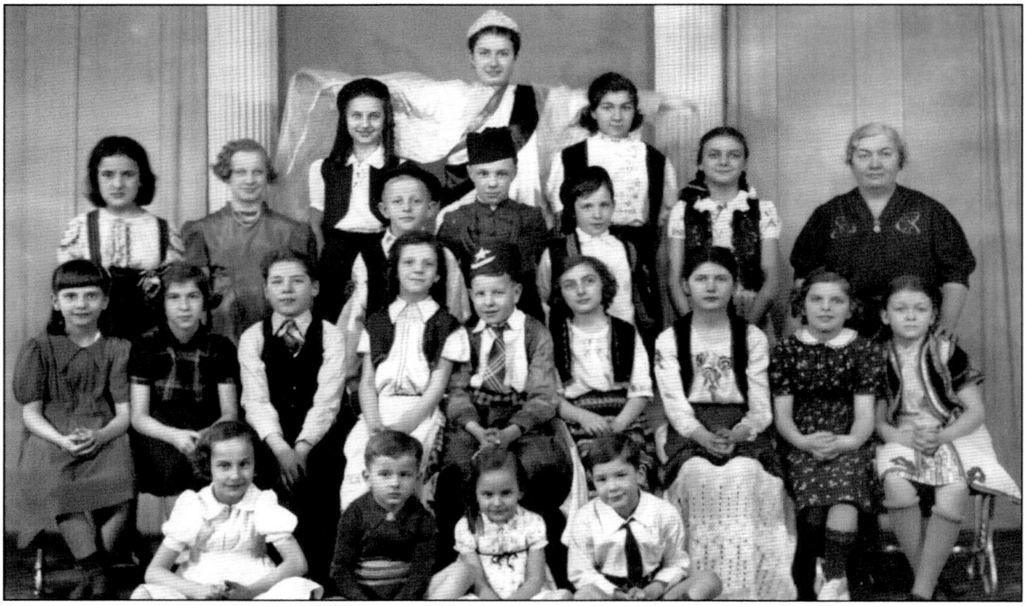

Ljubica Popovich (third row, right) directed the St. Archangel Michael Serbian Orthodox Church's plays in the 1940s and made some of the costumes. Her daughter Sophie is in the top row, and her other daughter, Mary, is in the first row, third from left. Also pictured is Eli Grba (left of Mary), who played professional baseball for the New York Yankees and Los Angeles Angels. (Courtesy of Dorothy Lalich.)

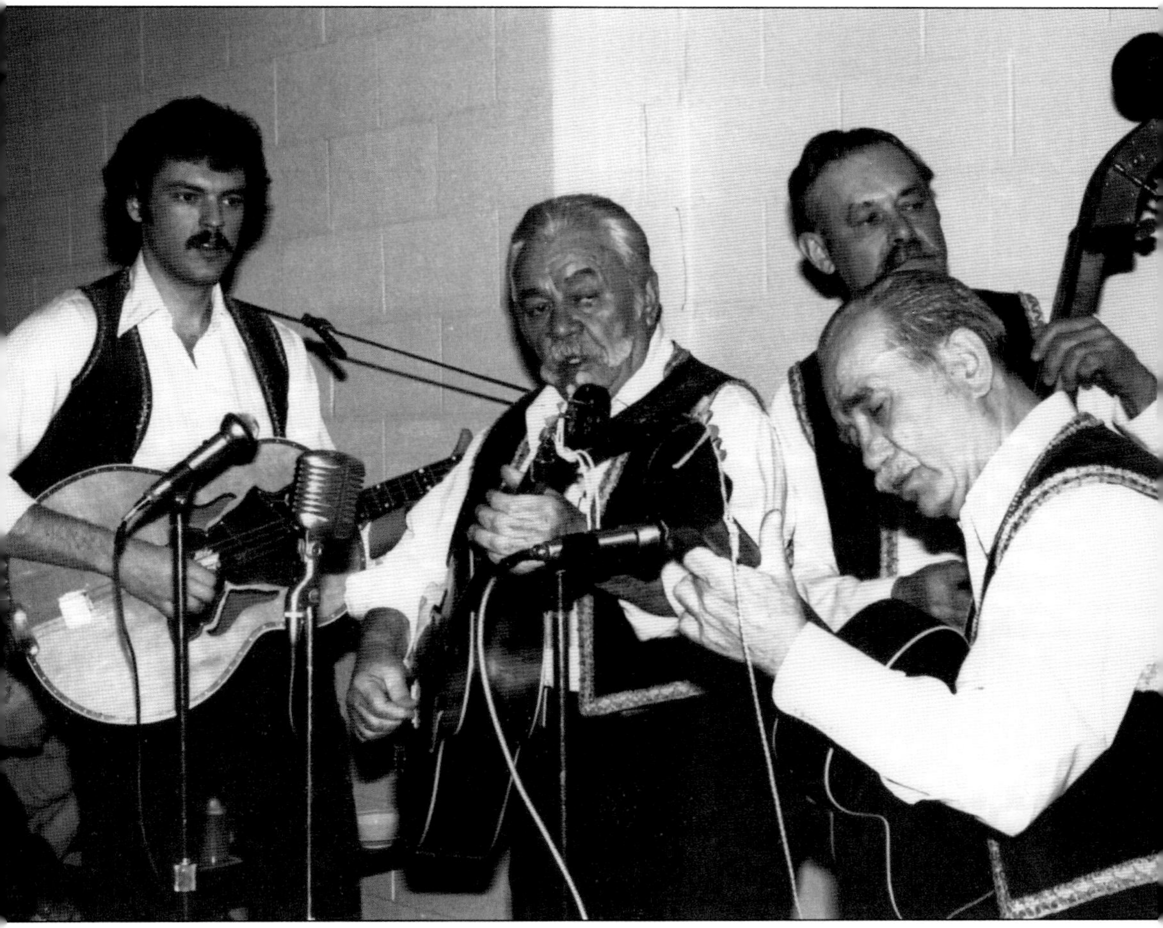

Serbians have a rich musical tradition and history. Among the most recognized and popular musicians were the Popovich Brothers, who played tambura concerts around the world starting in 1926. A tambura is the basic instrument of traditional Serbian folk music, and the music is usually performed by small groups of tambura players. Pictured in traditional nošnje are, from left to right, Bob Lalich, Ted Popovich, Pete Mistovich, and Adam Popovich performing at the St. Elijah Serbian Orthodox Church in Merrillville, Indiana, in 1979. Mistovich started playing with the group when brother Eli Popovich joined the Central Intelligence Agency in the late 1940s. He played with the Popovich Brothers Tamburitza Orchestra for more than 50 years. Lalich was asked to join the Popovich Brothers in January 1978, when Marko Popovich died, and played with them regularly—including at a 1982 performance in Washington, DC, where Adam Popovich received the National Endowment for the Arts Fellowship in Folk Heritage. (Courtesy of Dorothy Lalich.)

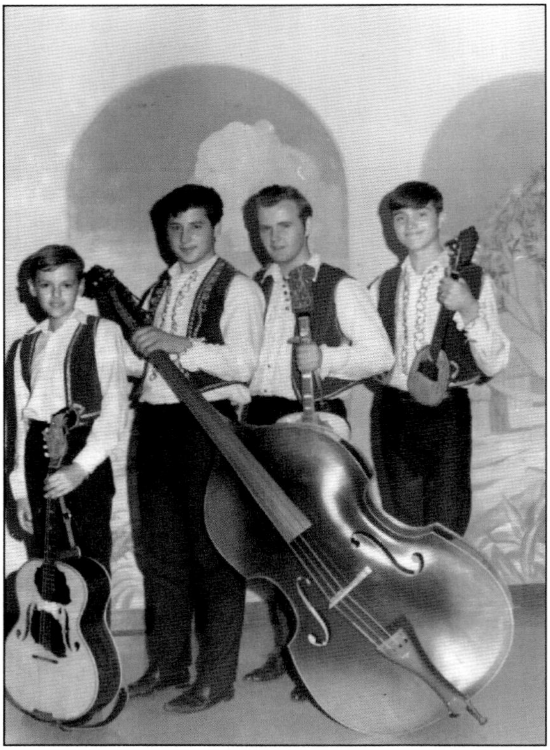

Bob Lalich (left) started playing tambura when he was eight years old. He joined the Popovich Brothers in 1978 and played with them for more than 20 years. Lalich and his fellow Mladi Becari (Young Fellows), pictured here from left to right, Scott Barach, Carl Schutzman Jr., and John Zevkovich, were all part of the St. Archangel Michael Junior Tamburitza group. They are pictured at Milan's Restaurant in 1967. (Courtesy of Dorothy Lalich.)

Thanks to the popularity of the Popovich Brothers and other traditional Serbian folk musicians, young groups of tambura players emerged across the Chicagoland area. One such group is the Mladi Becari—pictured here at the late 1970s wedding of Scott Barach—which performed at various functions for many years. (Courtesy of Dorothy Lalich.)

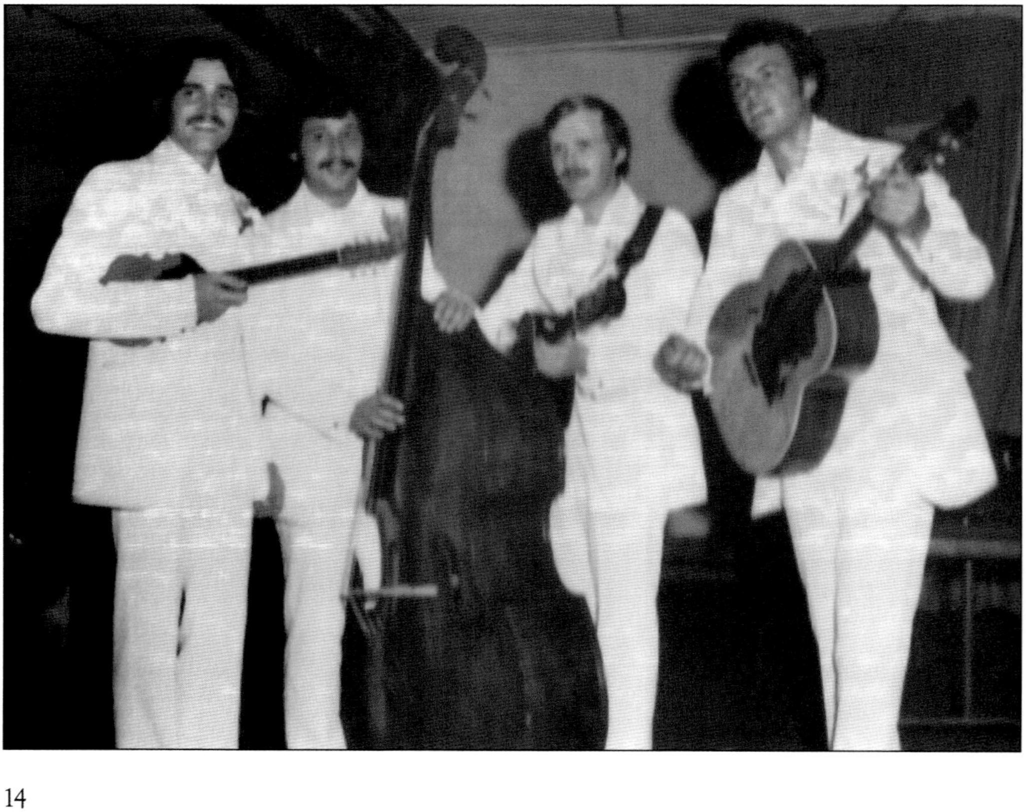

The Mladi Becari took their musical act on the road. This poster is for a concert in Minnesota, at a Serbian Orthodox church there. Pictured from left to right are Bob Lalich, Scott Barach, John Zevkovich, and Carl Schutzman Jr. Lalich started playing tambura when he was eight years old, and he continues to organize events at the St. Archangel Michael Serbian Orthodox Church in Lansing, Illinois. (Courtesy of Dorothy Lalich.)

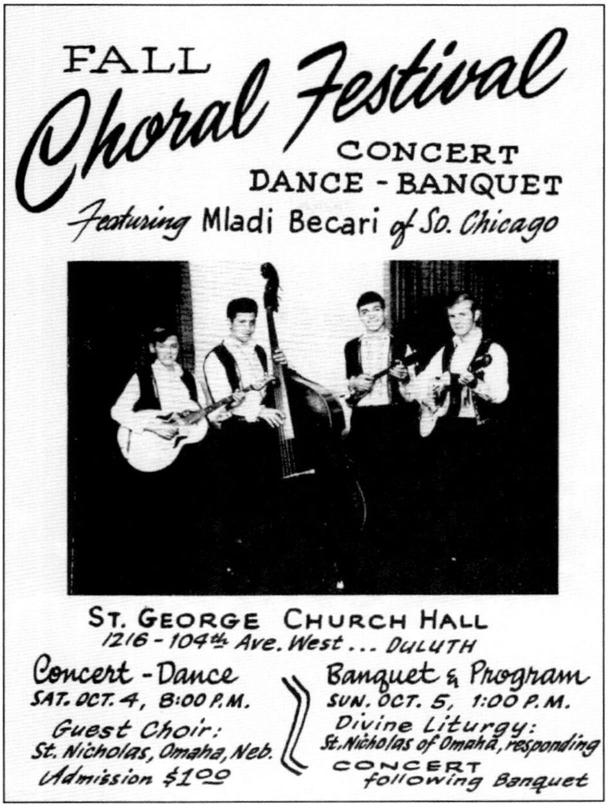

The love of Serbian music and instruments was instilled early among Serbian Americans. Pictured here is a youth tambura group, from the St. Sava Serbian Orthodox Church in Gary, Indiana. Playing traditional Serbian instruments are, from left to right, (first row) Nick Lacanski and Bob Mandich; (second row) Paul and Karen Gojkovich. (Courtesy of St. Sava Serbian Orthodox Church, Merrillville, Indiana.)

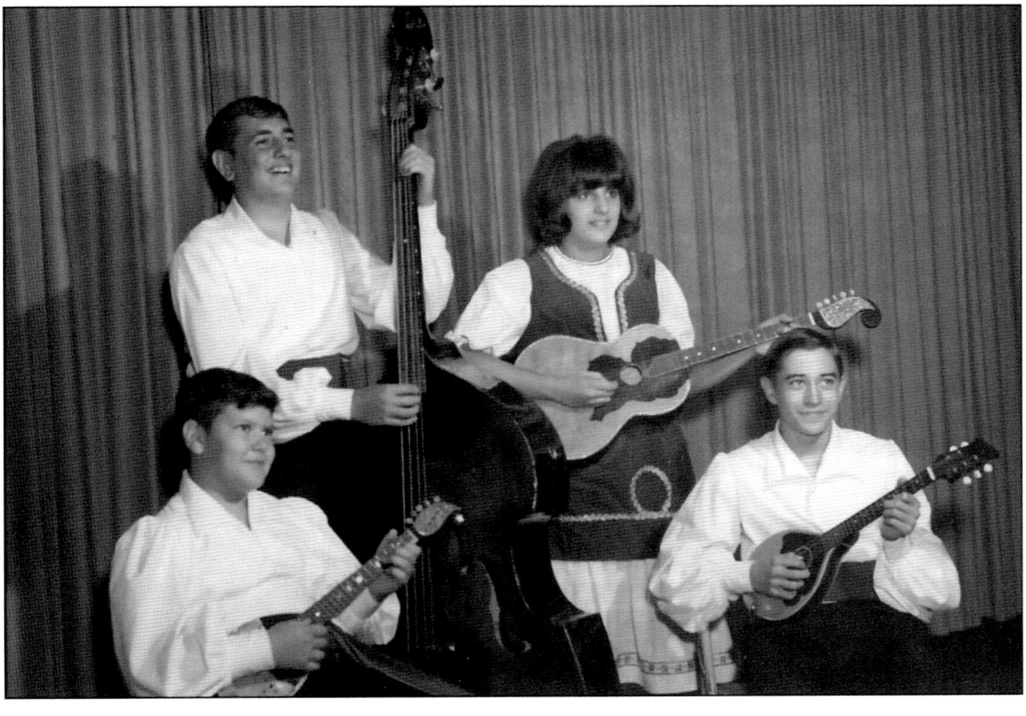

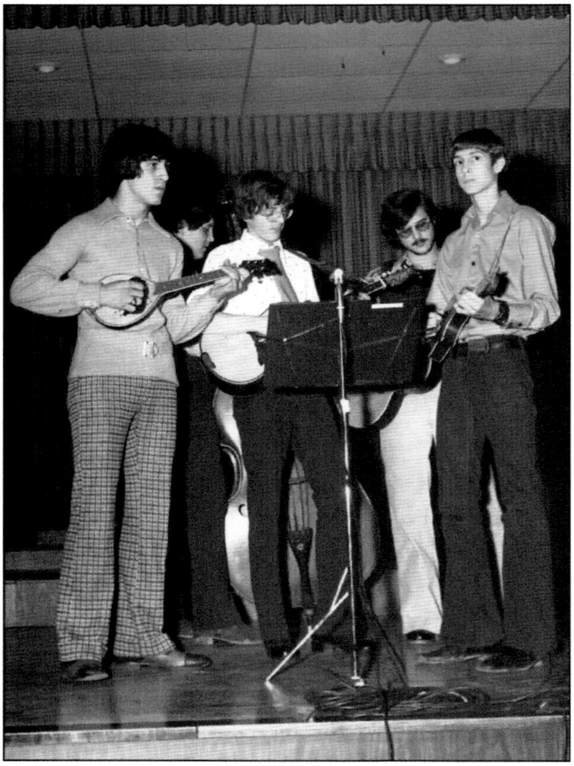

The various youth groups and orchestras would perform for parishioners during special celebrations. Nick Sever (left) was particularly active in the St. Sava Serbian Orthodox Church organizations. Here, he is playing with a youth group during a church celebration. (Courtesy of St. Sava Serbian Orthodox Church, Merrillville, Indiana.)

John "Bato" Hayden, a member of the St. Archangel Michael Serbian Orthodox Church in Lansing, Illinois, performed with the St. Elijah Serbian Orthodox Jr. Tammies in Alquippa, Pennsylvania, in 1959. Hayden was named the Serb National Federation's man of the year in 2014. He served as the building chairman of the Serbian Social Center in Lansing, Illinois, when the St. Archangel Michael Serbian Orthodox Church moved from South Chicago to Lansing. (Courtesy of Ljubi Ostoich Hayden.)

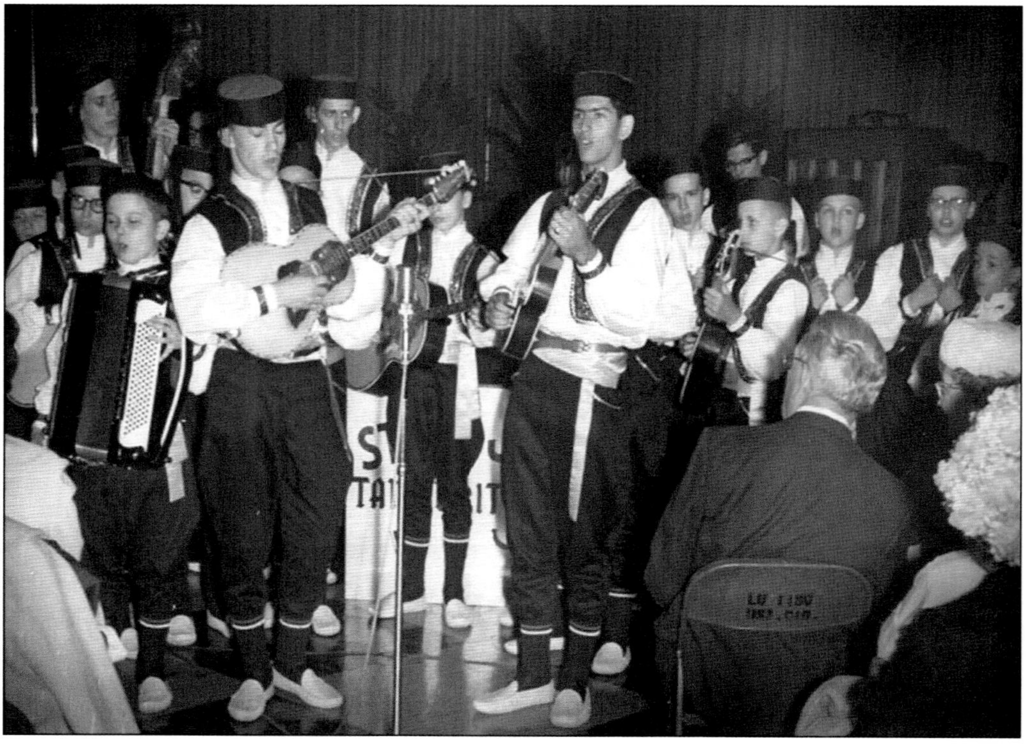

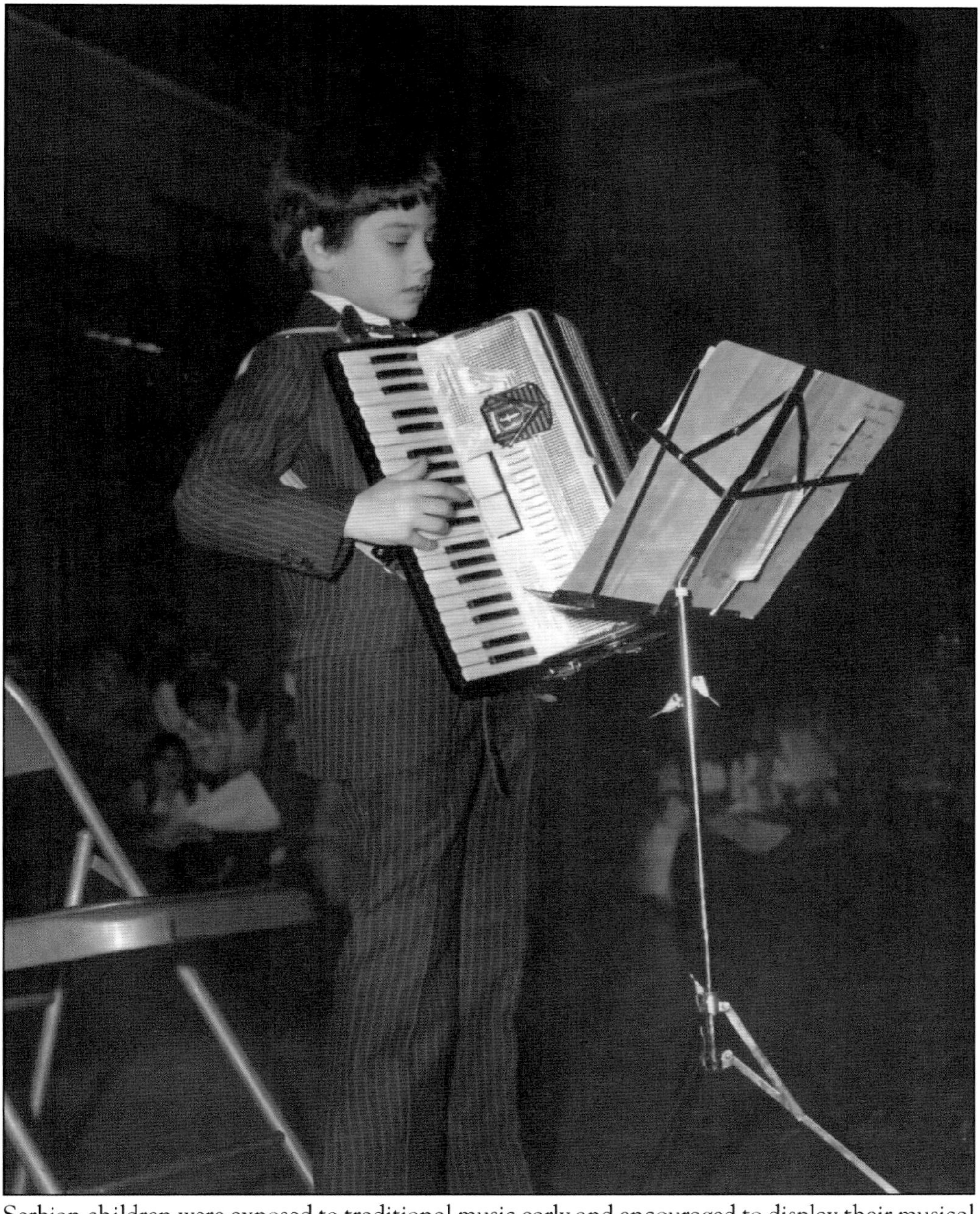

Serbian children were exposed to traditional music early and encouraged to display their musical skills at a variety of Serbian events. In this photograph from the early 1970s, an unidentified child plays the accordion as part of a St. Sava Day celebration at the St. Sava Serbian Orthodox Church, when it was located in Gary, Indiana. The accordion is played in many countries. In Serbia, is has primarily been used to play traditional folk music, although it can also be found in some popular music. The child is most likely playing a cultural song to honor St. Sava, who is considered the patron saint of children. He performed in front of other children and the parishioners who celebrate St. Sava every January. (Courtesy of St. Sava Serbian Orthodox Church, Merrillville, Indiana.)

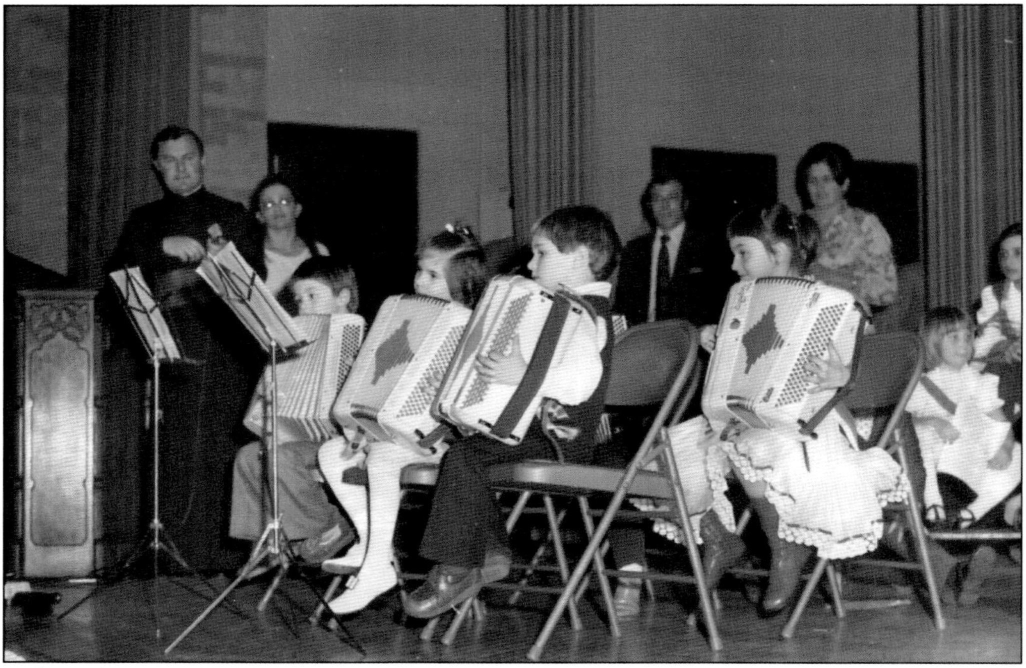

Kids perform on the accordion as part of a St. Sava Day presentation at the St. Sava Serbian Orthodox Church in the early 1970s. (Courtesy of St. Sava Serbian Orthodox Church, Merrillville, Indiana.)

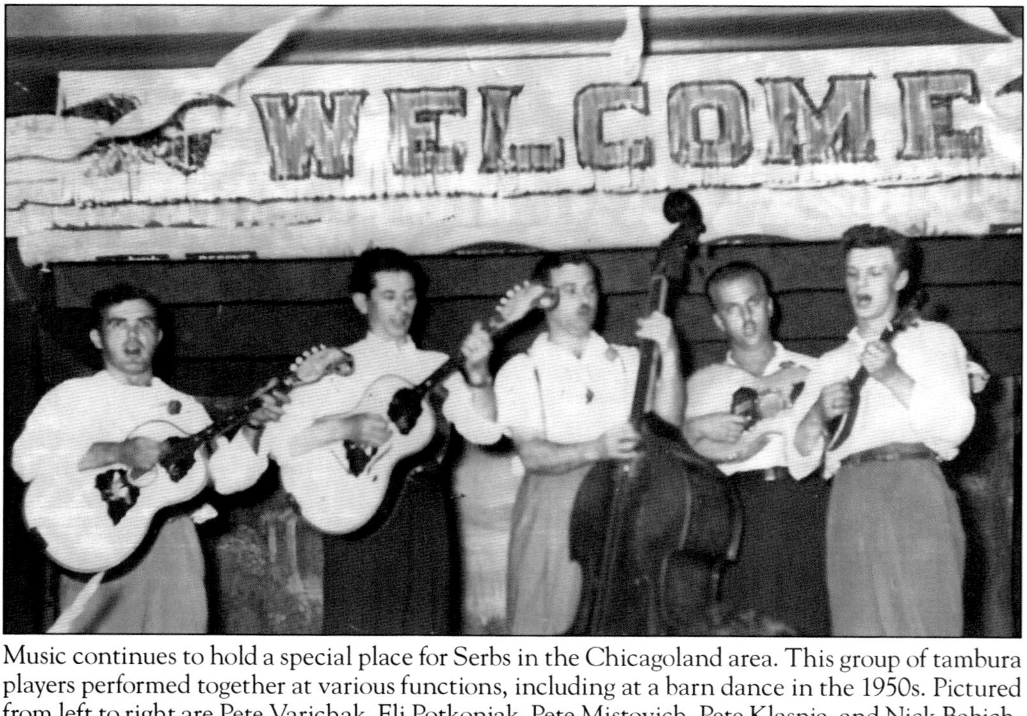

Music continues to hold a special place for Serbs in the Chicagoland area. This group of tambura players performed together at various functions, including at a barn dance in the 1950s. Pictured from left to right are Pete Varichak, Eli Potkonjak, Pete Mistovich, Pete Klasnja, and Nick Babich. The name of the orchestra was Kosovo. (Courtesy of Dorothy Lalich.)

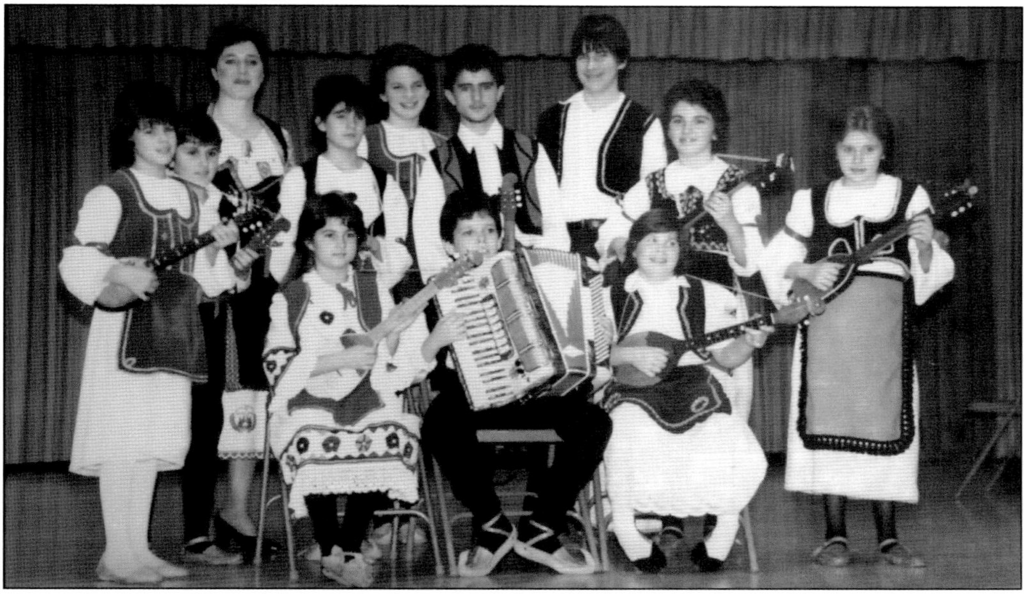

Pictured are members of the St. Archangel Michael Serbian Orthodox Church youth tambura group, from when the church was located in South Chicago. The members wore their nošnje, with each representing a different region of Serbia. The group's longtime leader, Nancy Colaković (back row, left), was a daughter of the priest at the time, Rev. Bozidar Dragicevich. (Courtesy of Marija Mihajlović.)

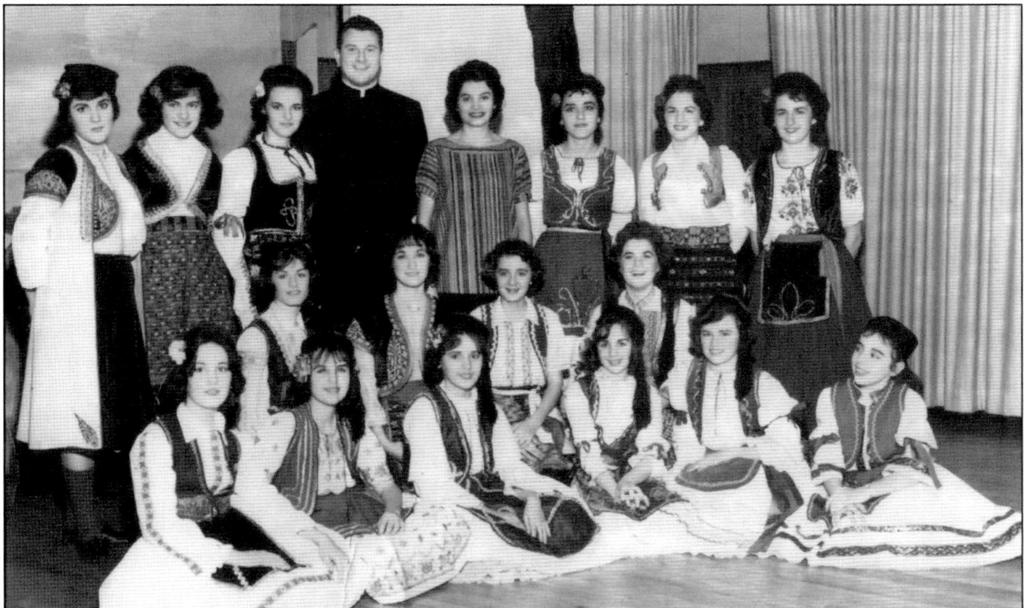

Kolo is a folk dance that is performed in a circle with several dancers. It is very common in Serbia, and groups have been formed at virtually every Serbian church. Pictured is the first dance group at the St. Sava Serbian Orthodox Church in Gary, Indiana. The priest's wife, Ljubinka Petakovich (back row, fifth from left), established the group in 1960. (Courtesy of St. Sava Serbian Orthodox Church, Merrillville, Indiana.)

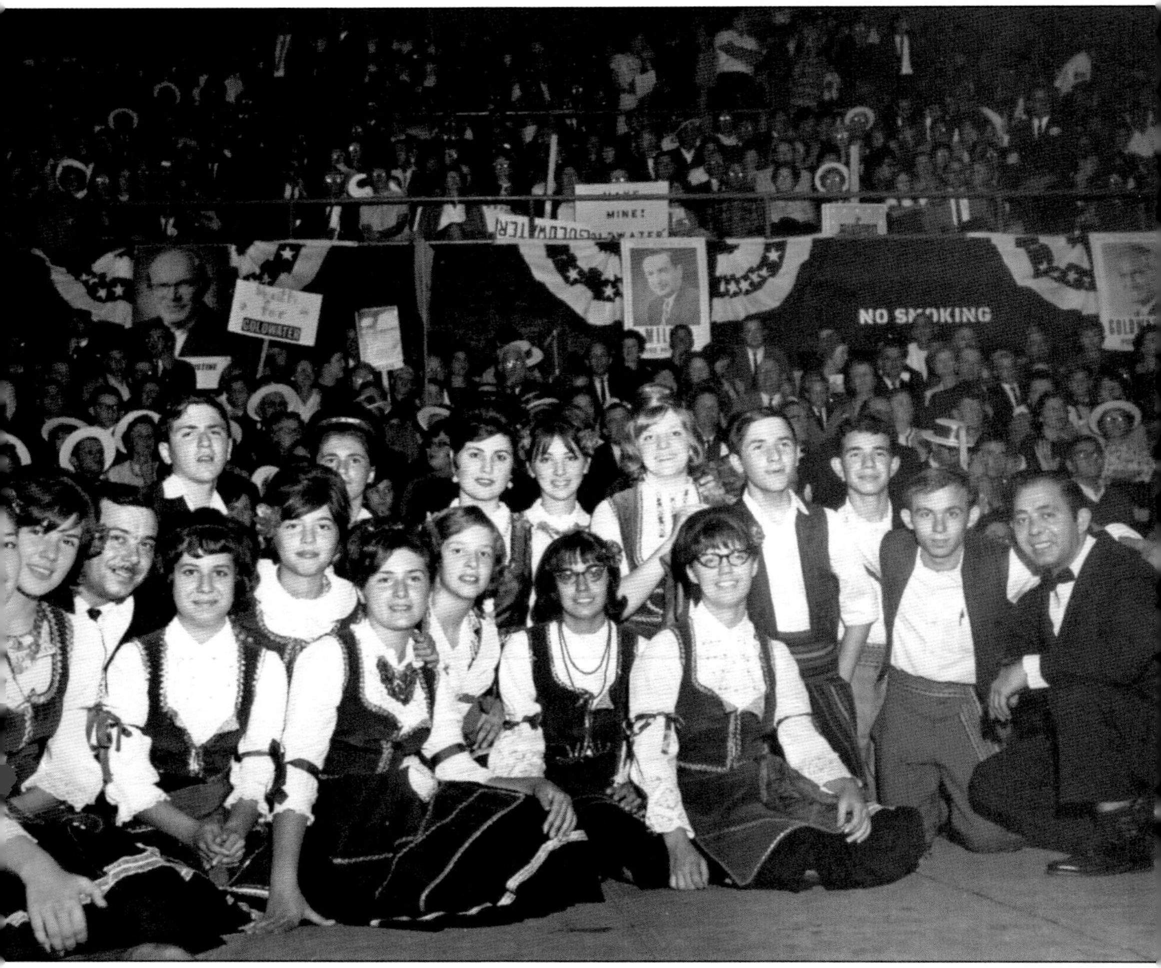

The folk dancing group from the St. George Serbian Orthodox Church in East Chicago, Indiana, was invited to perform during a Barry Goldwater presidential campaign stop and rally in Northwest Indiana in 1964. (Courtesy of St. George Serbian Orthodox Church, East Chicago, Indiana.)

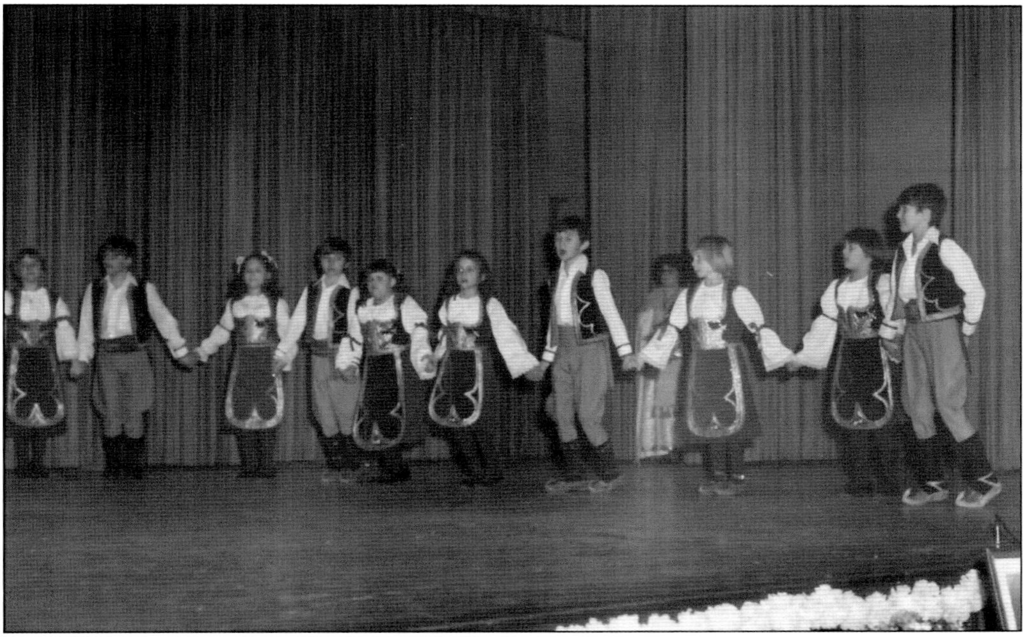

Kids perform a traditional kolo for their families and friends at the St. Sava Serbian Orthodox Church's hall, on Forty-ninth Avenue in Hobart, Indiana. Folk dancing performances take place regularly at Serbian churches throughout the Chicagoland area. (Courtesy of St. Sava Serbian Orthodox Church, Merrillville, Indiana.)

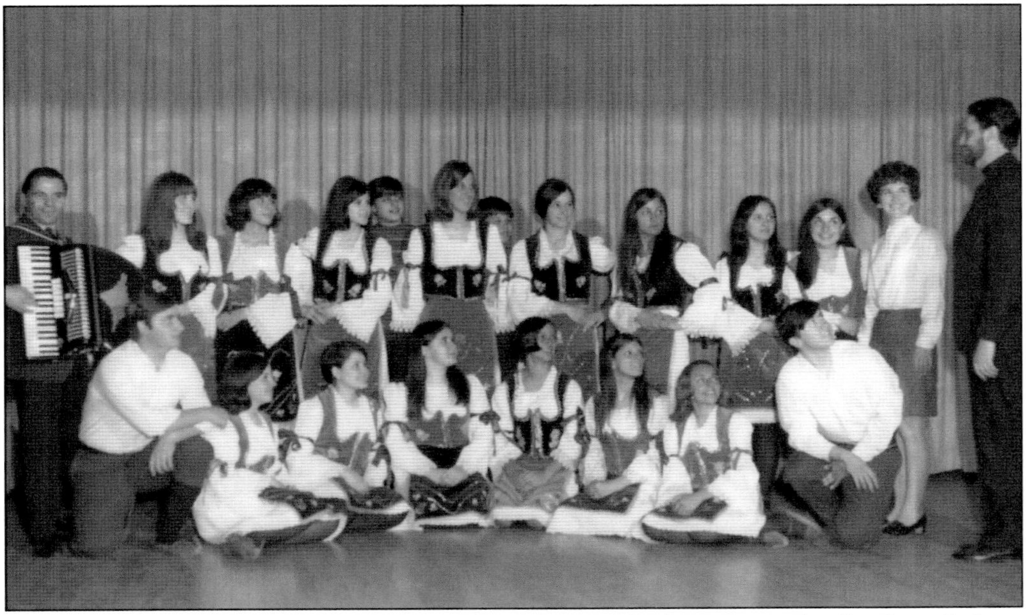

In this photograph from the 1960s, accordion player Mile Antić joins the St. Sava Serbian Orthodox Church folklore group. Accordions are a very popular and common instrument in the traditional Serbian music that accompanies kolo dances. Dessa Vrtikapa—the folklore group's instructor—and Rev. Peter Bankerovich are also pictured. (Courtesy of St. Sava Serbian Orthodox Church, Merrillville, Indiana.)

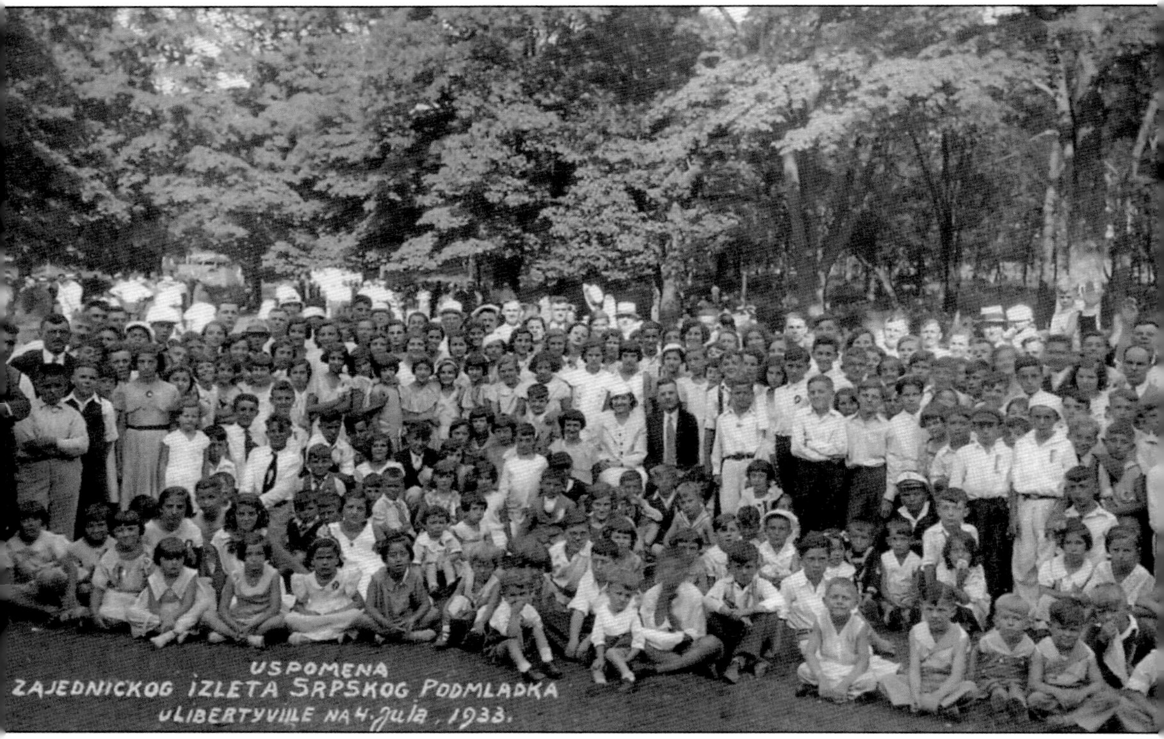

Taken on July 4, 1933, this photograph shows a gathering of the Serb National Federation's (SNF) Junior Order of Circle at the St. Sava Monastery in Libertyville, Illinois. Most, if not all, Serbian Orthodox churches had lodges or clubs. Younger members would join the junior lodges and older members formed senior clubs. These clubs provided people of Serbian descent a chance to spend social time with other Serbs. The clubs also helped maintain Serbian traditions and customs. The members shown here are gathering to celebrate the Fourth of July—honoring their Serbian heritage while also respecting their new home in the United States. Serbs continue to gather at St. Sava Monastery every Fourth of July for food, drink, song, and dance. (Courtesy of Serb National Federation, Pittsburgh, Pennsylvania.)

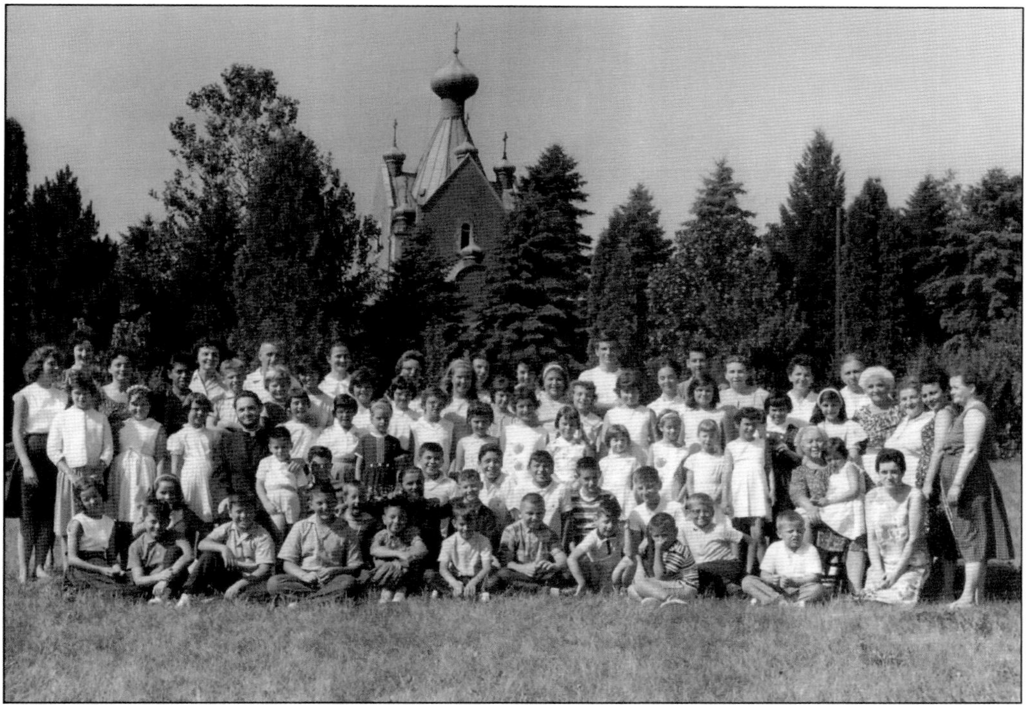

The St. Sava Serbian Orthodox Monastery in Libertyville, Illinois, has housed a children's summer camp since 1942. Kids who attend the camp enjoy a variety of activities in and around the monastery's grounds. This group of campers from the late 1950s pose with Rev. Peter Bankerovich, of St. Sava Serbian Orthodox Church in Gary, Indiana. (Courtesy of St. Sava Serbian Orthodox Church, Merrillville, Indiana.)

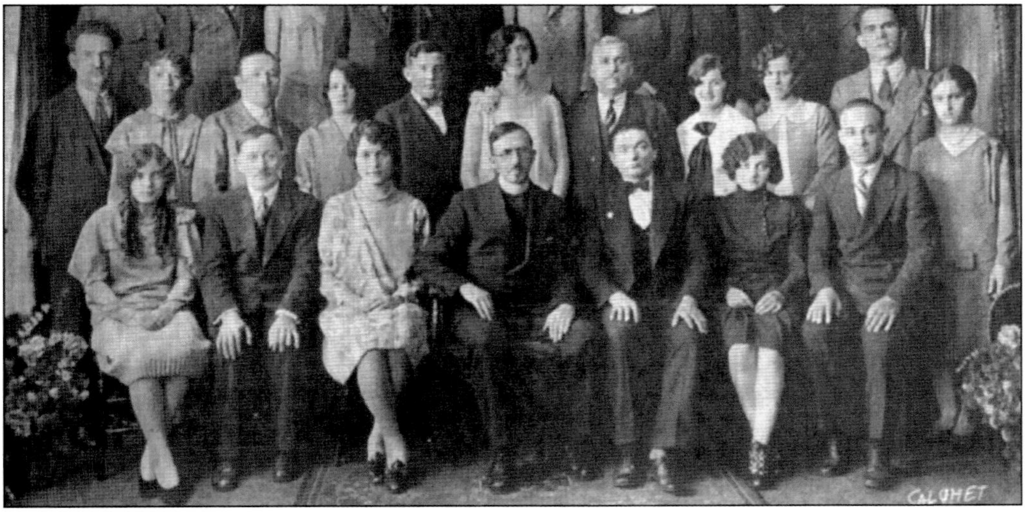

The Serbian singing society Sloboda (Freedom) of the St. Archangel Michael Serbian Orthodox Church posed for a photograph in 1927—the year it was organized. Over the years, the group sang in church and for church functions, competed in singing competitions, and performed around the country. The group is still active today and can be found singing at St. Archangel Michael every Sunday. (Courtesy of Ljubi Ostoich Hayden.)

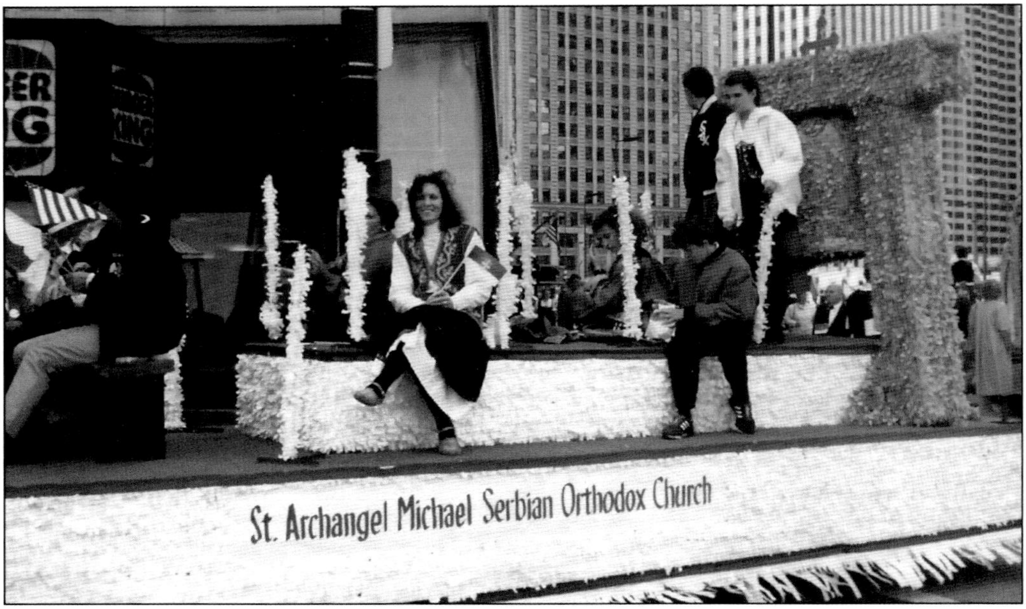

There was a significant amount of negative media coverage of Serbs during the Balkan wars in the early 1990s. In response, Serbs in the Chicagoland area organized a parade through the streets of downtown Chicago to demonstrate their pride in being Serbian. Several area churches, including St. Archangel Michael Serbian Orthodox Church, participated in the 1993 parade. (Courtesy of Ljiljana Dobrosavljević.)

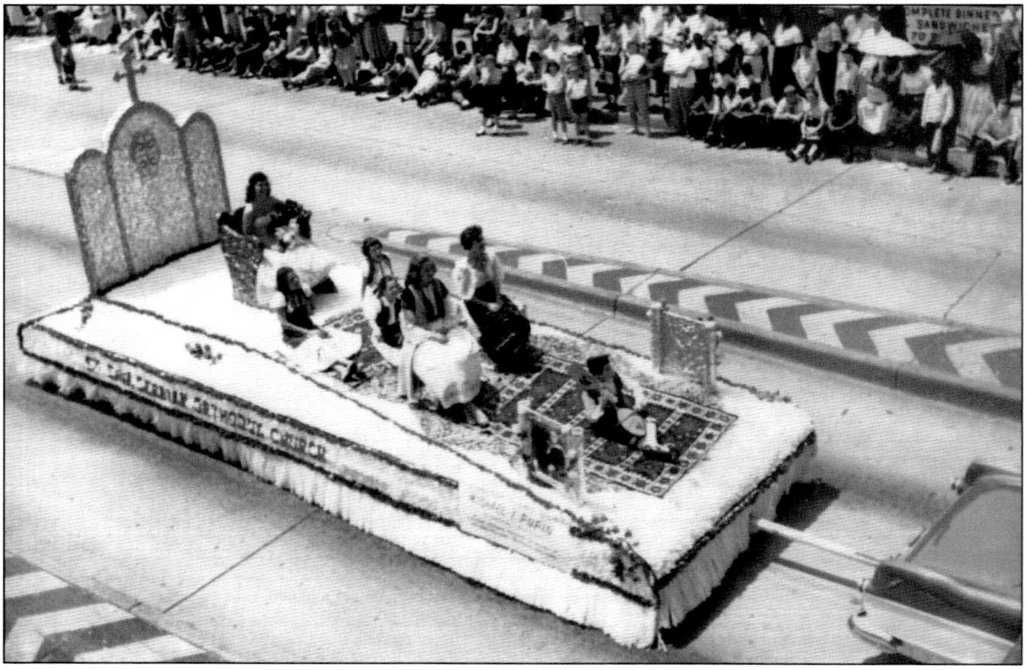

Dorothy (Nestorovich) Medich represented St. Sava Serbian Orthodox Church as its parade float princess. The parade was part of the Gary's Golden Jubilee celebration in 1956. (Courtesy of St. Sava Serbian Orthodox Church, Merrillville, Indiana.)

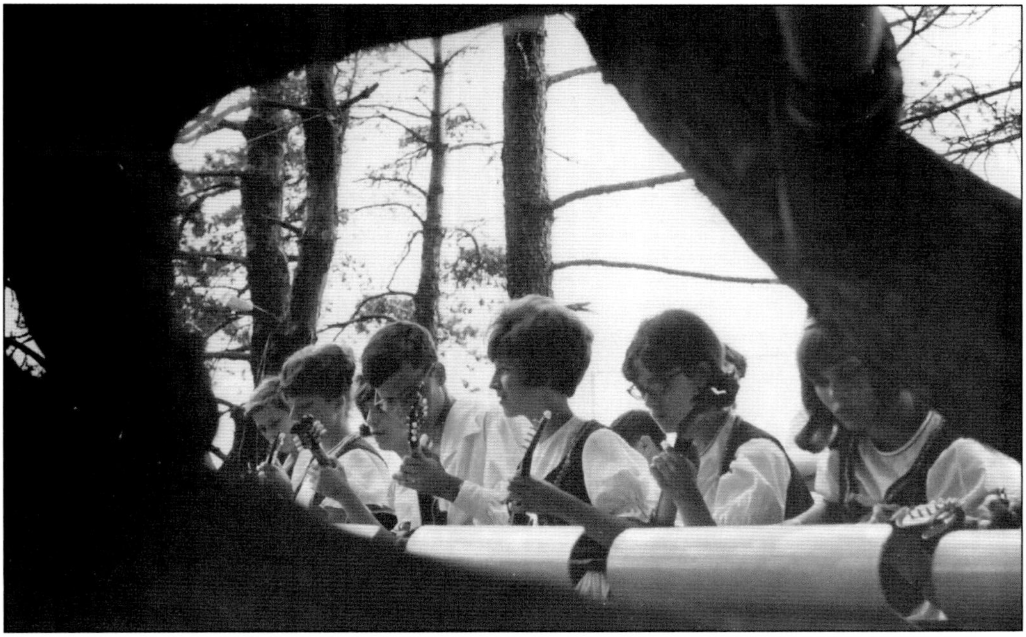

Serbian churches would often host gatherings at picnic grounds located at or near the church. Here the St. Sava youth tambura group performs at a Youth Day event at the St. Sava Serbian Orthodox Monastery in Libertyville, Illinois, in the 1960s. (Courtesy of St. Sava Serbian Orthodox Church, Merrillville, Indiana.)

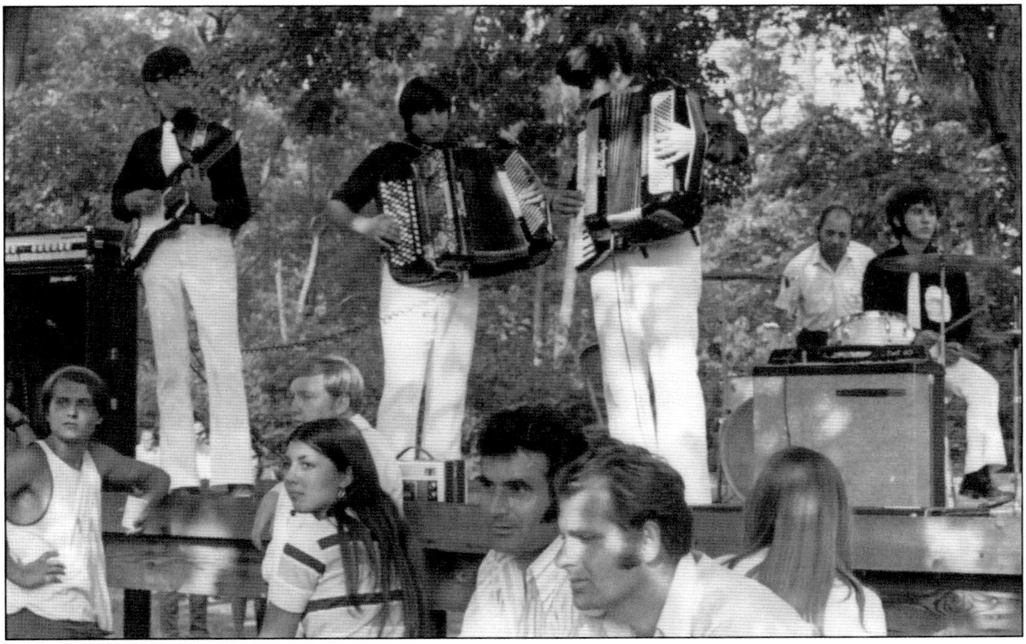

A youth group Mlada Srbadija entertains guests at the St. Sava Serbian Orthodox Monastery in Libertyville, Illinois, in the early 1970s. The musicians are playing an accordion, which is a very common instrument used to play Serbian folk music. (Courtesy of St. Sava Serbian Orthodox Church, Merrillville, Indiana.)

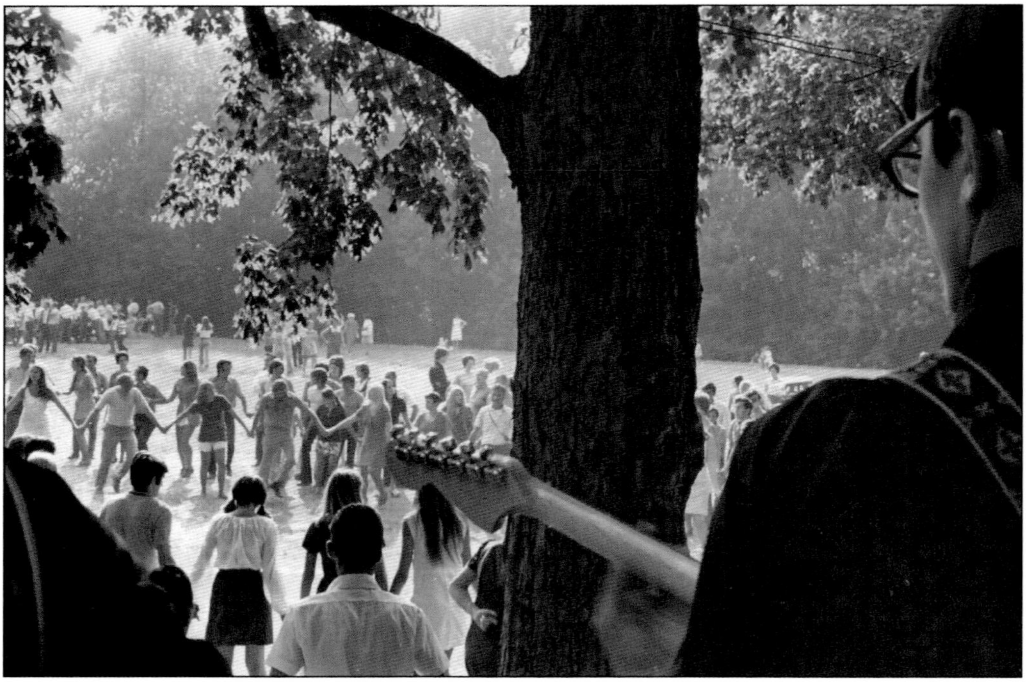

A group of Serbian Americans dance a kolo to traditional Serbian folk music performed by a youth group. The event took place in the 1970s at the St. Sava Serbian Orthodox Monastery in Libertyville, Illinois. These dances were brought over from Serbia and continue to serve as the hallmark of Serbian dancing at cultural celebrations. (Courtesy of St. Sava Serbian Orthodox Church, Merrillville, Indiana.)

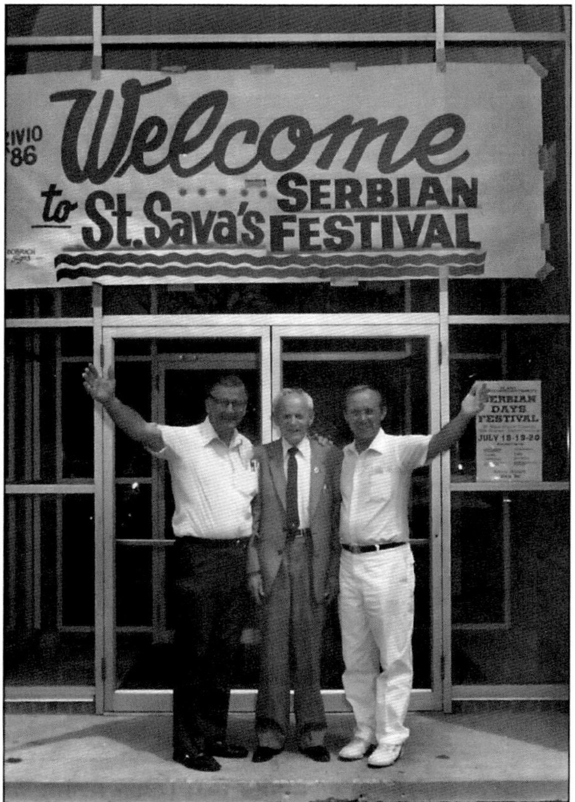

To celebrate and honor their Serbian heritage, Serbian Orthodox churches throughout the Chicagoland area hold Serb Fest events. These events bring together parishioners in a fun atmosphere and help keep the culture and traditions alive through food, music, and crafts. Pictured here, from left to right, are the organizers of the 1986 festival: Gordon Gerbick, Vlado Zegarac, and Ted Erceg. (Courtesy of St. Sava Serbian Orthodox Church, Merrillville, Indiana.)

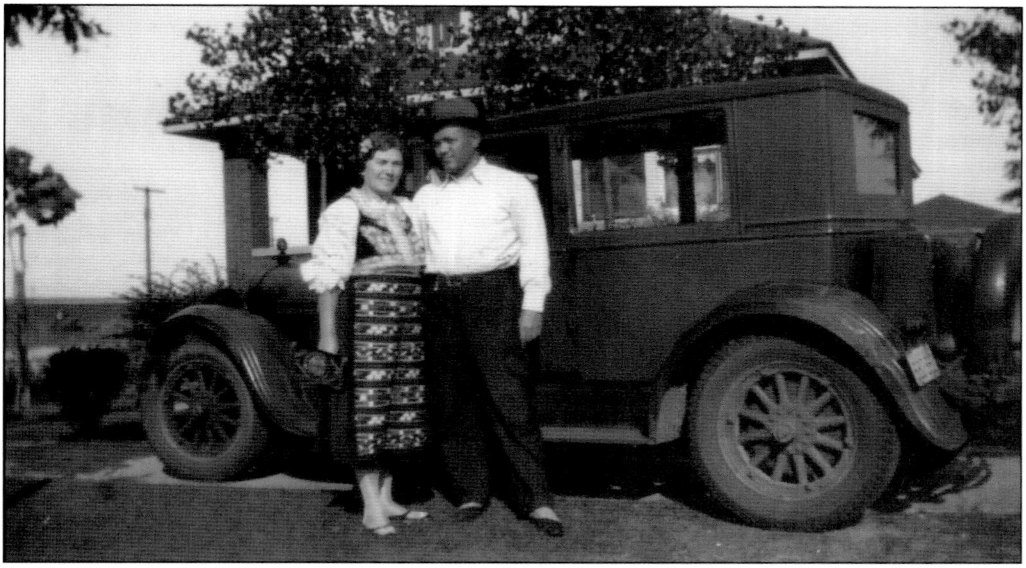

Godparenthood (*kumstvo*) holds a unique place in Serbian history and traditions. Its chief role is to educate the child in the ways of the religion, and in some Serbian Orthodox families, *kumovi* relationships can be traced through many generations. In this photograph from the 1920s, Dorothy (Babich) Lalich's godmother (*kuma*) Djordjevich is seen wearing a traditional *nošnja*. (Courtesy of Dorothy Lalich.)

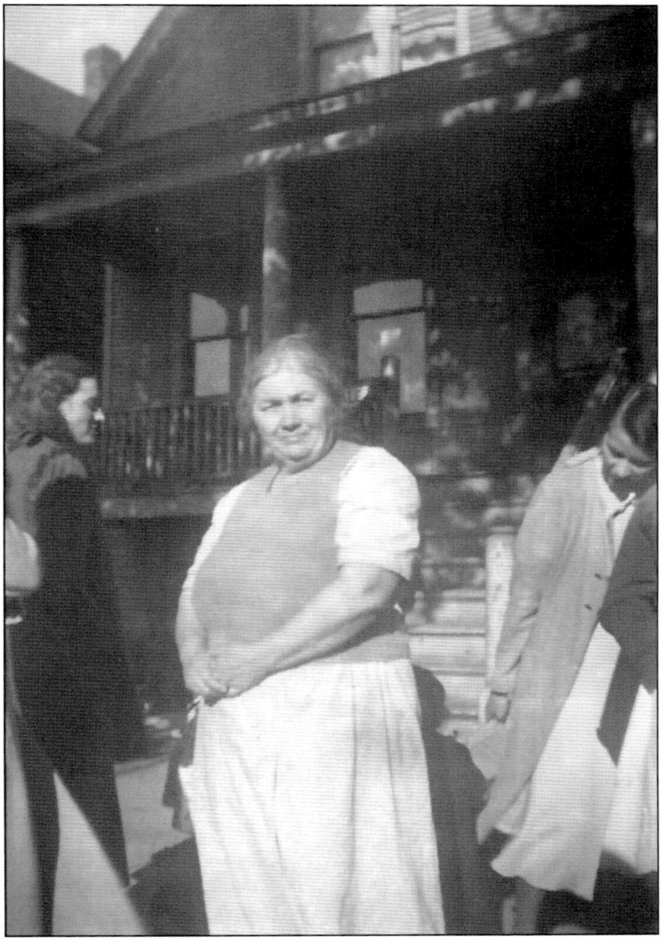

Ljubica (Lalich) Popovich stands in front of her house on Exchange Avenue in South Chicago. Many Serbian families lived in South Chicago, due to its proximity to several Serbian Orthodox churches and the steel mills where countless Serbs worked when they immigrated to the United States. (Courtesy of Ljubi Ostoich Hayden.)

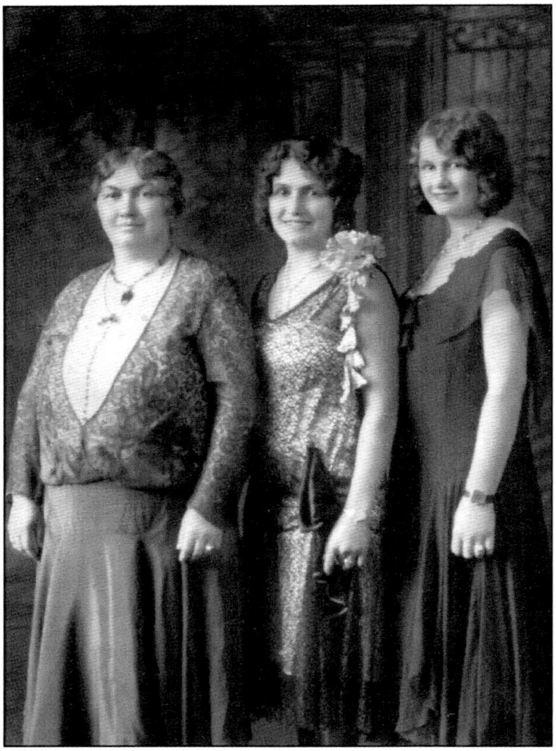

Wearing clothing associated with the times, three Serbian women pose in 1929 for a photograph. From left to right are Ljubica (Lalich) Popovich and her daughters, Cvjeta (Popovich) Knez, and Eva (Popovich) Grba. Popovich is the mother of the Popovich Brothers, world-renowned Serbian musicians, while Grba is the mother of Eli Grba—a former Major League Baseball pitcher who played for the New York Yankees and Los Angeles Angels. (Courtesy of Ljubi Ostoich Hayden.)

Funeral attendees in the 1920s posed for a photograph before proceeding to the cemetery for a burial. Serbian Orthodox tradition includes a wake the day before the burial, and a funeral service in a church prior to the burial service. A meal (*daca*) is held after the burial, and memorial services (*parastos*) are traditionally held 40 days, six months, and one year after burial. (Courtesy of St. George Serbian Orthodox Church, East Chicago, Indiana.)

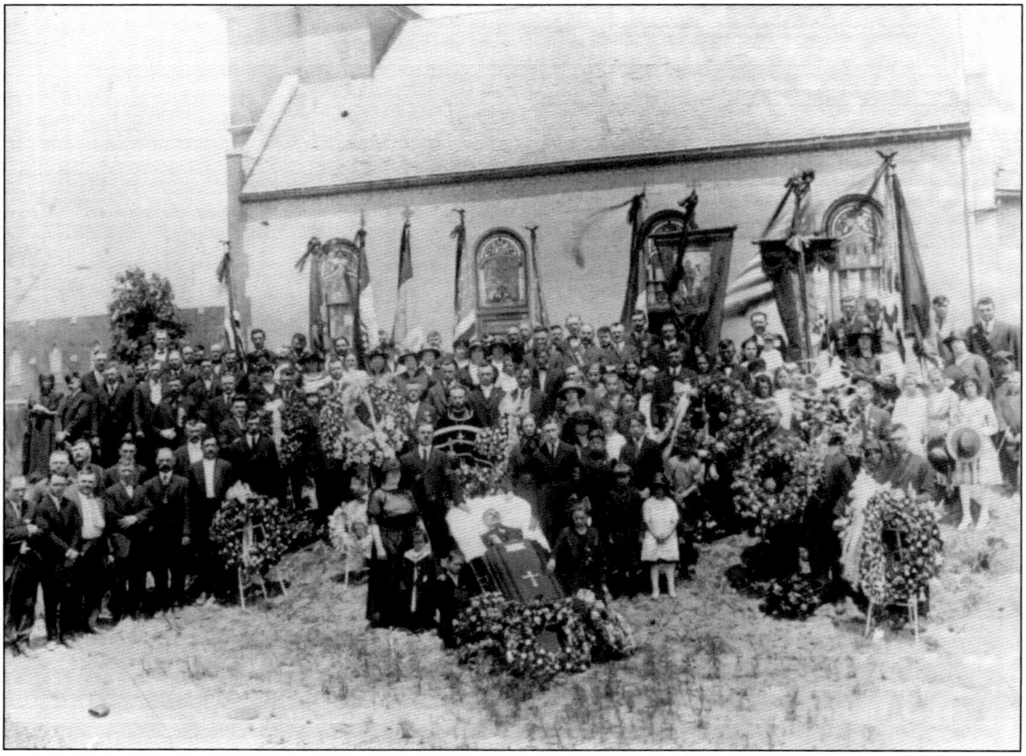

Two

Our People

With hundreds of thousands of Serbs having lived in the Chicagoland area throughout the years, it is no wonder that some have gone on to find fame, while others—who had already found it—shared their experiences with fellow Serbs in Chicago.

Immigrants inherently have an adventurous spirit, leaving behind families and friends for the promise of a better life in another country. It is, perhaps, this spirit that also encouraged them to explore entrepreneurial endeavors in their new countries. Throughout the Chicagoland area, Serbs have held leadership positions with various companies and owned businesses that cater to fellow Serbs and the community at large.

Serbs who lived in and around Chicago found ways to entertain their communities through song, dance, and drama, which help to define the Serbian identity. Even among the earliest immigrants to the Chicagoland area, Serbian plays, music, and songs were critical to maintaining the culture and traditions that honored their homeland. These performances fostered a love of the stage that helped to produce award-winning actors and musicians of Serbian descent.

Chicago has also witnessed its share of Serbian royalty. A member of the Serbian monarchy visited the city—and was once buried here—and the unofficial king of electricity left his mark in a very visible way in Chicago.

Most importantly, however, are the scores of unsung heroes in the Serbian American community in the Chicagoland area. These are the families who have lived in this area for generations and still maintain their Serbian culture and heritage. Some have never been to Serbia and yet the bond they have with their homeland is as strong as—and sometimes even stronger—than those who came after them. While their names and photographs may not appear on the following pages, they are represented throughout this book as the true picture of the Serbs of Chicagoland.

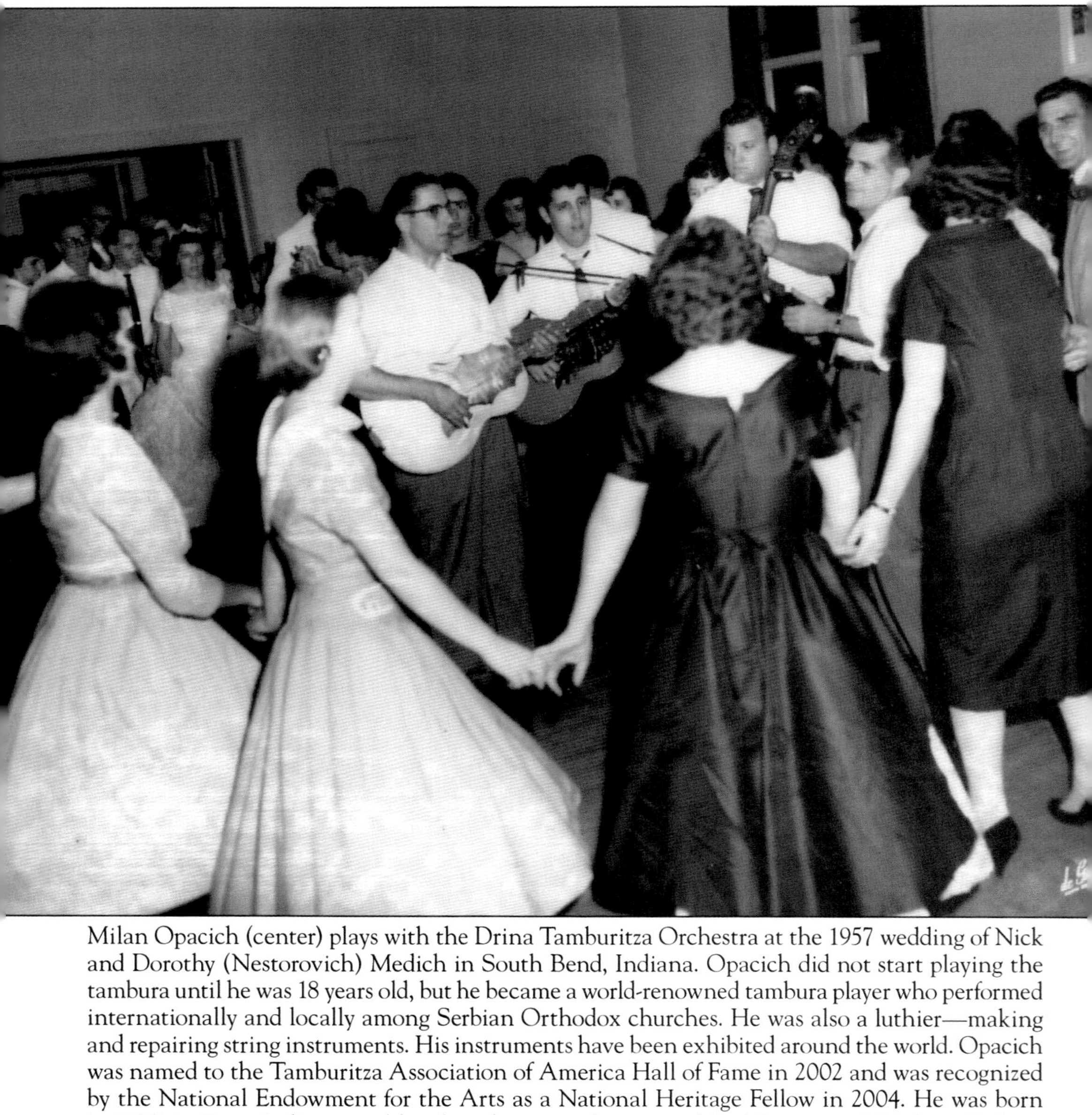

Milan Opacich (center) plays with the Drina Tamburitza Orchestra at the 1957 wedding of Nick and Dorothy (Nestorovich) Medich in South Bend, Indiana. Opacich did not start playing the tambura until he was 18 years old, but he became a world-renowned tambura player who performed internationally and locally among Serbian Orthodox churches. He was also a luthier—making and repairing string instruments. His instruments have been exhibited around the world. Opacich was named to the Tamburitza Association of America Hall of Fame in 2002 and was recognized by the National Endowment for the Arts as a National Heritage Fellow in 2004. He was born in 1928 in Gary, Indiana, and lived in the region his entire life. (Courtesy of St. Sava Serbian Orthodox Church, Merrillville, Indiana.)

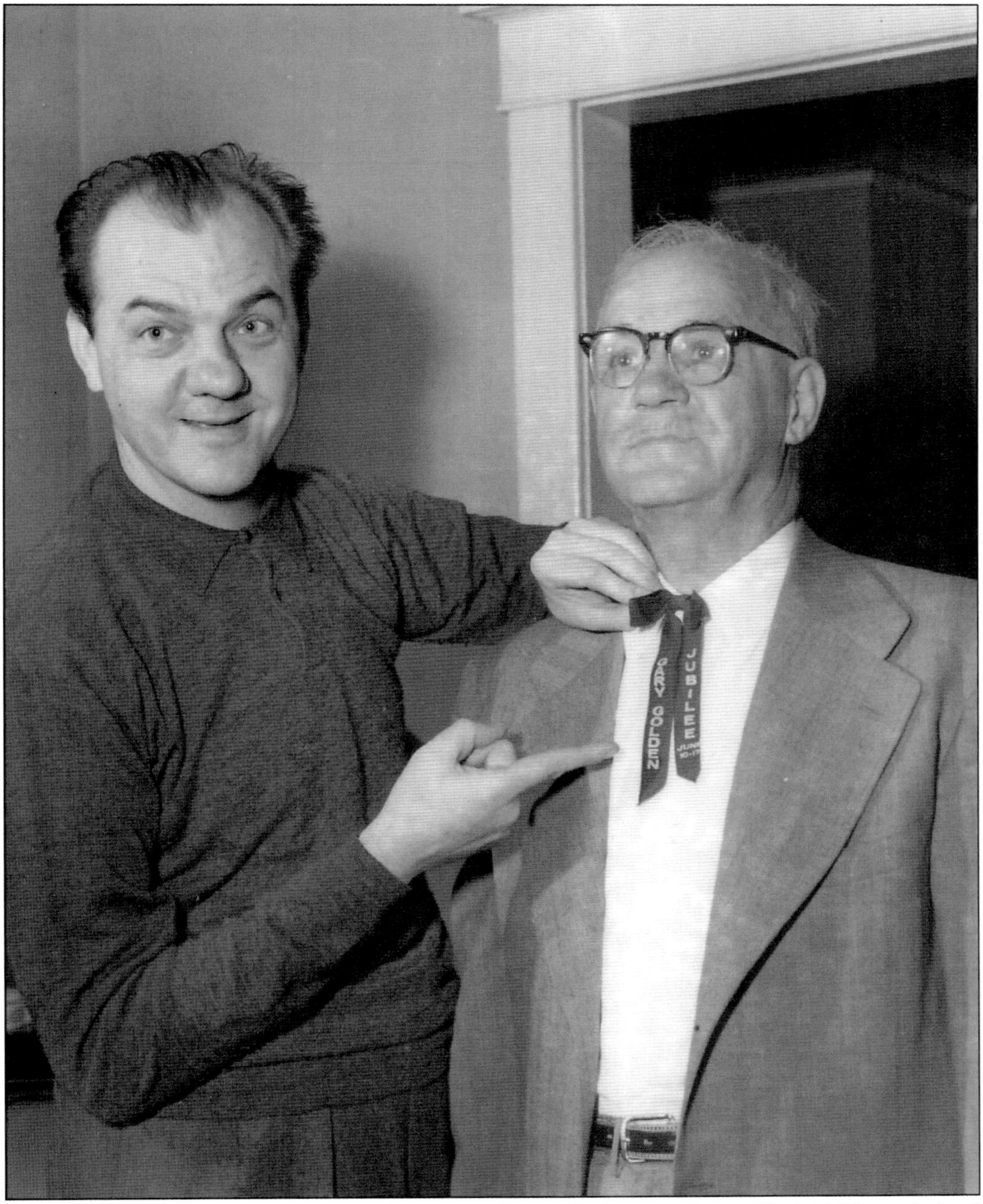

A young Mladen Sekulovich—better known to film and television fans as Karl Malden—helped his father, Petar, get ready for Gary's Golden Jubilee celebrations in 1956. Malden had already won an Academy Award for Best Supporting Actor for *A Streetcar Named Desire* when this photograph was taken. Malden was born in 1912 in Chicago and grew up in Gary, Indiana. For a few years, he worked in the same steel mills as his father before pursuing theater and acting full time. Malden was proud of his Serbian heritage and was very supportive of his family's church, St. Sava. Even after Malden became a famous actor, he returned to Gary and Northwest Indiana occasionally. In 1992, Malden and his family helped the church pay off its mortgage. (Courtesy of St. Sava Serbian Orthodox Church, Merrillville, Indiana.)

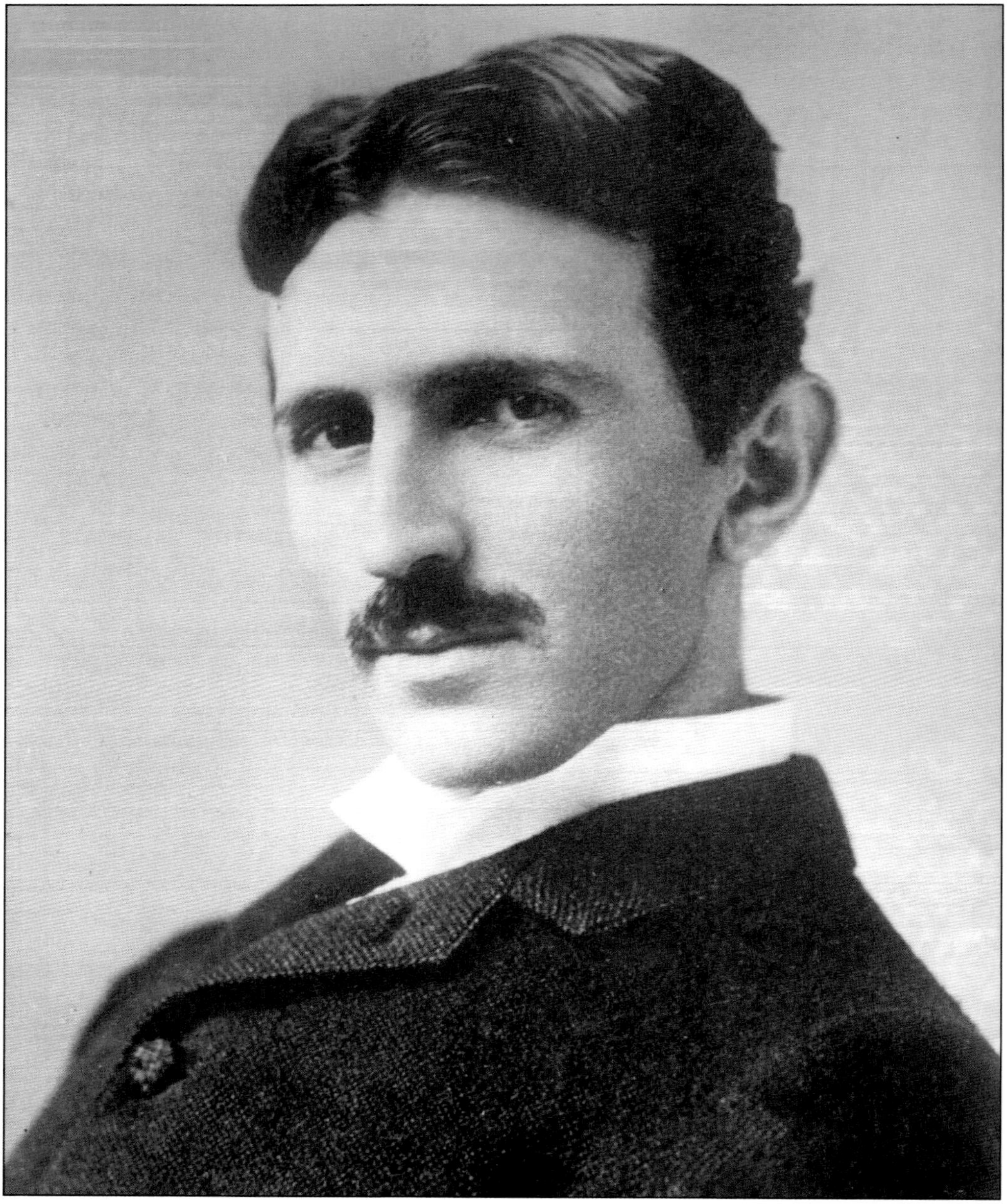

Born in 1856 to Serbian parents in modern-day Croatia, Nikola Tesla was an inventor and engineer who is most famous for the design of the alternating current electricity supply system. He moved to the United States as a young man and was working with George Westinghouse when Westinghouse won the contract to light the 1893 World's Columbian Exposition in Chicago with alternating current. At the exposition, Tesla demonstrated his invention. He became a naturalized United States citizen in 1891 and lived most of his life in hotels around New York. He never stopped inventing, and his experiments included early x-ray imaging and wireless products. He died in 1960, but has enjoyed a recent resurgence of interest and popularity thanks, in part, to Tesla Motors—whose name was inspired by the inventor. (Courtesy of Library of Congress, LC-B2- 1026-9 [P&P].)

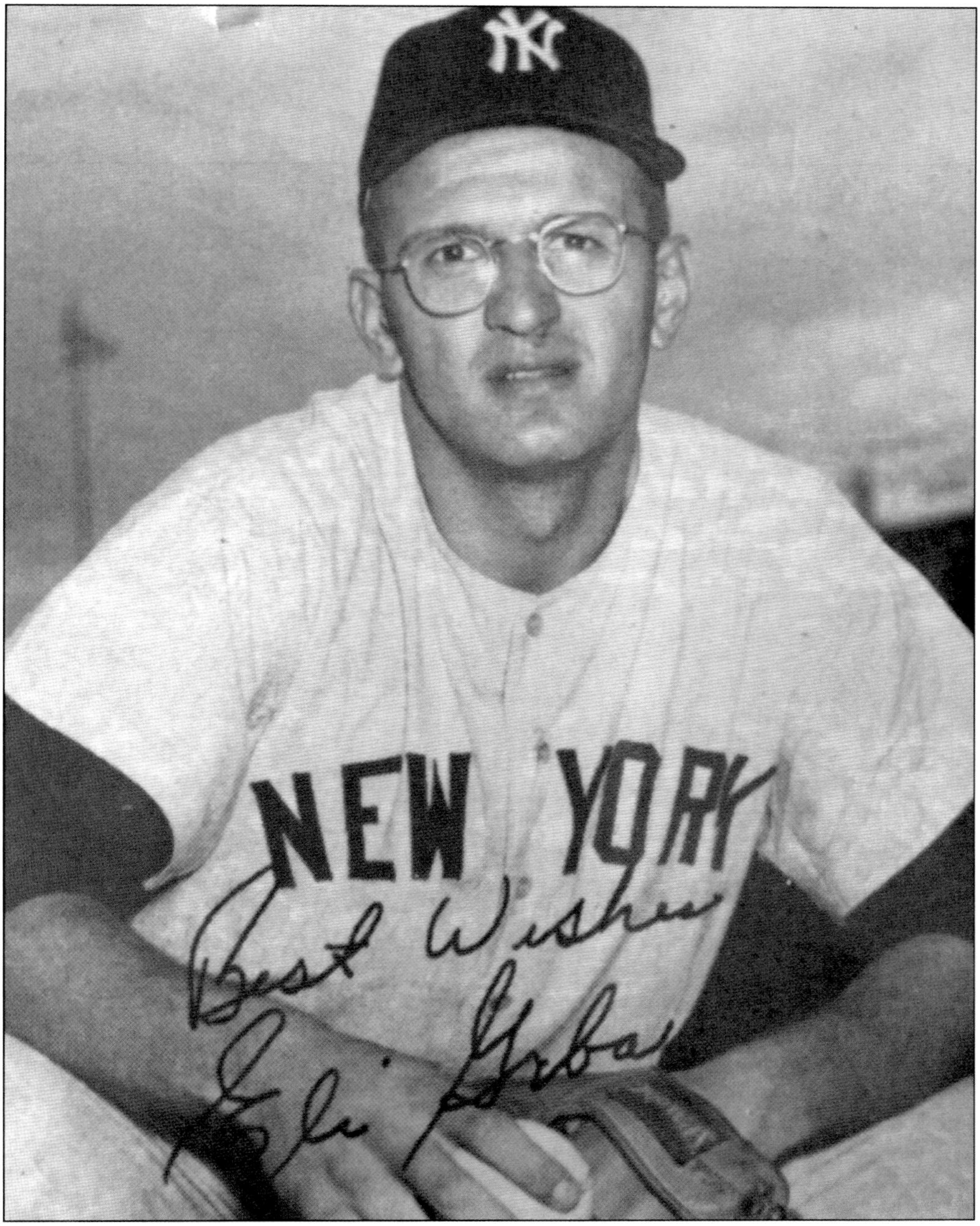

Eli Grba was born in Chicago to Serbian parents in 1934 and would go on to pitch for the New York Yankees and Los Angeles Angels between 1959 and 1963. He was a member of the 1960 American League champion New York Yankees team and was the first player drafted with the expansion Los Angeles Angels team. Whenever Grba played against the Chicago White Sox or Chicago Cubs, his Chicago-based family and friends came to watch. After he stopped playing baseball, he became a scout and coach before trying his hand at managing. As a child, Grba performed in church plays at the St. Archangel Michael Serbian Orthodox Church. (Courtesy of Dorothy Lalich.)

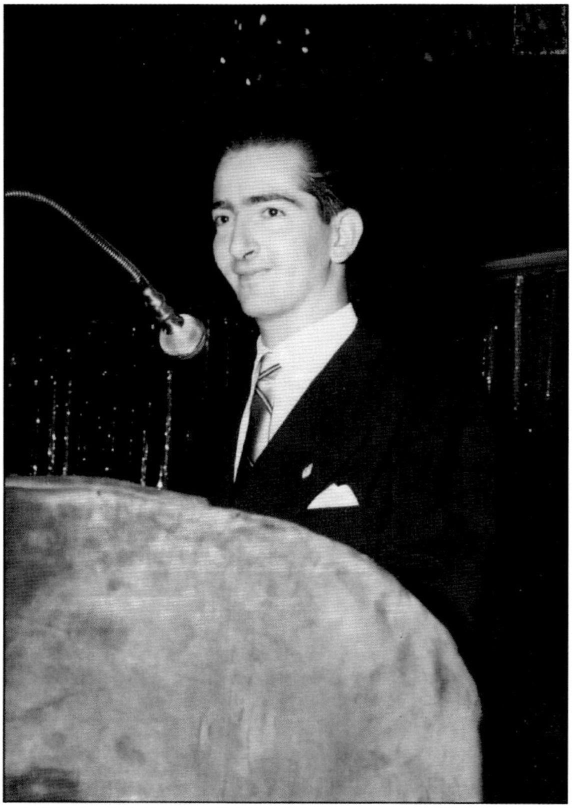

Peter II Karageorgevich (Karađorđević), the third and final king of Yugoslavia and last reigning member of the Karageorgevich dynasty, settled in the United States after being deposed by Yugoslavia's Communist Party in 1945. This photograph was taken during a visit to Chicago. He was buried at St. Sava Monastery in Libertyville, Illinois, until he was moved to Serbia in 2013 for reburial. (Courtesy of Dorothy Lalich.)

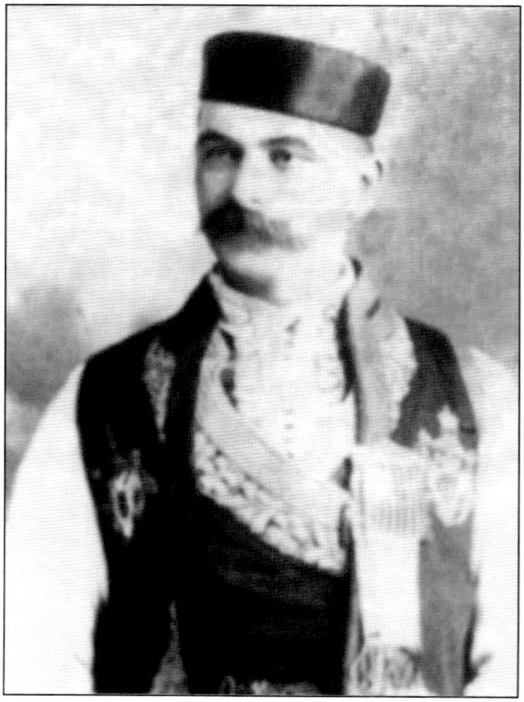

Ivan Vucetich was the first documented Serb to arrive in Chicago and remain here. Others came, but returned to Serbia or their villages. Ivan arrived in Chicago in July 1872, helped establish a variety of benevolent societies when the influx of Serbs arrived, and helped found the Holy Resurrection Serbian Orthodox Cathedral parish. (Courtesy of Holy Resurrection Serbian Orthodox Cathedral, Chicago, Illinois.)

Among the most recognized and popular Serbian musicians were the Popovich Brothers, who played tambura concerts around the world starting in 1926. Here, the Popovich Brothers entertain guests at a Serbian wedding in the early 1980s. Pictured are Bob Lalich, Ted Popovich, Pete Mistovich, and Adam Popovich, who also directed the Serbian Singing Society, Sloboda (Freedom), at the St. Archangel Michael Serbian Orthodox Church. (Courtesy of Dorothy Lalich.)

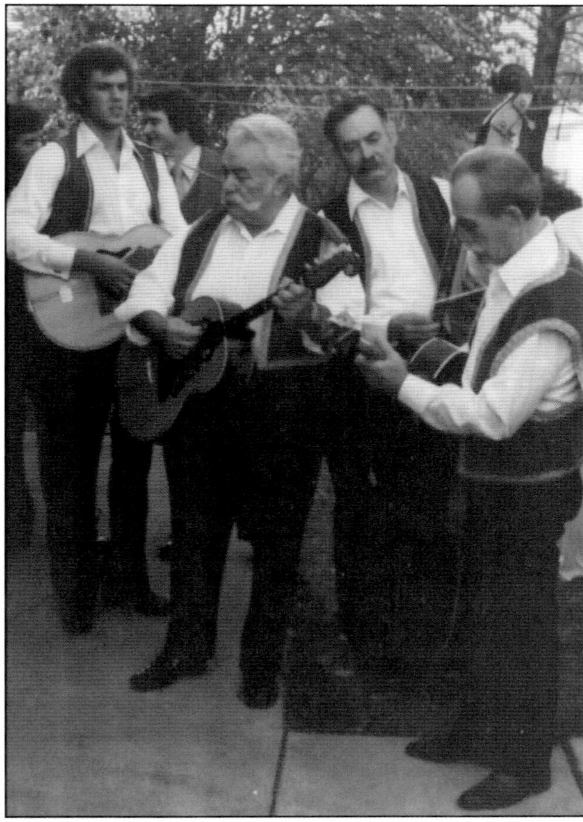

Sava Vrtikapa was very active in the St. Sava Serbian Orthodox Church in Gary, Indiana. In 1971, he was awarded the highest award that a layman working for his church can receive from the Serbian Orthodox Diocese, for his commitment to the Serbian community. He received other honors, including this one from a Serbian choir and folk dancing group in California. (Courtesy of St. Sava Serbian Orthodox Church, Merrillville, Indiana.)

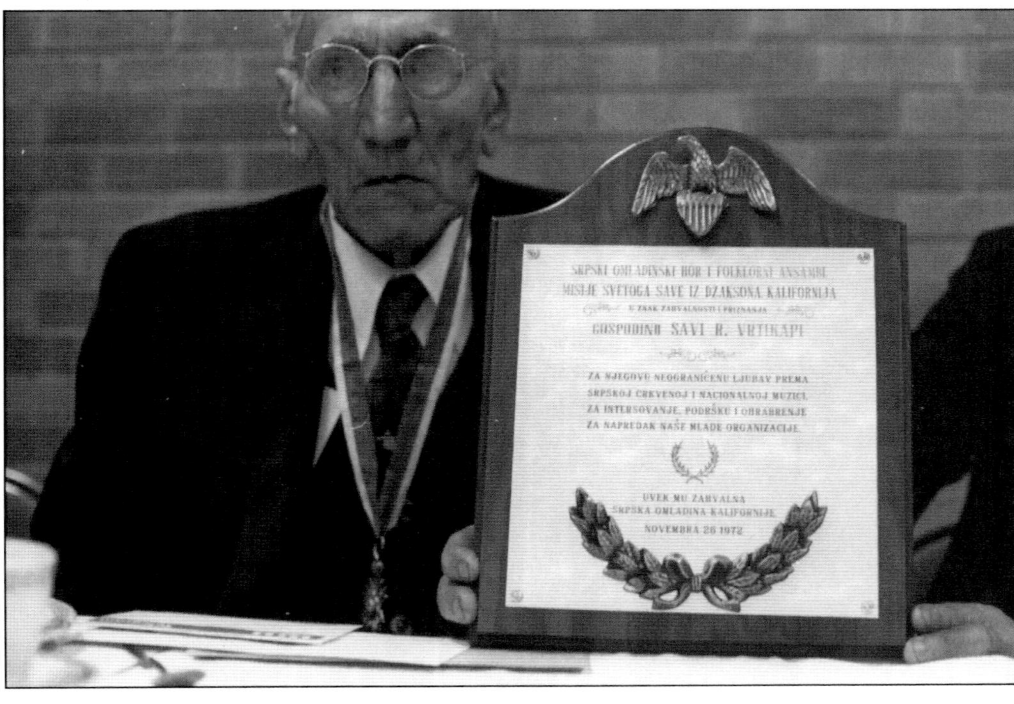

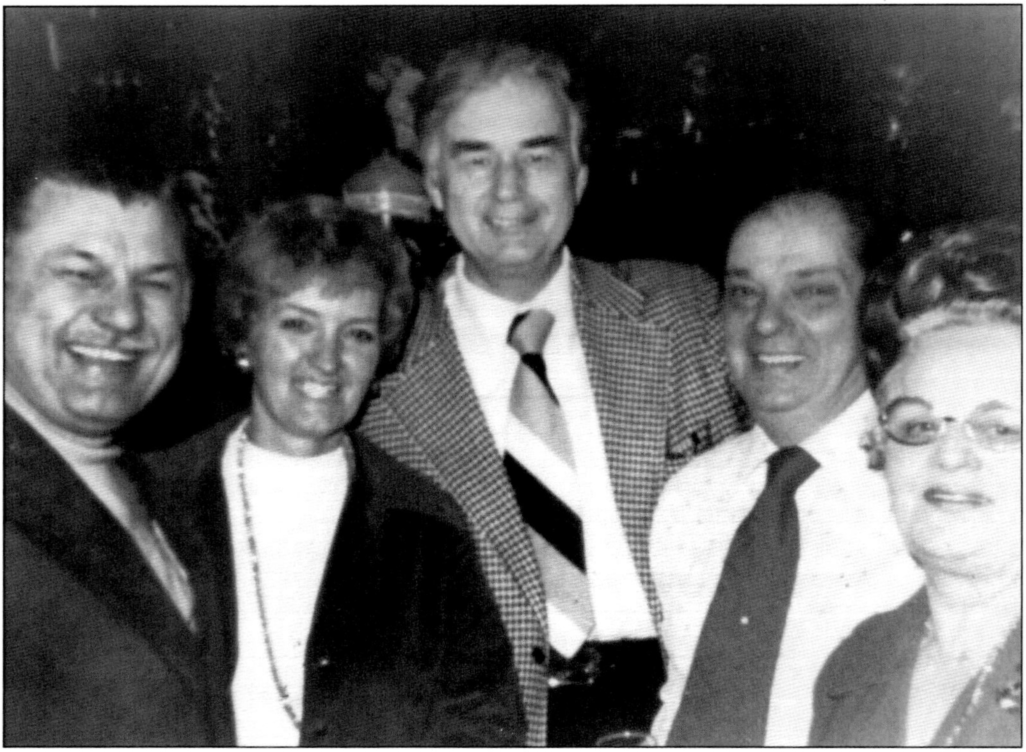

William "Bill" George Salatich, center, was born to Serbian immigrants in Chicago and became the president of Gillette North America. He received many commendations and awards, including one for instituting job training and opportunities for women and minorities in the 1970s. Salatich grew up on the north side of Chicago in a Serbian neighborhood and remained active with the Serbian American community. Pictured from left to right are Svetozar "Swats" Sarovich, Dorothy Lalich, Salatich, Kojo Klasnja, and Violet Klasnja. (Courtesy of Dorothy Lalich.)

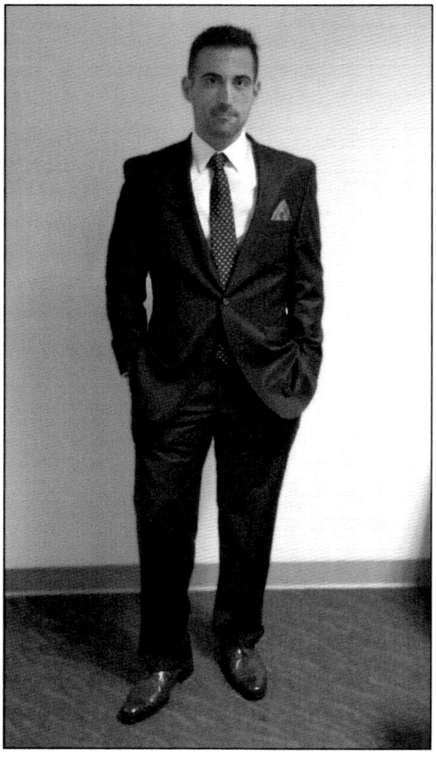

Toma Dobrosavljević was born in South Chicago, Illinois, to Serbian parents who immigrated to the United States in the mid-1970s. Dobrosavljević competed on and won Season 16 of the reality television series *The Biggest Loser*. He and his family belong to St. Archangel Michael Serbian Orthodox Church in Lansing, Illinois. (Courtesy of Toma Dobrosavljević.)

Three

Our Work

At the end of the 19th century, and well into the 20th, the steel mills that lined Lake Michigan lured in many immigrants with plentiful and well-paying jobs. Despite the long hours and oftentimes dangerous work, Serbs arriving in the Chicagoland area were eager to find a job that would support their families in the United States and, many times, back home.

Serbs also tapped into the familiar—catering to the increasing number of Serbian immigrants arriving in the Chicagoland area. They opened stores that carried Serbian goods, and restaurants that served Serbian food. Immigrants who didn't speak English well were able to meet others who could provide help and guidance.

Serbs who owned their own businesses often hired other Serbs, giving them a chance at improving their own station in life. In addition, part of the American dream included owning something of one's own. For some, owning a business fulfilled that promise—proving that the struggle of moving to a new country was worth it. Today, there are a variety of businesses throughout the Chicagoland area that cater to Serbs and those who enjoy Serbian food and music.

Over time, as more and more Americans of Serbian descent grew up in the United States, their professions have expanded. They have served in public office, worked as doctors and scientists, entertained the masses on stage and screen, and made a living to support their families like any other citizen.

The new wave of immigrants may face some of the same challenges as those who came a century before them. If the success stories of those before them are any indication, however, they too will find ways to build their lives here.

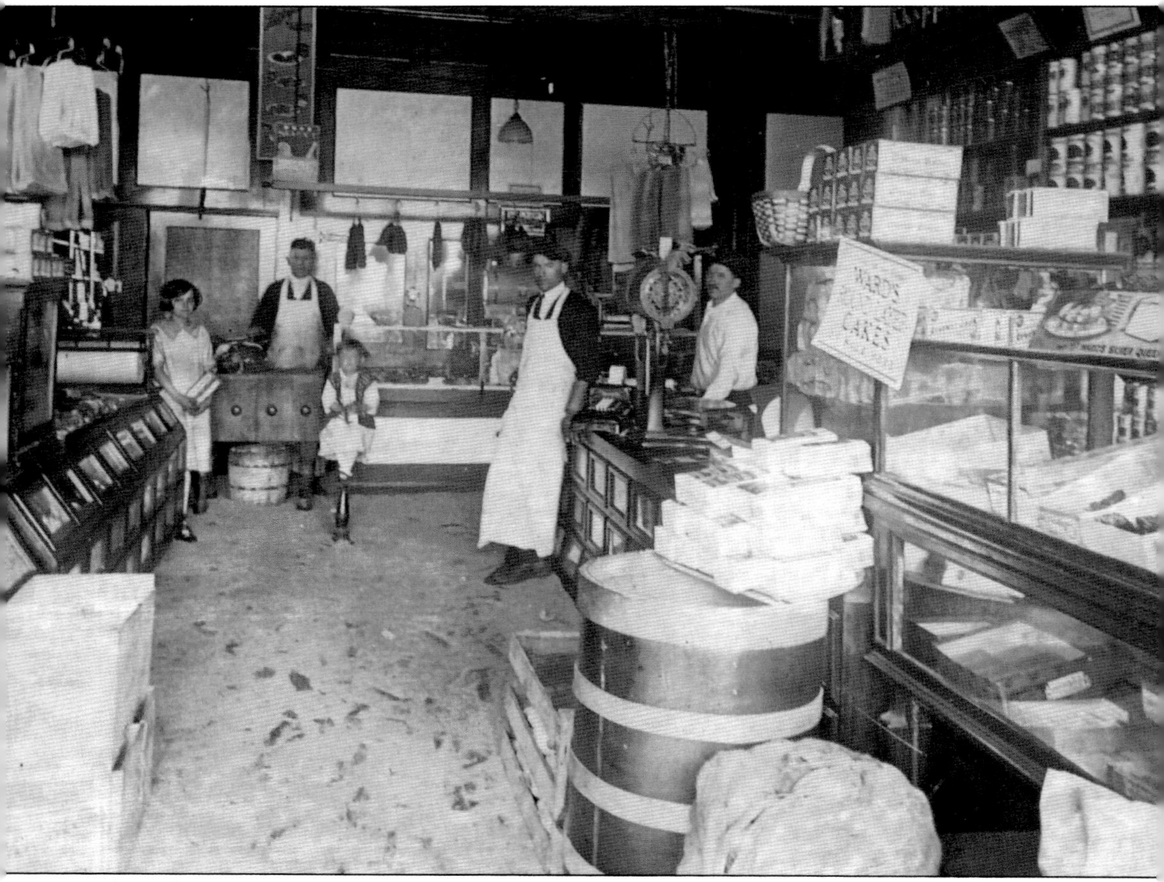

The Adamovich family opened a general store and delicatessen next door to their saloon, where customers could purchase Serbian food as well as school supplies, ice cream, and candy. Many Serbs settled in the area and would shop at Serbian-owned stores or stores with employees who spoke Serbian. The Adamovich family lived directly behind the store. Both buildings are still located in the same spot and are occupied by other businesses. (Courtesy of Dorothy Lalich.)

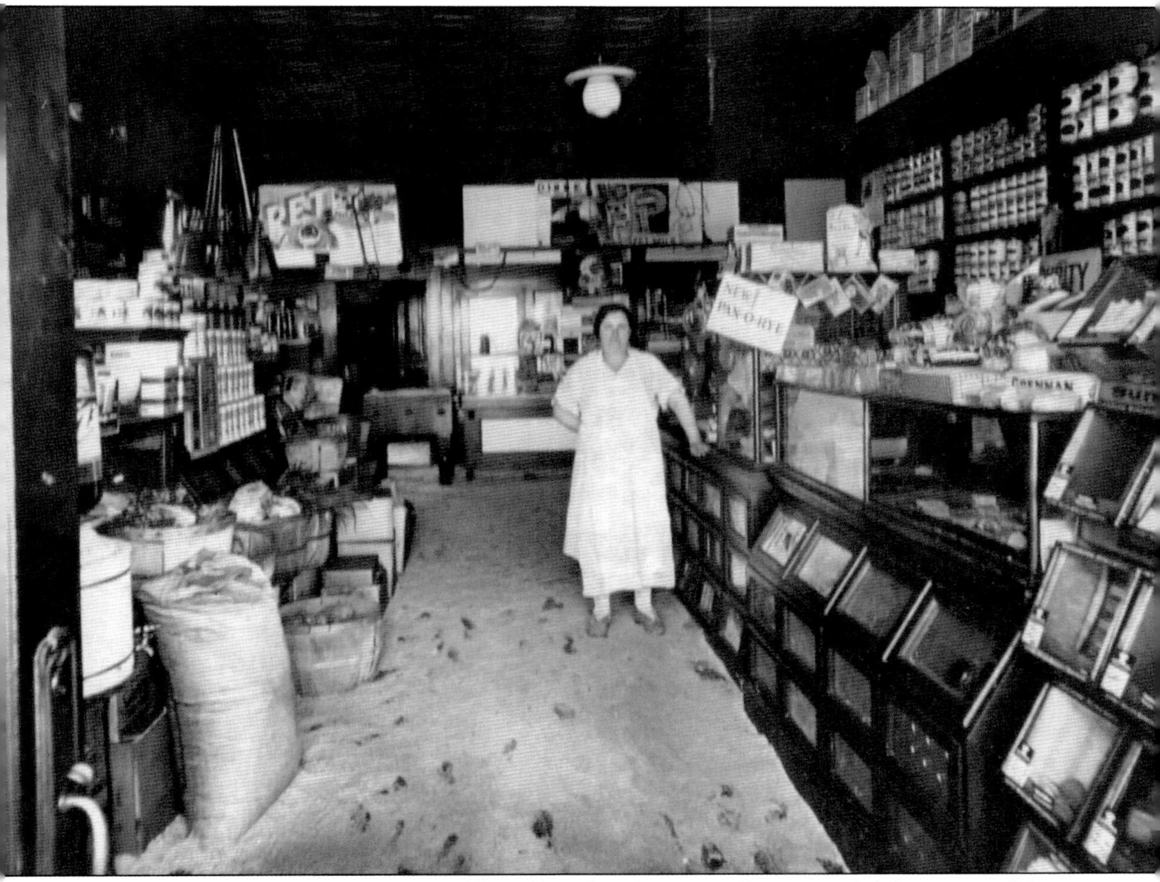

Vasilija Adamovich stands in the middle of her family's general store and delicatessen. Many Serbian immigrants lived near the store, which was located near one of the largest Serbian Orthodox churches in the area. Stores like this were a welcome place for immigrants who did not speak English well. (Courtesy of Dorothy Lalich.)

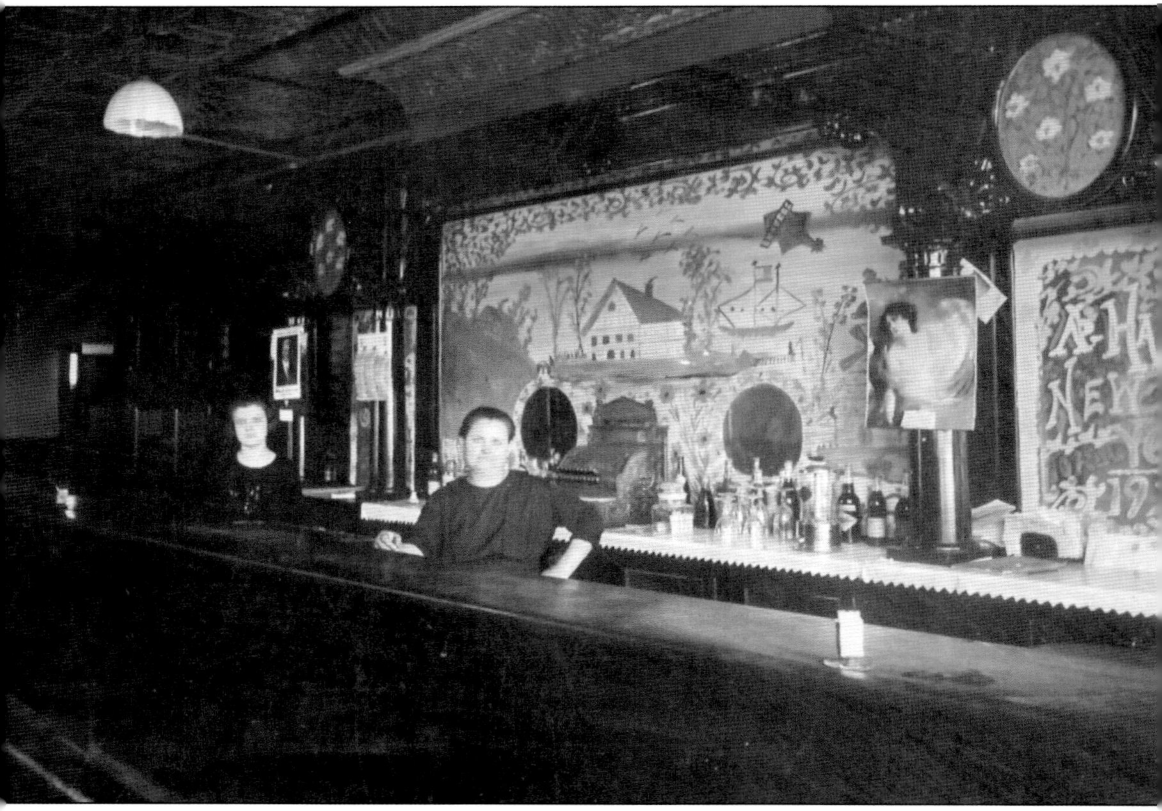

The Adamovich family owned a saloon in South Chicago near many Serbs—and blocks away from the St. Archangel Serbian Orthodox Church. The family lived behind the saloon. After Nick Adamovich died in 1923, his wife, Vasilija Adamovich (right), took over the saloon in order to keep it open. Also pictured is their daughter Milka Adamovich. (Courtesy of Dorothy Lalich.)

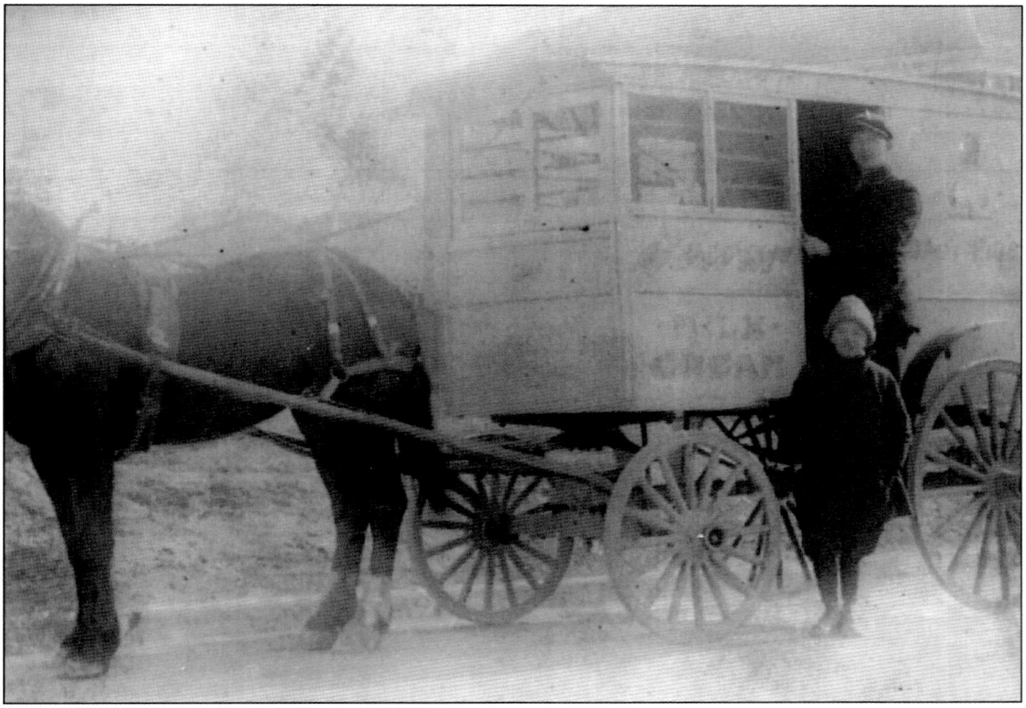

Serbian immigrants worked a variety of jobs. This photograph, taken on April 18, 1932, shows Daniel Narancich and Rudy Kovachević, who delivered Cloverfield Dairy's milk by horse and buggy in Gary, Indiana. Mitchell Duchich, a prominent Serbian leader and former Gary, Indiana, alderman, owned the company and helped to hire Serbs looking for employment. (Courtesy of St. Sava Serbian Orthodox Church, Merrillville, Indiana.)

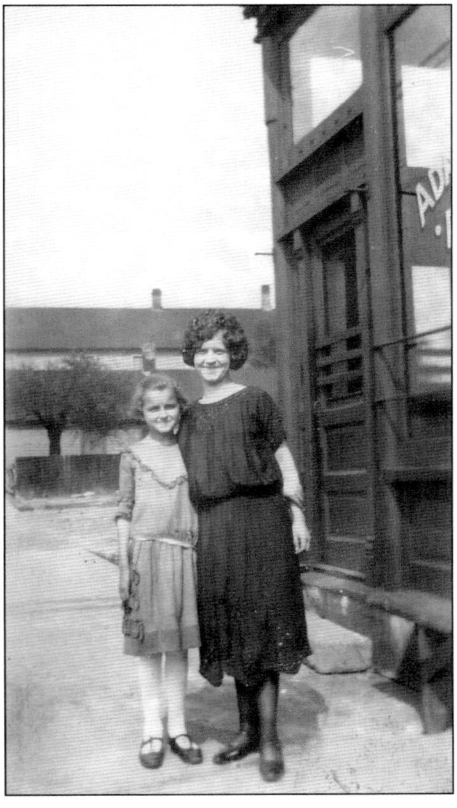

Milka Adamovich (right) stands in front of her family's store and saloon in South Chicago in the late 1920s. Also pictured is her sister, Bea (Adamovich) Anderson. Serb-owned stores often hired Serbs, and employees spoke Serbian to help immigrants who were not yet fluent in English. In the background is a building owned by their uncle, Petar Krneta, who also operated a saloon in part of the building. (Courtesy of Dorothy Lalich.)

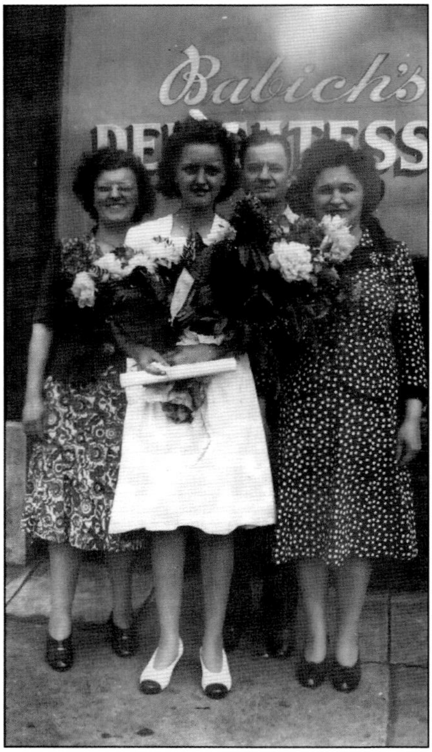

When Milka (Adamovich) Babich (left) married Stanko "Sam" Babich (second from right), they took over the Adamovich store and renamed it Babich's Delicatessen. Also pictured is their daughter, Dorothy Babich, on her eighth grade graduation day in 1944 and her kuma, Dorothy Adich—after whom Dorothy was named. (Courtesy of Dorothy Lalich.)

This is a 1928 view of a typical Chicago street in the South Chicago neighborhood near where many Serbians lived and worked. This photograph looks east along Ninety-second Street, from a point east of Commercial Avenue. Lining the streets are various businesses run by immigrants from all over the world. (Courtesy of Dorothy Lalich.)

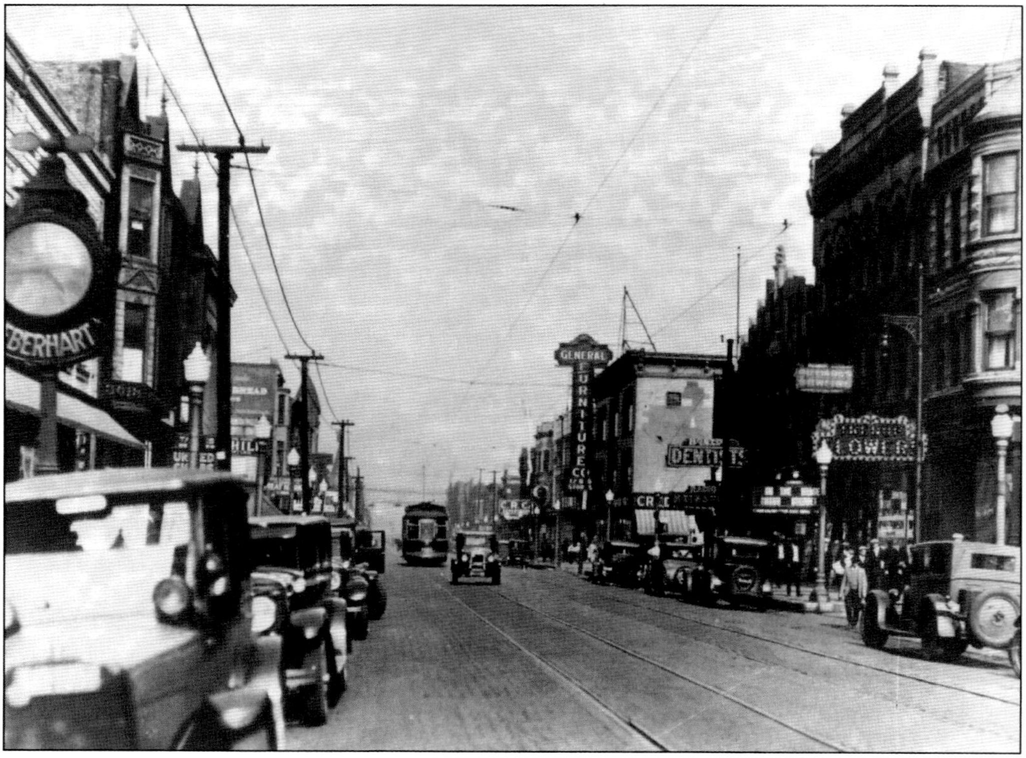

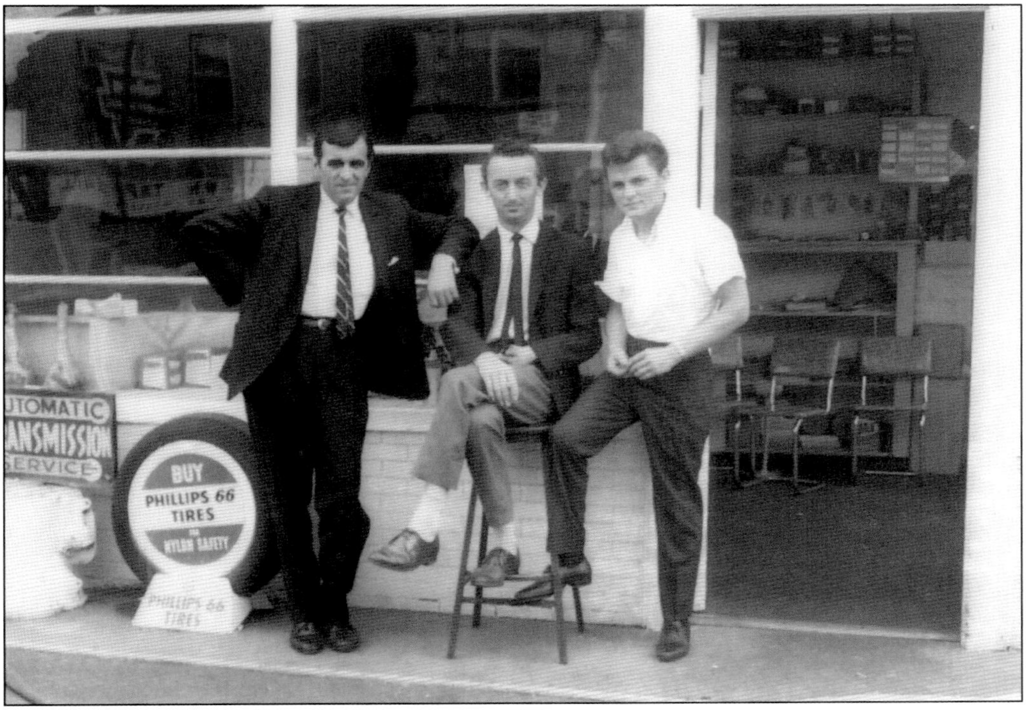

In the 1950s, the Kukrika family owned a gas station and car repair business in Gary, Indiana. Many Serbian American immigrants had an entrepreneurial spirit and opened their own businesses throughout the region. Pictured from left to right are Djuro Kukrika, Boro Ilich, and Milos Bogdanich. (Courtesy of St. Sava Serbian Orthodox Church, Merrillville, Indiana.)

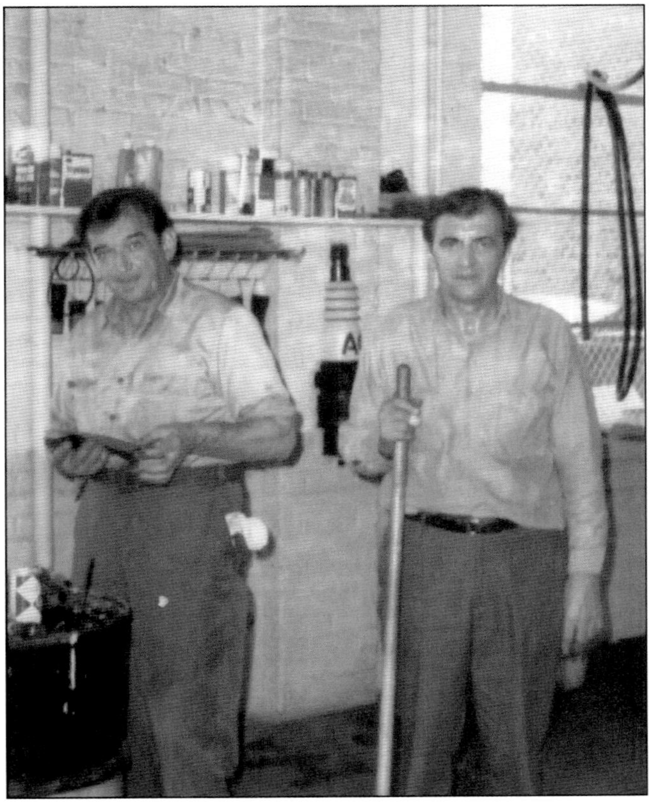

Family businesses were passed down from generation to generation. Here, the Kukrika family provides car care services to the Gary, Indiana, community in the 1960s. Pictured are Petar Kukrika (left) and his brother Djuro Kukrika. (Courtesy of St. Sava Serbian Orthodox Church, Merrillville, Indiana.)

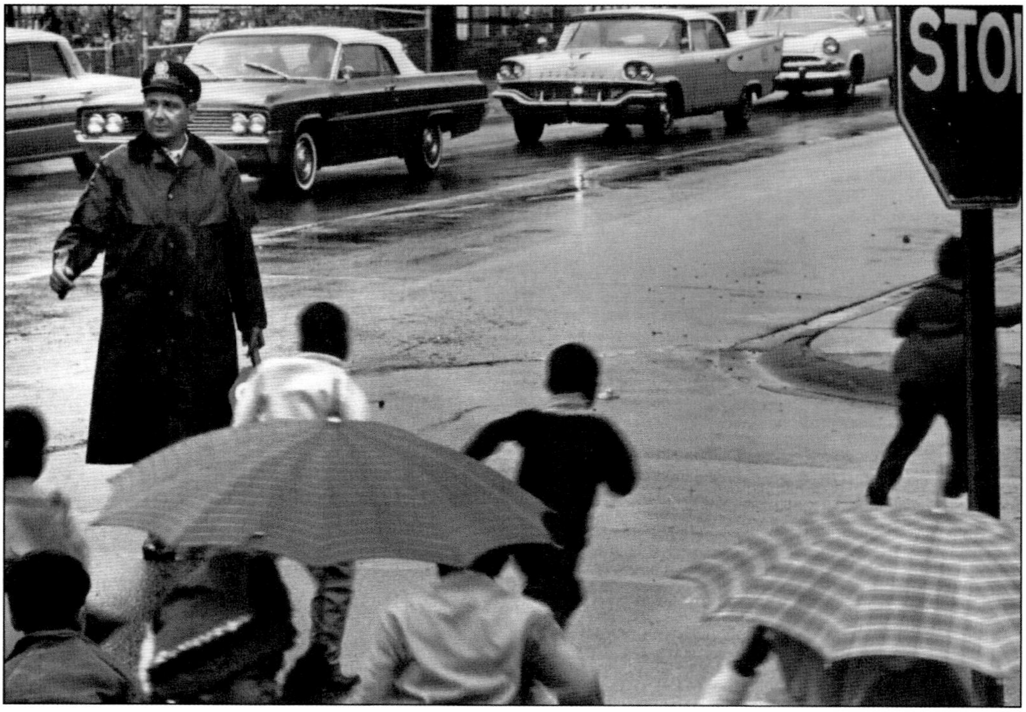

As more Serbian Americans were born and raised in Chicago, they found jobs outside the steel mills. Some worked as public servants and police officers. Pictured here is Donald Sekulich, a Serbian American police officer in the 1950s in Gary, Indiana. (Courtesy of St. Sava Serbian Orthodox Church, Merrillville, Indiana.)

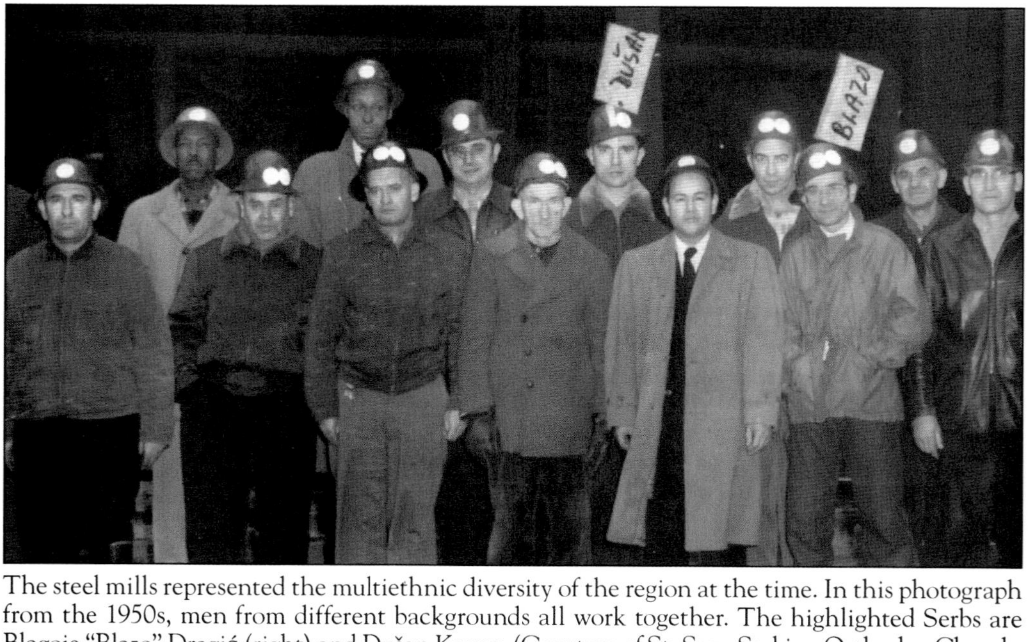

The steel mills represented the multiethnic diversity of the region at the time. In this photograph from the 1950s, men from different backgrounds all work together. The highlighted Serbs are Blagoje "Blazo" Dragić (right) and Dušan Kovac. (Courtesy of St. Sava Serbian Orthodox Church, Merrillville, Indiana.)

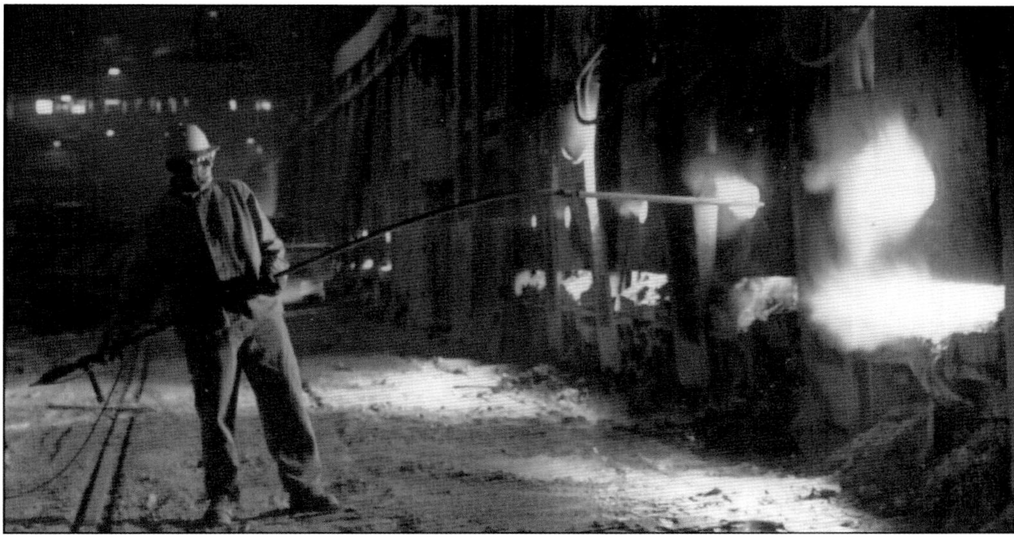

Working in a steel mill was dangerous. For Serbian immigrants to Chicago, however, it represented a chance at a better financial life for themselves and their families. Untold numbers of Serbs, including Stevo Rodich (pictured), worked at the many different steel mills located throughout the Chicagoland area. (Courtesy of St. Sava Serbian Orthodox Church, Merrillville, Indiana.)

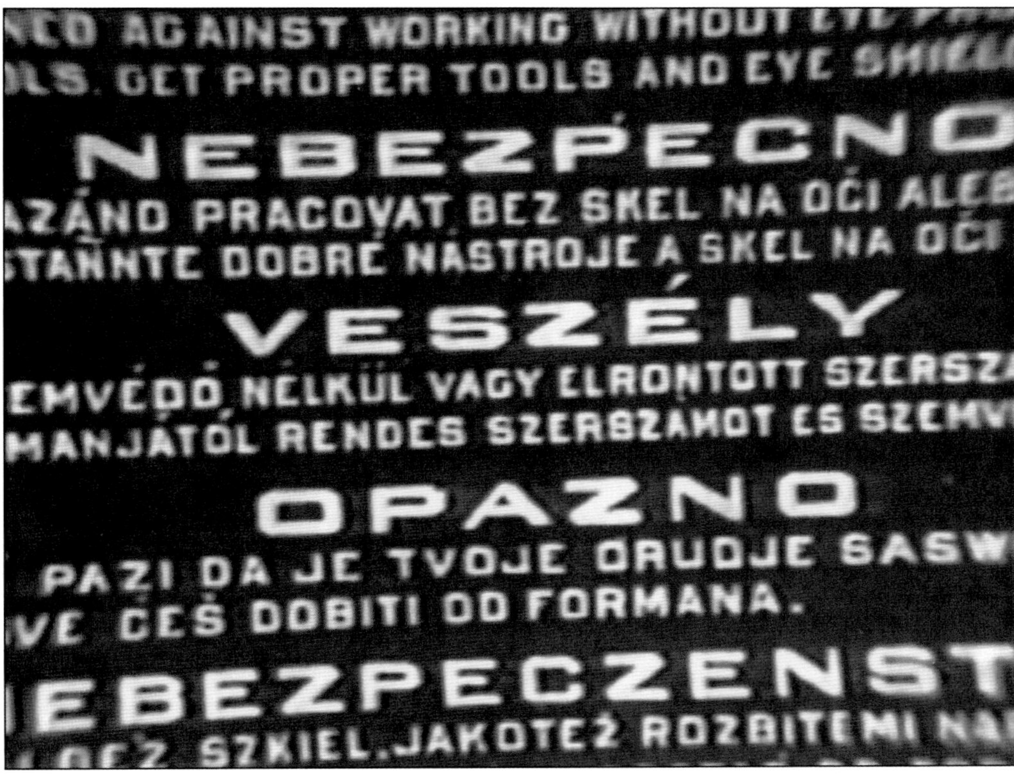

It was common to see instructions and information printed in the many different languages of immigrant workers at the steel mills. Pictured here is a poster that includes a warning (*opazno*) in Serbian for workers to be aware of a danger. (Courtesy of Calumet Regional Archives.)

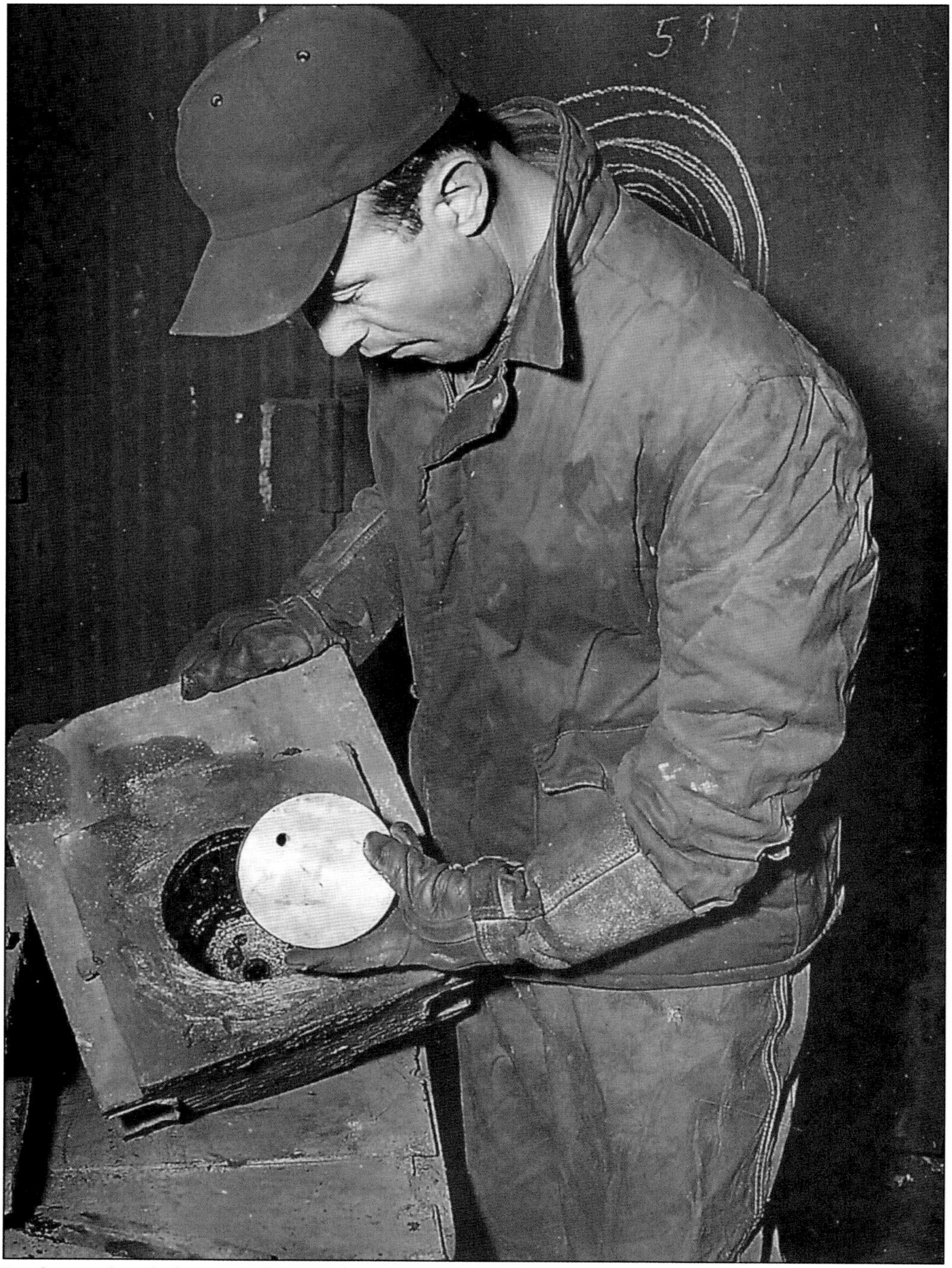

In this undated photograph, a Serbian man works at a steel mill in the Chicagoland area. The steel mills represented an opportunity for men arriving from Serbia and looking to improve their economic outlook and send money back home to relatives. Among the steel companies operating at the time were U.S. Steel, Republic Steel, Inland Steel, and Wisconsin Steel. (Courtesy of St. Sava Serbian Orthodox Church, Merrillville, Indiana.)

Four

Our Organizations

Serbs began to form fraternal, youth, and women's organizations almost as soon as they arrived in the United States at the end of the 19th century. These societies provided a way for newly arrived immigrants to meet other Serbs and preserve their culture and language. It was also a way for them to rely on each other in a new land.

Among the earliest organizations was the Serb National Federation, whose roots date back to 1901. Initially called Srbobran, the organization merged over time with similar fraternal organizations such as Sloga, Sloboda, and others before officially incorporating as the Serb National Federation (SNF) in 1929. At least two other societies, Obilich and Jedinstvo, have merged with SNF over the years—forming the oldest and largest Serbian fraternal organization. In its earliest days, the SNF provided critical sick and death benefits to its members, who often did not have insurance. Today, the member-supported organization continues to provide life insurance. Socially, the SNF hosts annual athletic tournaments in a variety of sports that rotate among Serbian churches across North America.

There were also independent women's organizations founded by Serbian women. The leading group was the Circle of Serbian Sisters (Kolo Srpskih Sestara), which was originally established in Belgrade in 1903 and helped maintain and encourage Serbian culture. Regional offices were set up at Serbian Orthodox churches in many cities, including in Chicago. The society was banned in Serbia in 1941 but was restored in 1990. Members then resumed visiting and caring for the elderly, sick, poor, and vulnerable. In the United States, the Circle of Serbian Sisters remained active without interruption, with some groups dating back more than 85 years. The group continues to raise funds to support churches and various church activities, as well as raise awareness of Serbian culture and traditions.

Today, new generations of Serbs are forming additional societies in fields such as medicine and law, which honor Serbian heritage while also reflecting the changing professions of those with Serbian ancestry.

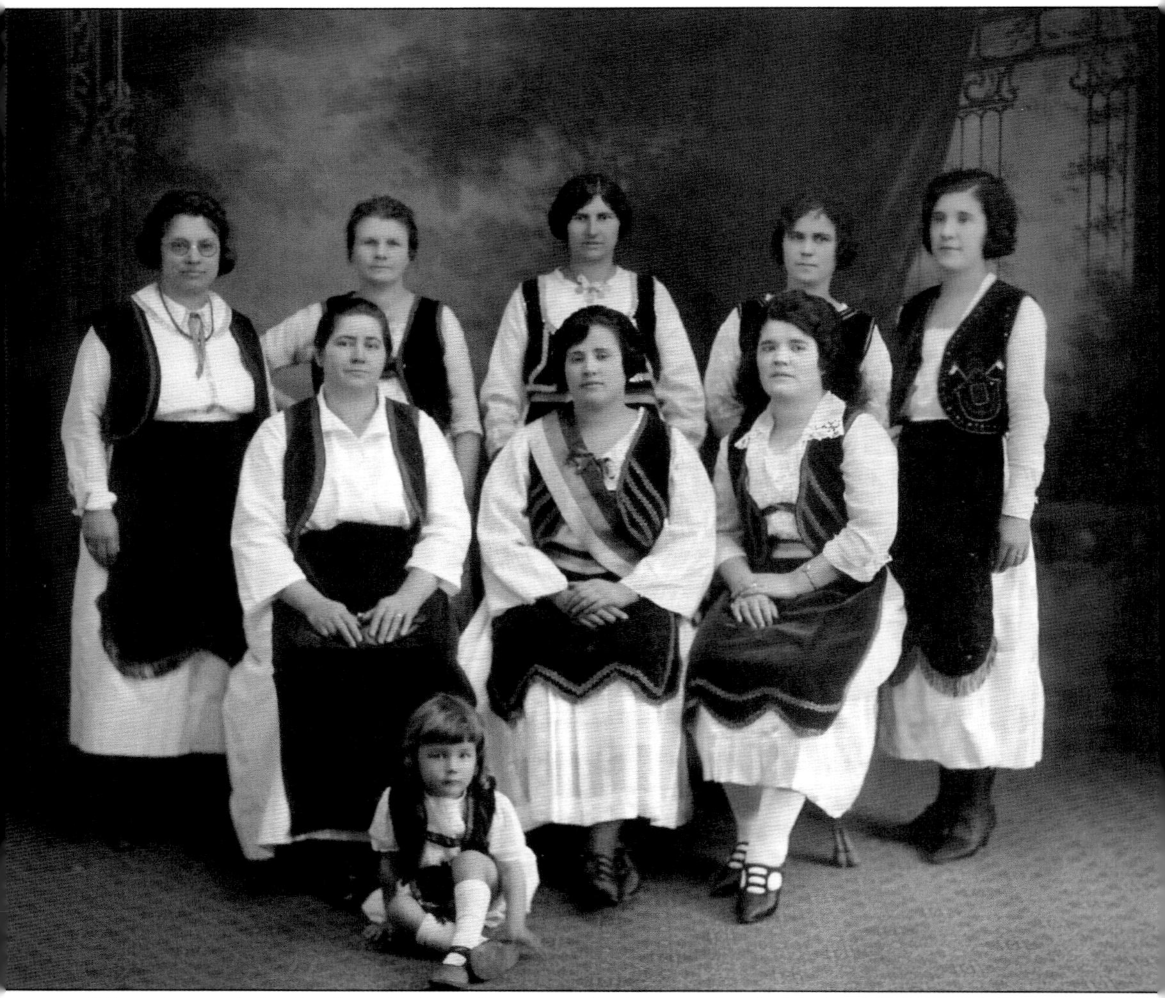

The origins of the Circle of Serbian Sisters in the Chicagoland area date back to the 1920s. The Circle of Serbian Sisters is a charitable society that is credited with helping to maintain Serbian culture and pride while also raising money for worthwhile causes both inside and outside the church. Membership in the group grew incrementally over the years. Today, the Circle of Serbian Sisters is still active in most, if not all, of the Serbian Orthodox churches in the Chicagoland area. Here, the group from St. Sava Serbian Orthodox Church in Gary, Indiana, pose in the 1920s with the group's leader—their kuma, Milka Rapaich (center), who also served as president of the organization. The members are wearing traditional Serbian nošnje, which members are known to still wear for special occasions. (Courtesy of St. Sava Serbian Orthodox Church, Merrillville, Indiana.)

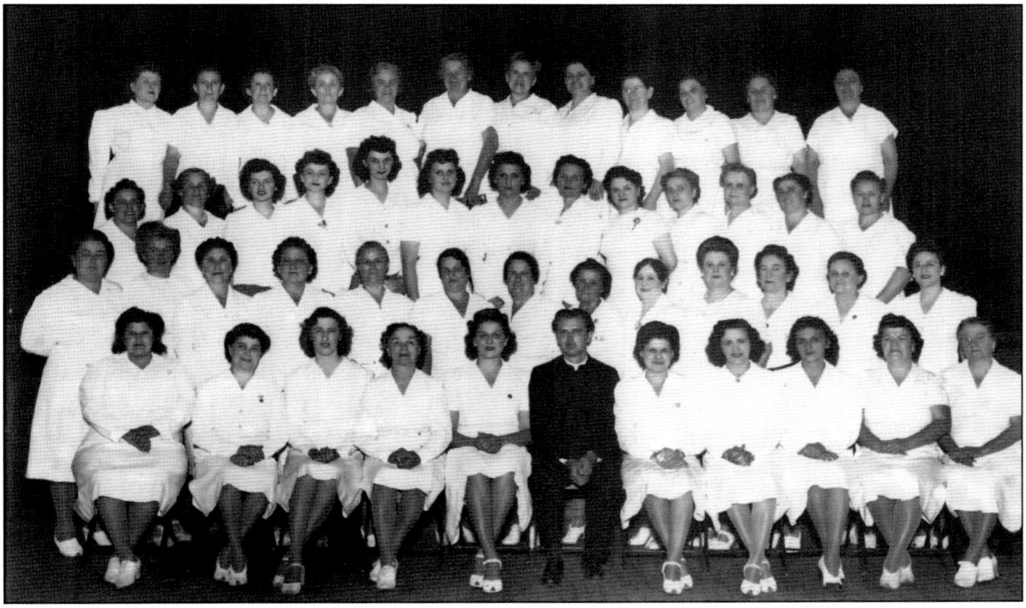

A big part of a Serbian Orthodox church's financial success rested on the shoulders of the Circle of Serbian Sisters, which raised money to support different initiatives at the church. In 1933, Rev. Vladimir Mrvichin poses with members of the group from the St. Sava Serbian Orthodox Church, who were very active at the church and in the community. (Courtesy of St. Sava Serbian Orthodox Church, Merrillville, Indiana.)

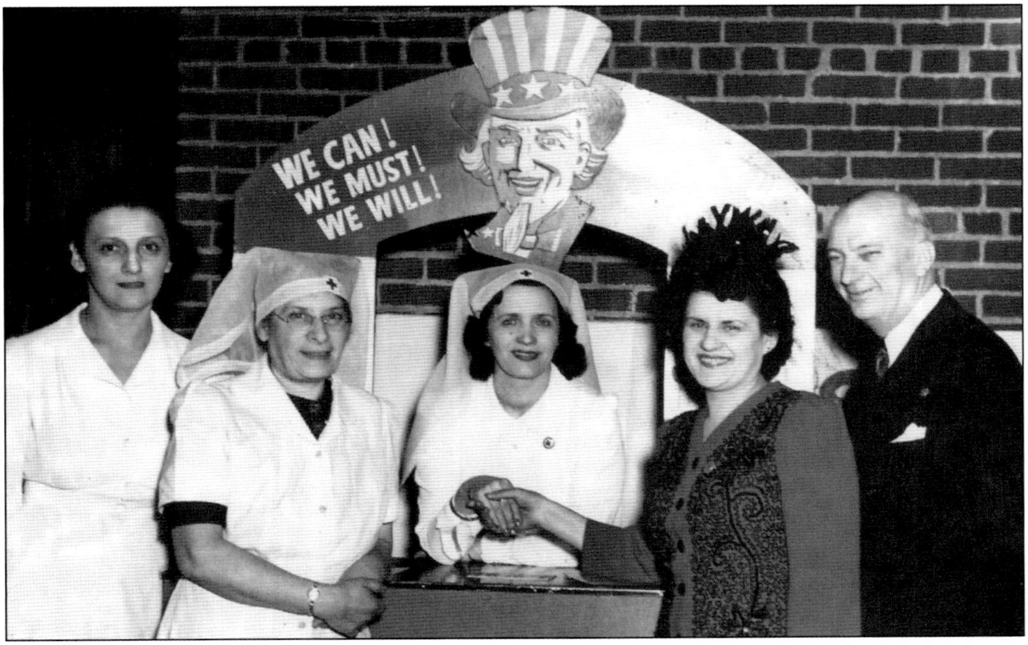

Serbian American parishioners were members of the Circle of Serbian Sisters, which helped raise money for war bonds. The Circle existed in part to help those in need. Volunteering with the Red Cross was a natural extension of the work the parishioners at St. Sava Serbian Orthodox Church were already doing. (Courtesy of St. Sava Serbian Orthodox Church, Merrillville, Indiana.)

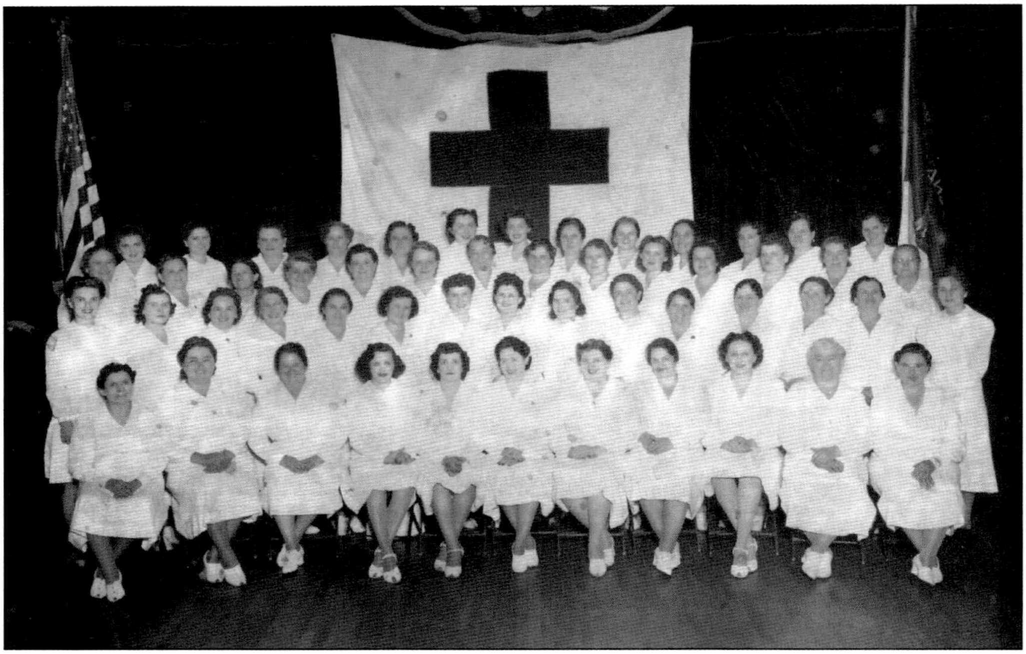

World War II presented an opportunity for the Circle of Serbian Sisters to put their skills to use and volunteer with the war effort. This photograph, taken between 1938 and 1940, includes a strong showing of members. (Courtesy of St. Sava Serbian Orthodox Church, Merrillville, Indiana.)

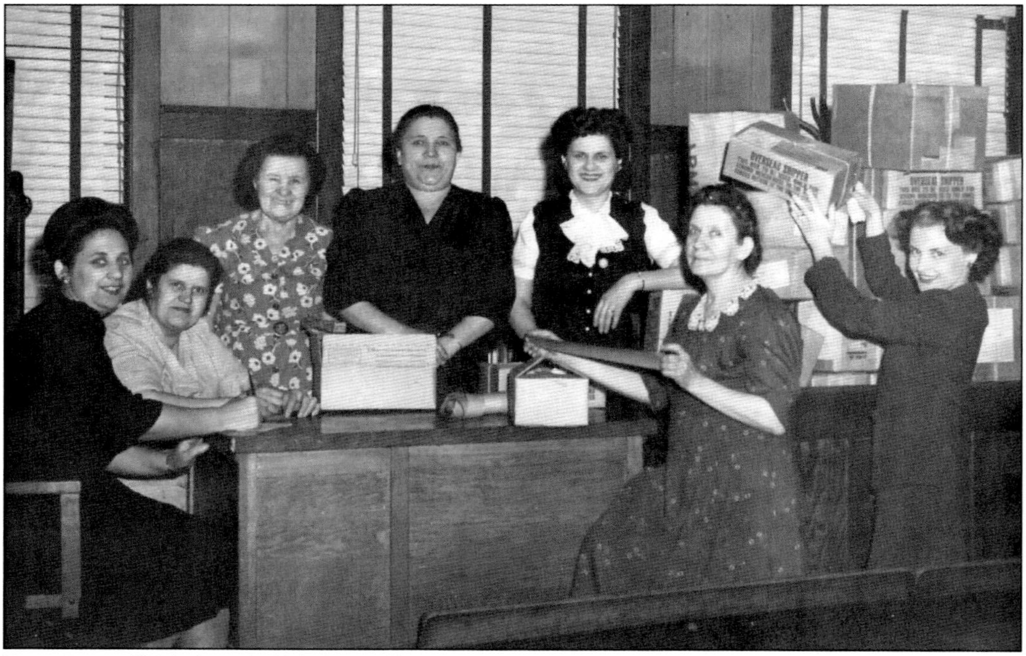

Ruza Sever (fifth from left) led an effort by the Circle of Serbian Sisters at the St. Sava Serbian Orthodox Church—packing and shipping care packages to soldiers and families in Europe during World War II. The group was very active then and during the Balkan wars in the late 1990s. (Courtesy of St. Sava Serbian Orthodox Church, Merrillville, Indiana.)

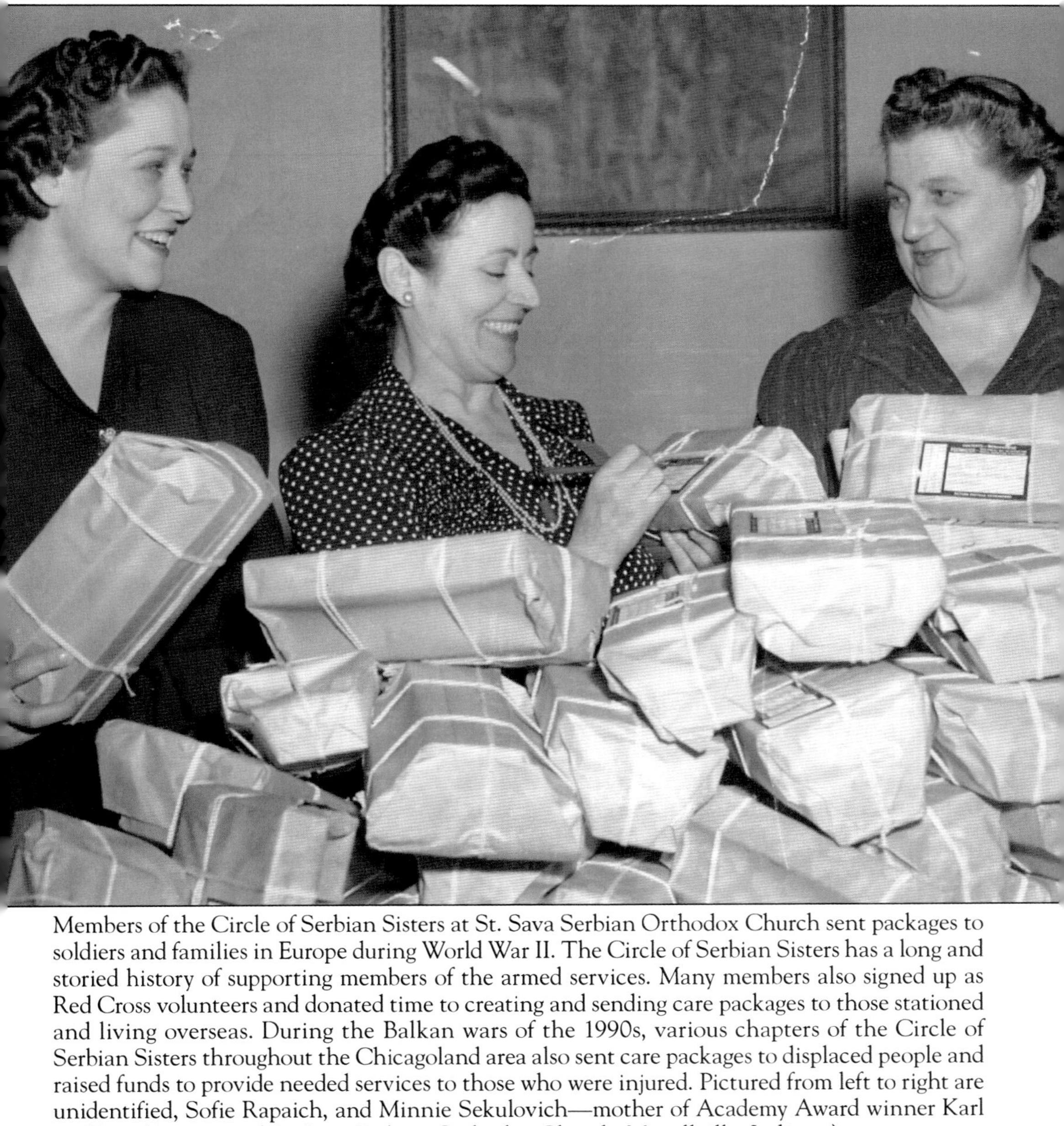

Members of the Circle of Serbian Sisters at St. Sava Serbian Orthodox Church sent packages to soldiers and families in Europe during World War II. The Circle of Serbian Sisters has a long and storied history of supporting members of the armed services. Many members also signed up as Red Cross volunteers and donated time to creating and sending care packages to those stationed and living overseas. During the Balkan wars of the 1990s, various chapters of the Circle of Serbian Sisters throughout the Chicagoland area also sent care packages to displaced people and raised funds to provide needed services to those who were injured. Pictured from left to right are unidentified, Sofie Rapaich, and Minnie Sekulovich—mother of Academy Award winner Karl Malden. (Courtesy of St. Sava Serbian Orthodox Church, Merrillville, Indiana.)

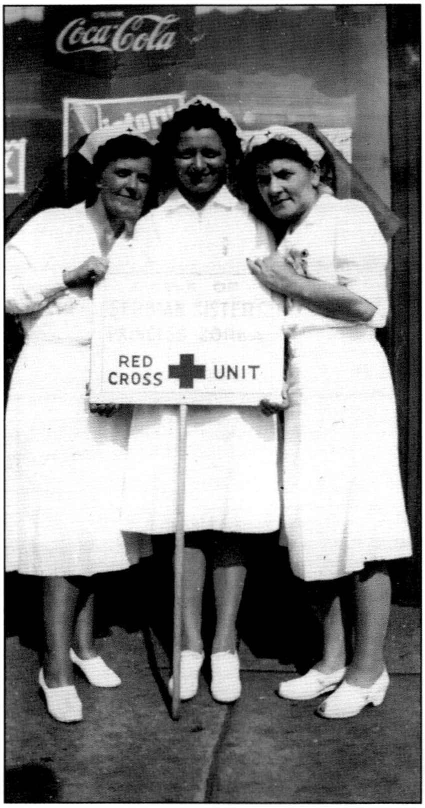

Milka Babich, Millie Chalich, and ? Krga joined the Circle of Serbian Sisters' Red Cross unit during World War II to help support the troops. The Circle of Serbian Sisters, established in 1903 in Belgrade, was a precursor of numerous Serbian women's humanitarian organizations. Today, the Circle of Serbian Sisters is active throughout the world—including in the Chicagoland region. (Courtesy of Dorothy Lalich.)

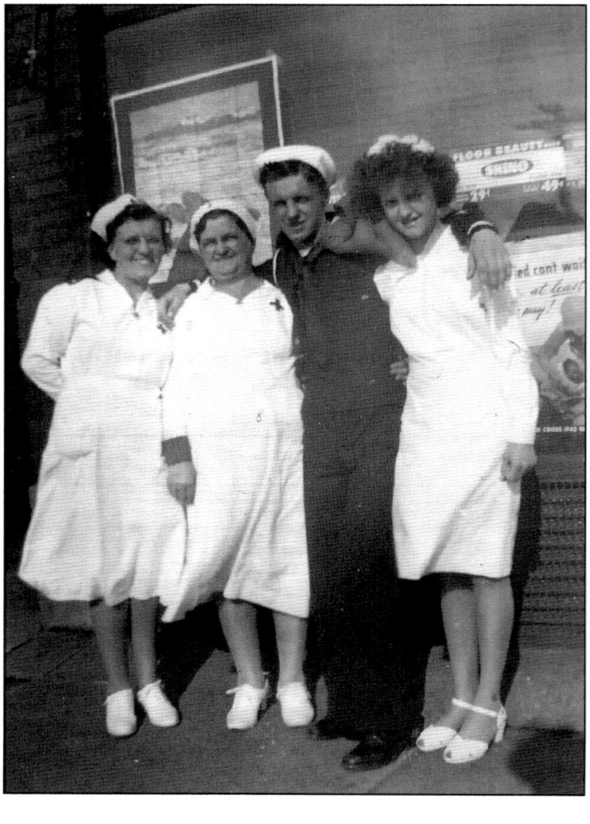

During World War II, many Serbian boys and men enlisted in the war, while Serbian girls and women joined Red Cross units through the Serbian churches and helped support those who enlisted. Seen here in 1944 are, from left to right, Milka (Adamovich) Babich, Vasilija (Adamovich) Sasic, Nick Babich, and Dorothy (Babich) Lalich. Babich, Sasic, and Lalich worked making bandages for the troops. (Courtesy of Dorothy Lalich.)

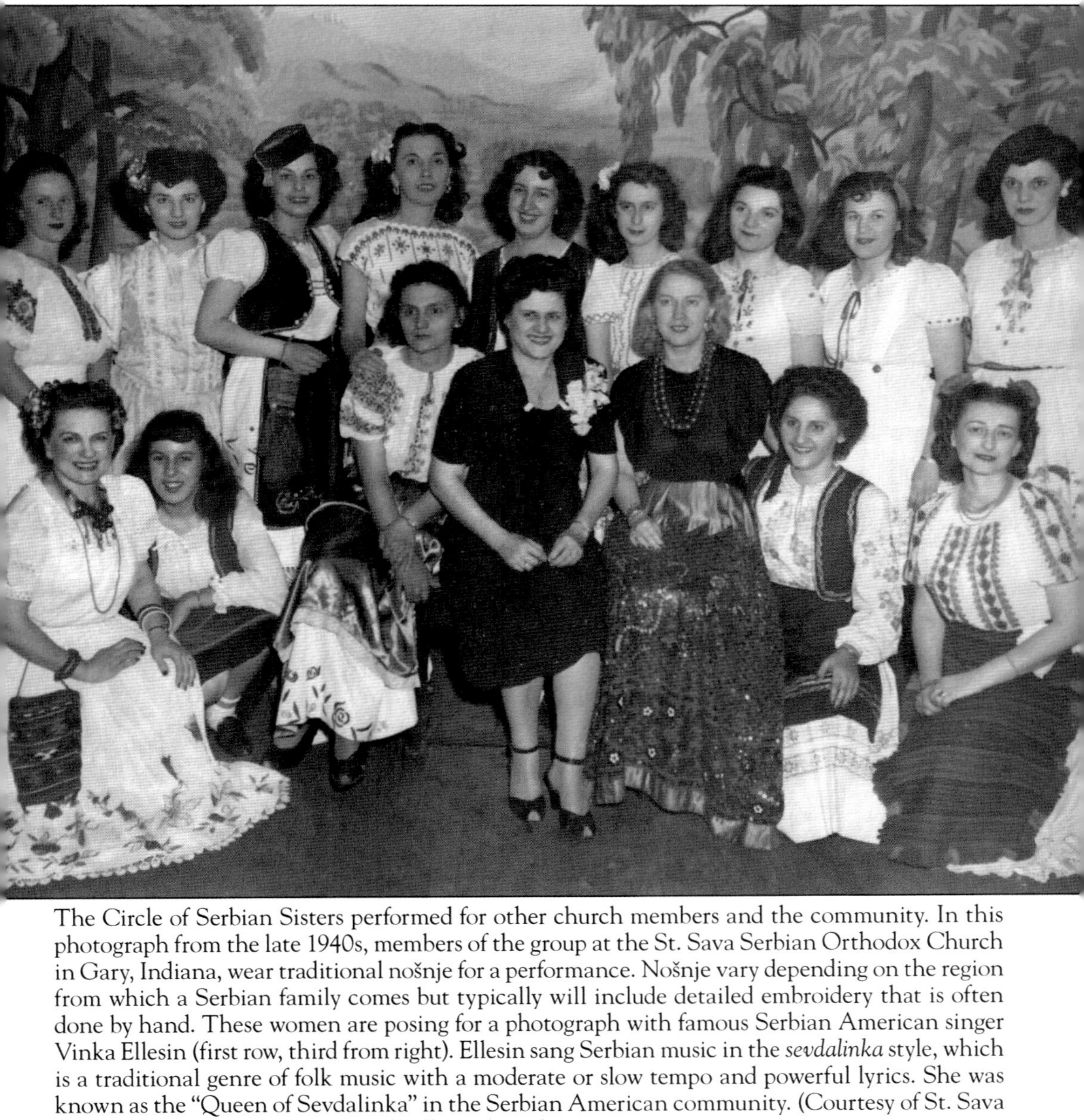

The Circle of Serbian Sisters performed for other church members and the community. In this photograph from the late 1940s, members of the group at the St. Sava Serbian Orthodox Church in Gary, Indiana, wear traditional nošnje for a performance. Nošnje vary depending on the region from which a Serbian family comes but typically will include detailed embroidery that is often done by hand. These women are posing for a photograph with famous Serbian American singer Vinka Ellesin (first row, third from right). Ellesin sang Serbian music in the *sevdalinka* style, which is a traditional genre of folk music with a moderate or slow tempo and powerful lyrics. She was known as the "Queen of Sevdalinka" in the Serbian American community. (Courtesy of St. Sava Serbian Orthodox Church, Merrillville, Indiana.)

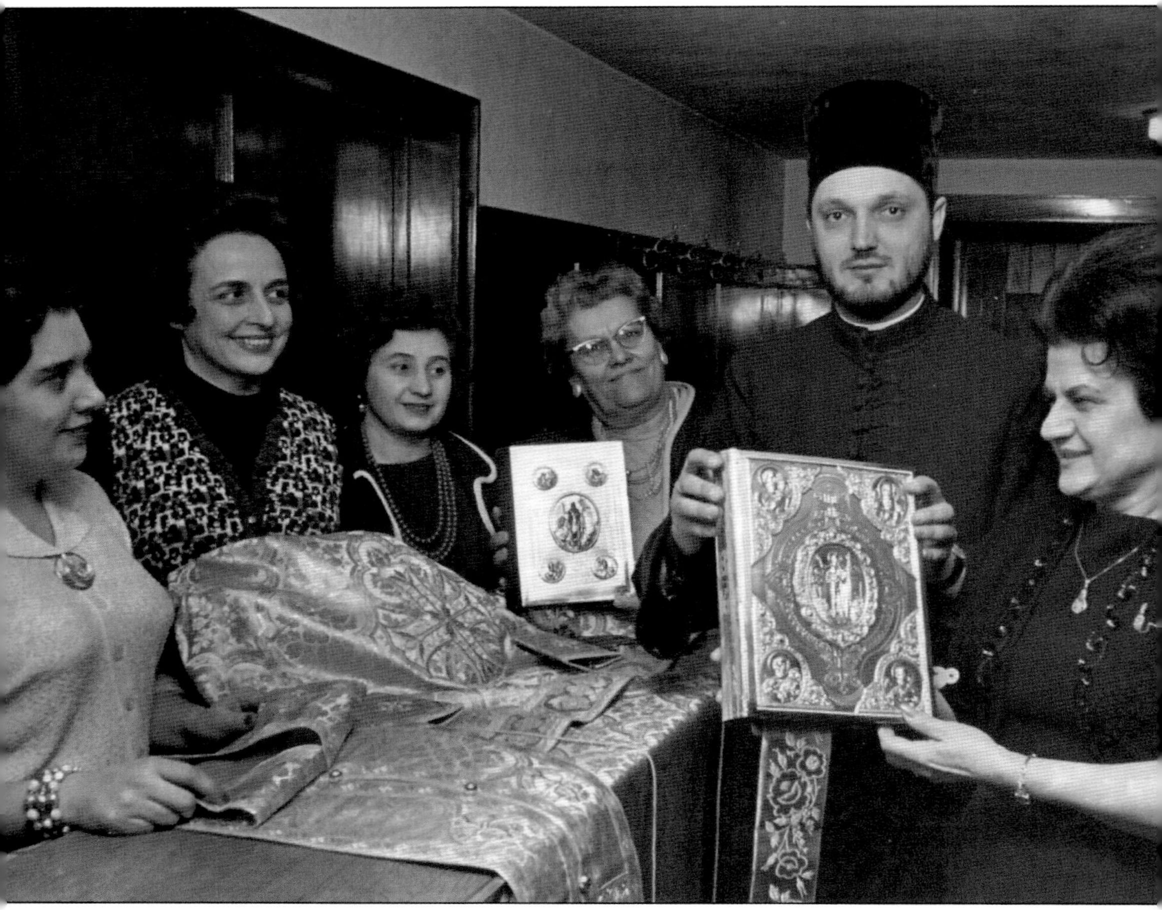

In 1964, Rev. Peter Bankerovich, of the St. Sava Serbian Orthodox Church, received new vestments and bibles from the Circle of Serbian Sisters. Holding the vestment is Helen Bogdanich—mother of Pulitzer Prize–winning investigative journalist Walt Bogdanich—while Stana Nahud holds the bible at center and Ruza Sever holds the bible at right. In addition to the general fundraising that the Circle of Serbian Sisters did, the organization also raised money to purchase these culturally significant items for the church. A priest's vestment set includes an embroidered tunic, stole, belt, and other pieces—each with important meaning. Serbian Orthodox priests wear vestments for all church services, from weekly services to special occasions like weddings and christenings. (Courtesy of St. Sava Serbian Orthodox Church, Merrillville, Indiana.)

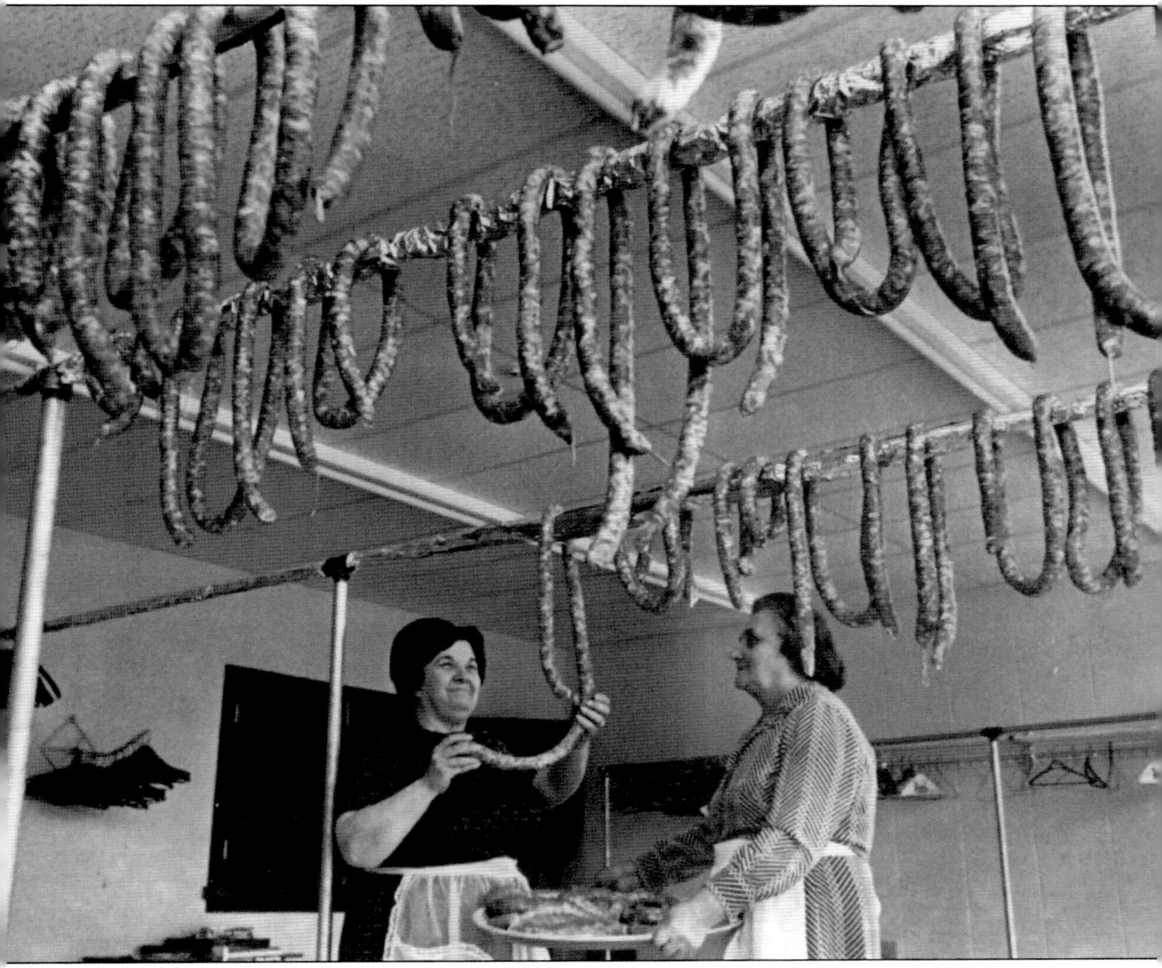

Violet Golub (left) and Smilja Orlich make sausages in the late 1960s at the St. Sava Serbian Orthodox Church hall, on Forty-ninth Avenue in Hobart, Indiana. The sausages were sold at Serbian functions at the hall, which hosted events like Serbian weddings, christenings, and events booked by non-Serbs. Like many nationalities, Serbians place a strong emphasis on plentiful food, which, along with Serbian drinks, form the cornerstone of tradition for Serbs here and abroad. While several foods are common for people of Serbian descent, meat—and especially sausages—is omnipresent at events at homes, churches, and restaurants. Golub and Orlich were members of the Circle of Serbian Sisters at the St. Sava Serbian Orthodox Church of Gary, Indiana. (Courtesy of St. Sava Serbian Orthodox Church, Merrillville, Indiana.)

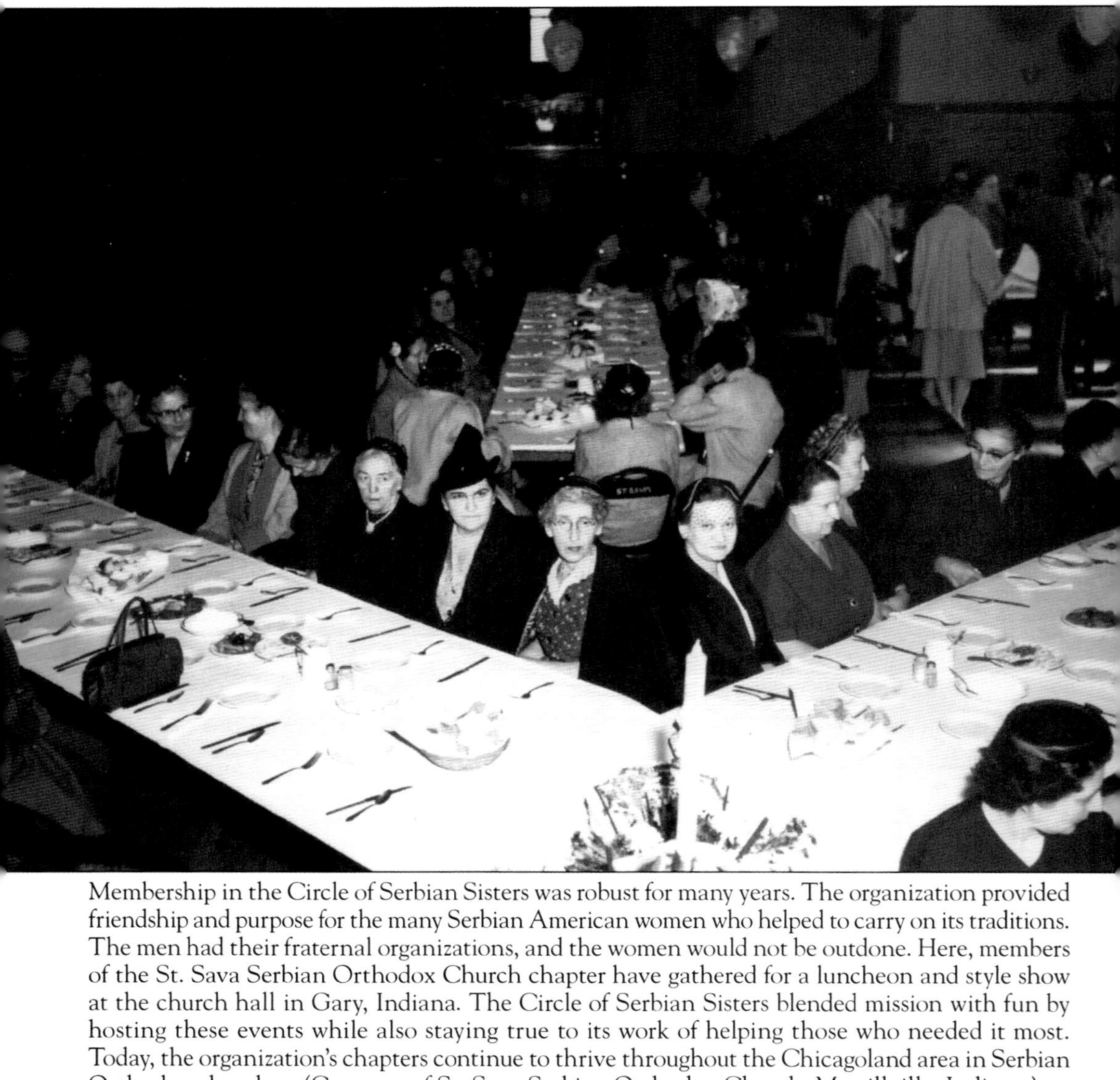

Membership in the Circle of Serbian Sisters was robust for many years. The organization provided friendship and purpose for the many Serbian American women who helped to carry on its traditions. The men had their fraternal organizations, and the women would not be outdone. Here, members of the St. Sava Serbian Orthodox Church chapter have gathered for a luncheon and style show at the church hall in Gary, Indiana. The Circle of Serbian Sisters blended mission with fun by hosting these events while also staying true to its work of helping those who needed it most. Today, the organization's chapters continue to thrive throughout the Chicagoland area in Serbian Orthodox churches. (Courtesy of St. Sava Serbian Orthodox Church, Merrillville, Indiana.)

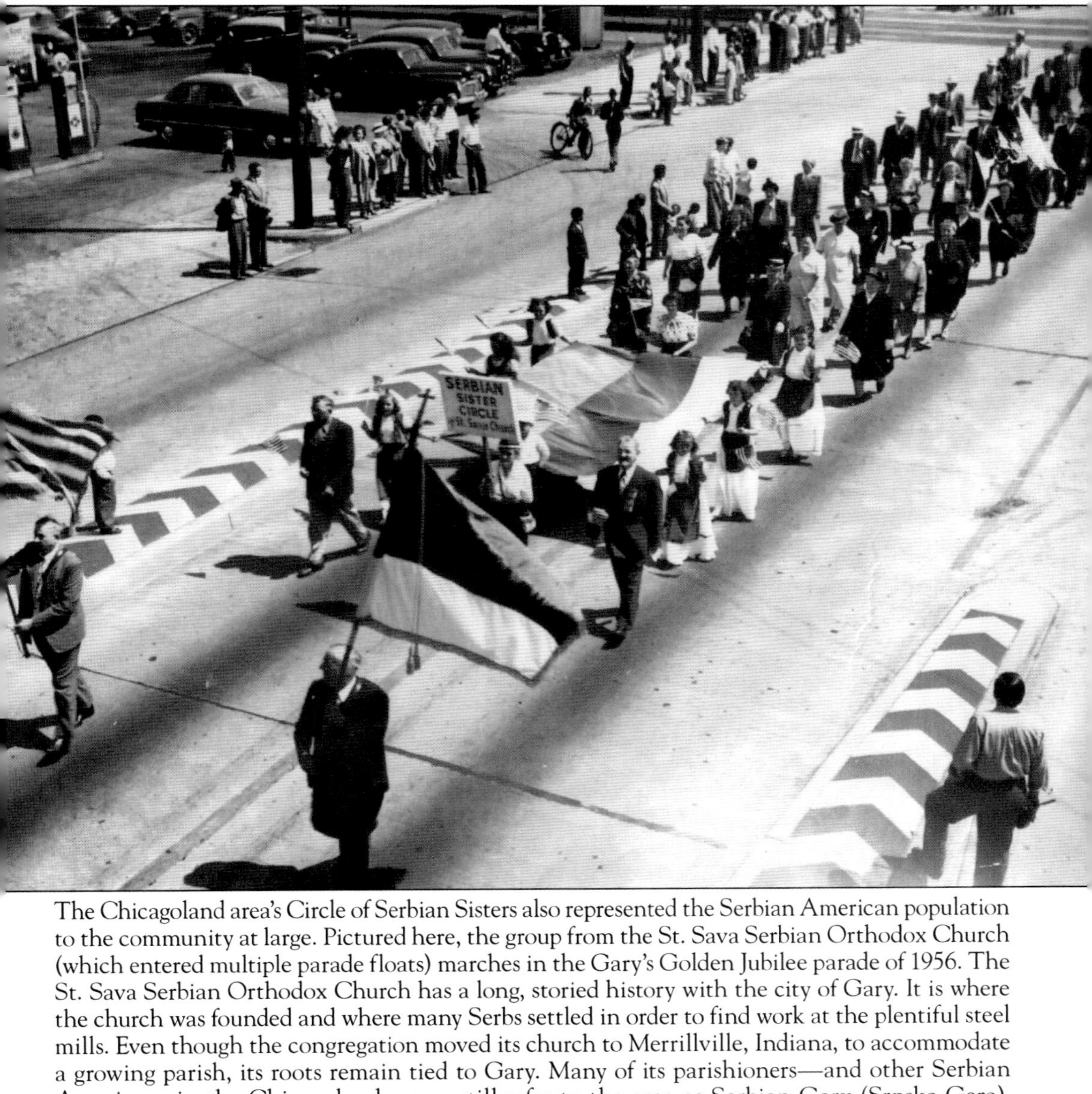

The Chicagoland area's Circle of Serbian Sisters also represented the Serbian American population to the community at large. Pictured here, the group from the St. Sava Serbian Orthodox Church (which entered multiple parade floats) marches in the Gary's Golden Jubilee parade of 1956. The St. Sava Serbian Orthodox Church has a long, storied history with the city of Gary. It is where the church was founded and where many Serbs settled in order to find work at the plentiful steel mills. Even though the congregation moved its church to Merrillville, Indiana, to accommodate a growing parish, its roots remain tied to Gary. Many of its parishioners—and other Serbian Americans in the Chicagoland area—still refer to the area as Serbian Gary (Srpska Gera). Holding the sign in the parade is Mileva Tandarich, who was a regular churchgoer and community supporter. (Courtesy of St. Sava Serbian Orthodox Church, Merrillville, Indiana.)

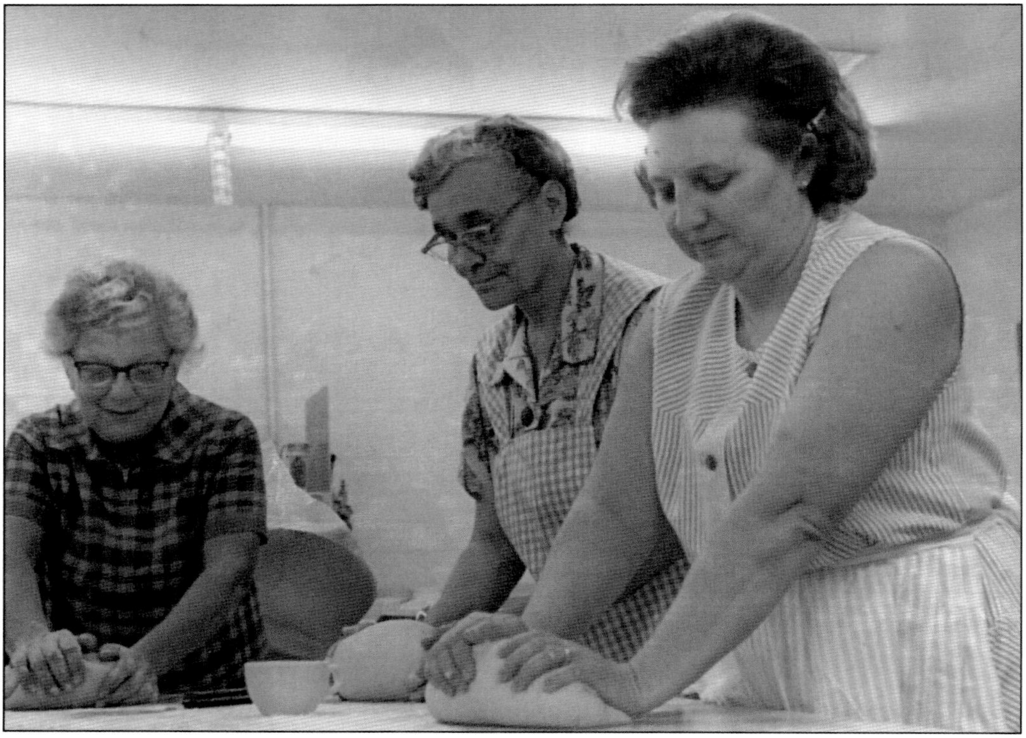

Members of the Circle of Serbian Sisters also made donuts (krofne) to sell at different church functions. Many Serbian desserts and foods are made with basic ingredients such as flour, sugar, and oil that were readily available to most everyone. (Courtesy of St. Sava Serbian Orthodox Church, Merrillville, Indiana.)

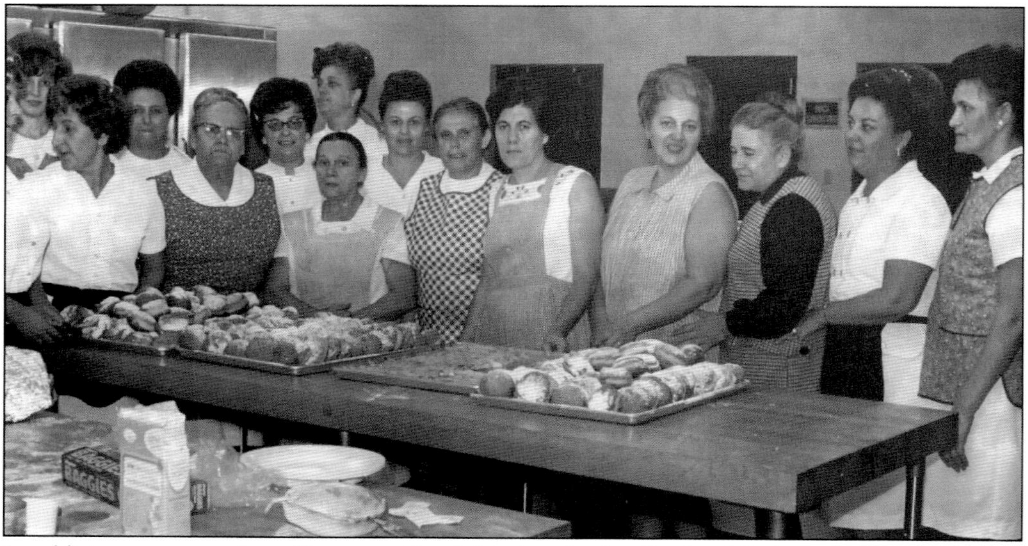

In addition to supporting efforts outside of the church, the Circle of Serbian Sisters also hosted bake sales and other fundraising events to help maintain the church. Pictured are women from St. Sava Serbian Orthodox Church catering staff, at its hall at Forty-ninth Avenue in Hobart, Indiana, in the late 1960s. (Courtesy of St. Sava Serbian Orthodox Church, Merrillville, Indiana.)

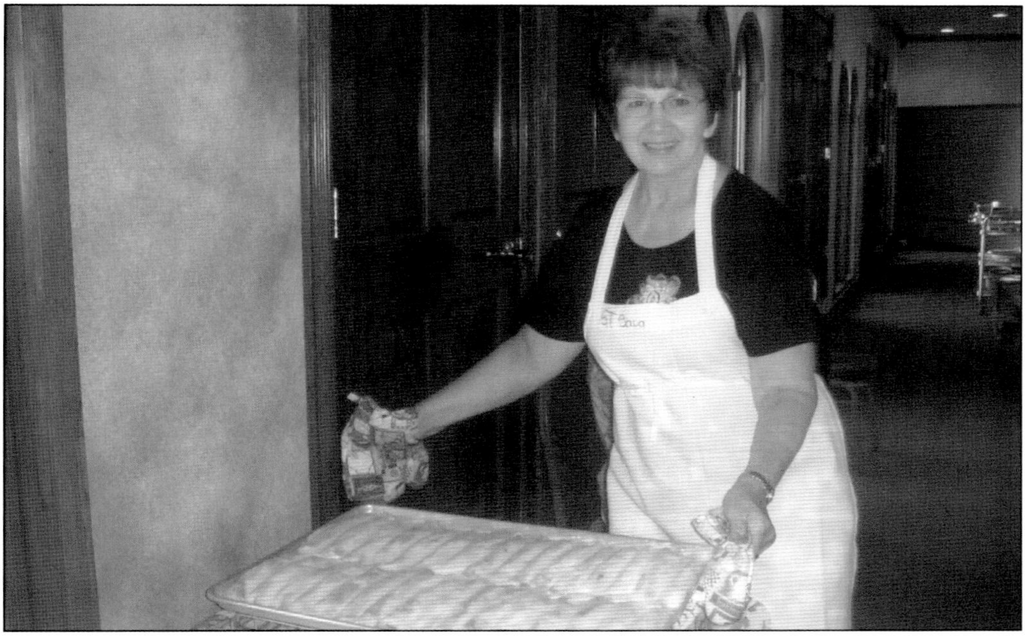

A past president of the Circle of Serbian Sisters at the St. Sava Serbian Orthodox Church, Milena "Beba" Rudman prepares a tray of palačinke—thin pancakes common in Serbia and similar to the French crepe—for Serb Fest. (Courtesy of St. Sava Serbian Orthodox Church, Merrillville, Indiana.)

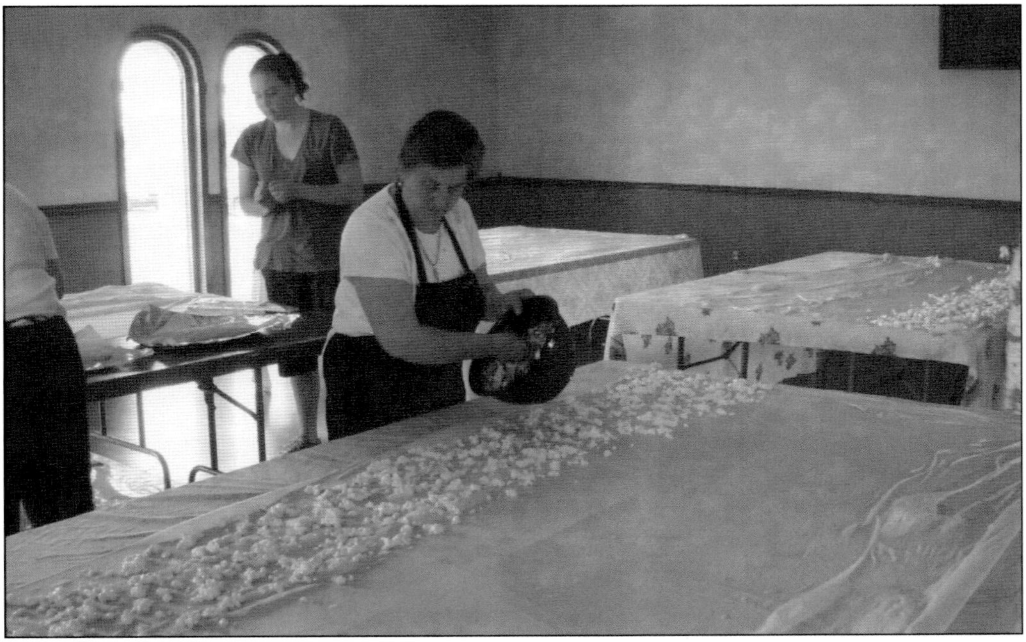

A traditional Serbian cheese strudel (*pita*) is still made the same way today as it has been for generations. Members of the Circle of Serbian Sisters make the strudel from scratch. Here, Zorka Glumac drizzles the cheese mixture over a recently hand-stretched sheet of dough. (Courtesy of St. Sava Serbian Orthodox Church, Merrillville, Indiana.)

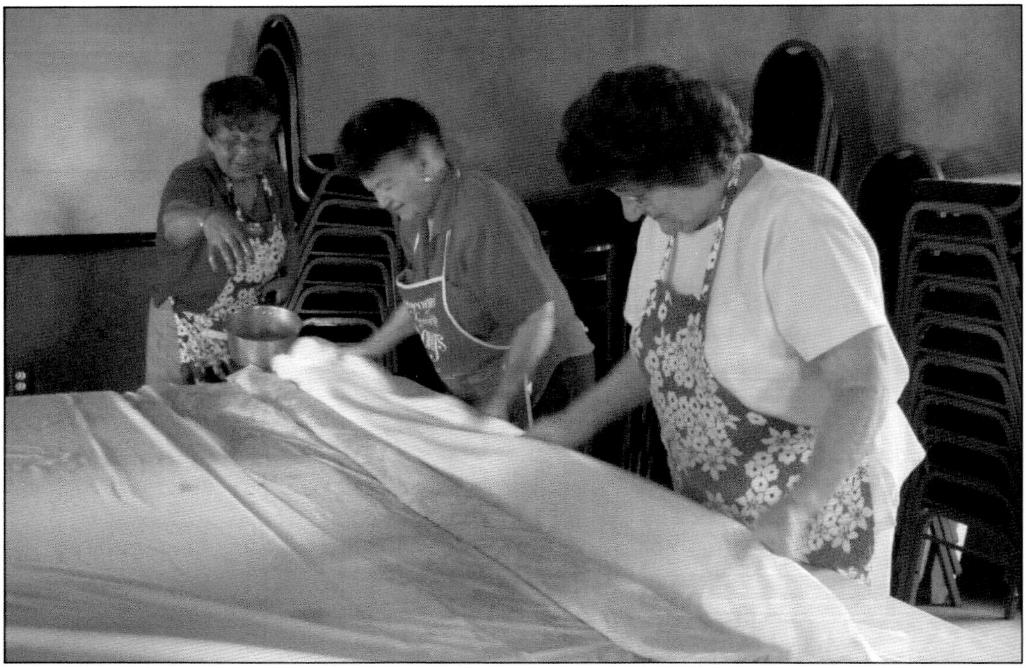

Members of the Circle of Serbian Sisters work together to make the dough for a traditional pita—stretching out the dough until it is thinner than a sheet of paper. Together, they roll the dough—after the cheese has been placed on the inside—and then bake it. Cheese strudel is a staple at virtually every Serbian function. (Courtesy of St. Sava Serbian Orthodox Church, Merrillville, Indiana.)

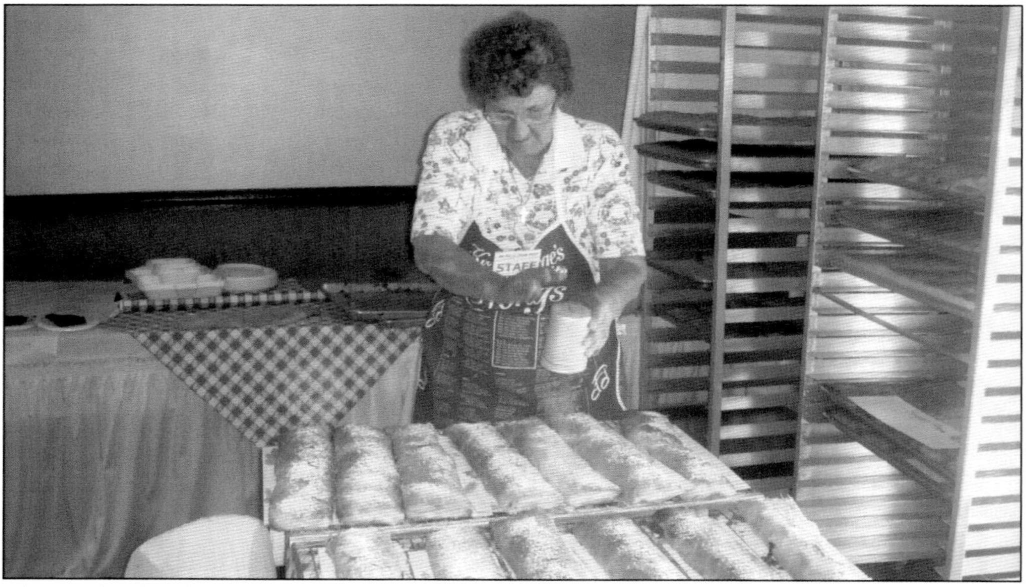

The Circle of Serbian Sisters helps raise money to support the church and its activities. One way the group does this is by hosting bake sales at the local Serbian churches with which each chapter is associated. Pictured is Millie (Tatalovich) Griggs, making a traditional fruit pita. (Courtesy of St. Sava Serbian Orthodox Church, Merrillville, Indiana.)

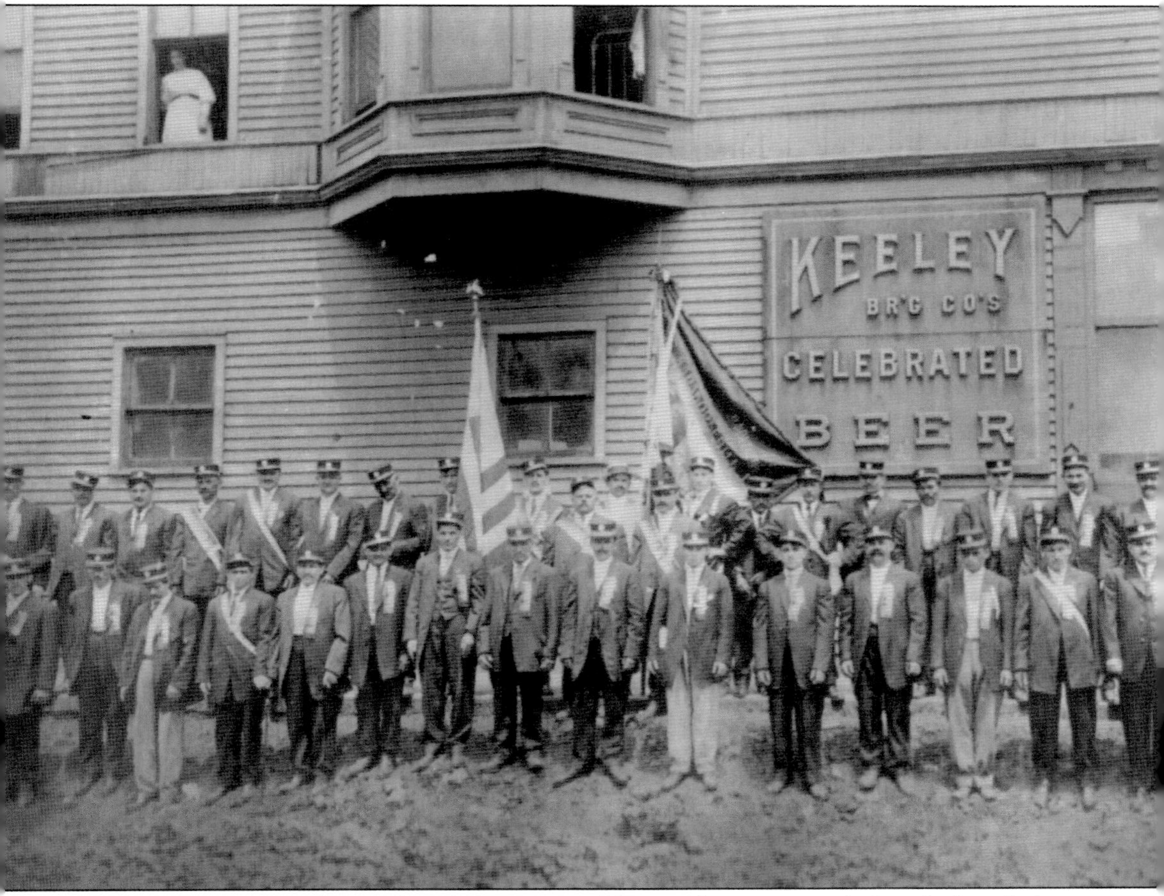

Serbian immigrants in Chicago founded a variety of fraternal societies, including Serbian lodges that helped maintain camaraderie and community. This 1912 photograph shows members of the Karageorgevich (Karađorđević) Lodge—under the Serb National Federation—from South Chicago. The group was originally founded in 1905 with a group of 200 men—none of them older than 25—from the St. Archangel Michael Serbian Orthodox Church. Over the years, the lodge has been very active in raising money to help support people back in the homeland. Karageorgevich has helped charitable organizations in their efforts, provided monetary assistance to young men going to war, and helped build monuments. Several wars claimed the lives of lodge members, but their memory continues in the work that the organization still does. Among the many members pictured is Bozidar Lalich (front row, ninth from the left), who immigrated to the United States. (Courtesy of Dorothy Lalich.)

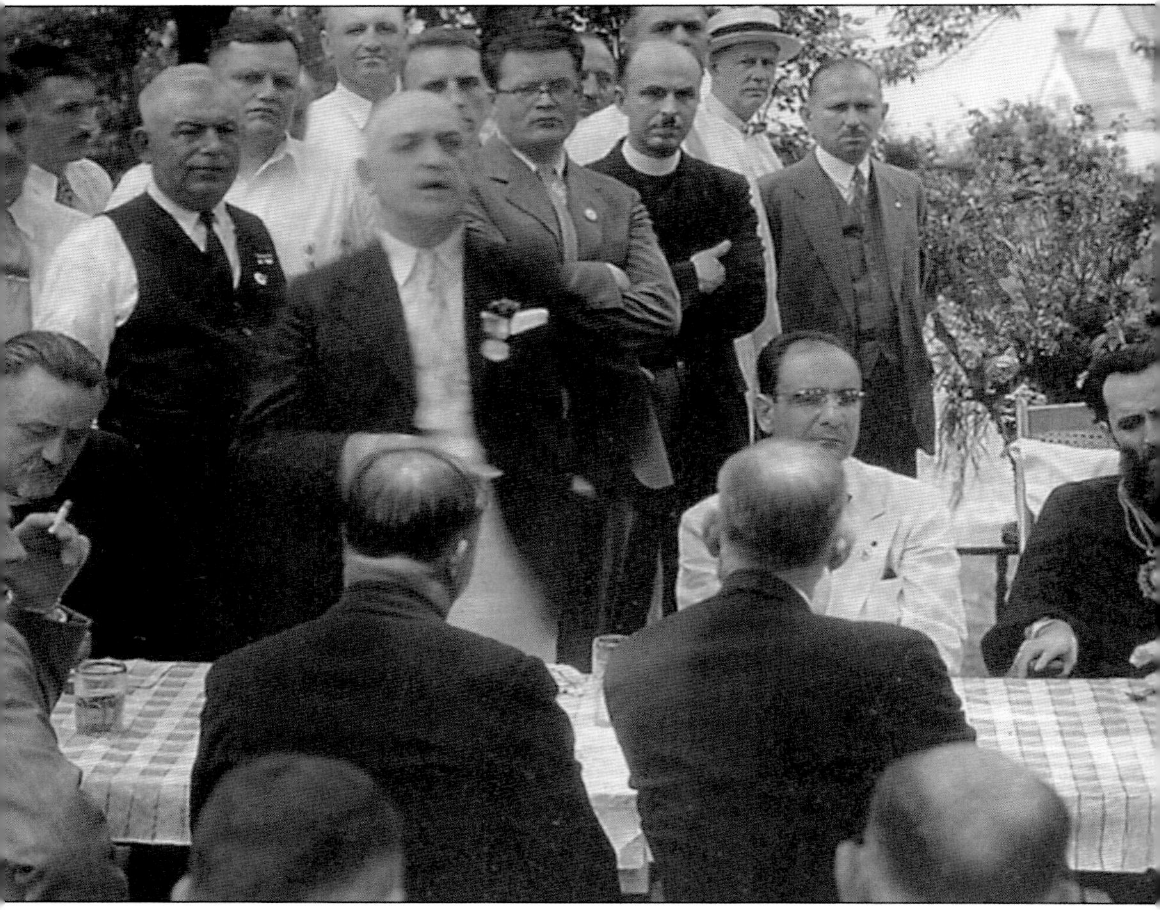

Bishop Mardarije (center) is among the delegates of the second Serb National Federation (SNF) convention attending a banquet in their honor at the St. Sava Monastery in Libertyville, Illinois, on July 4, 1935. SNF conventions still take place today. Bishop Mardarije was born in 1889 in Podgorica, Montenegro. He was the first Serbian Bishop of America and Canada. Bishop Mardarije worked relentlessly to establish a monastery in America and, in 1923, founded the St. Sava Serbian

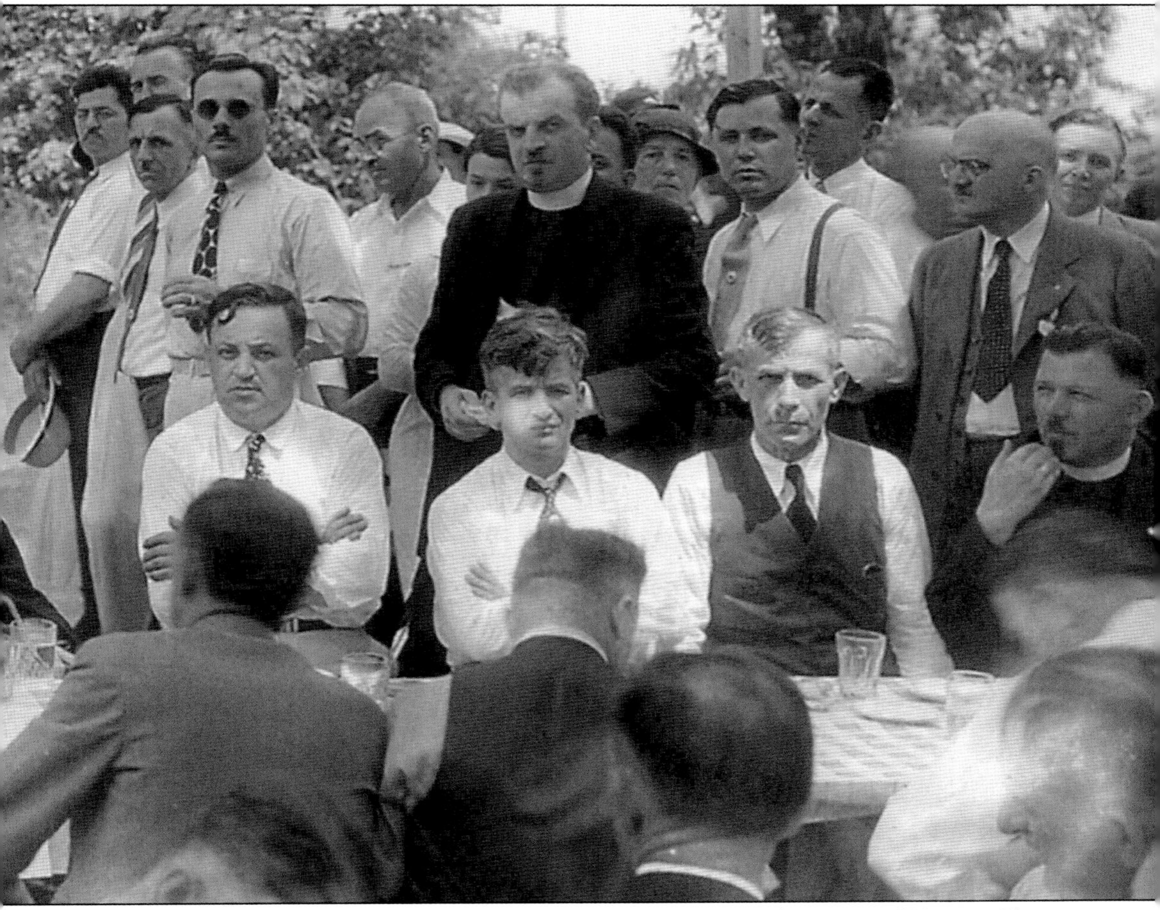

Orthodox Monastery. The monastery, which is listed on the National Register of Historic Places, maintains a symbolic importance for Serbs, Serbian culture, and the Serbian Orthodox church. Bishop Mardarije was only 46 years old when he died on December 12, 1935, and he was buried at St. Sava. (Courtesy of Serb National Federation, Pittsburgh, Pennsylvania.)

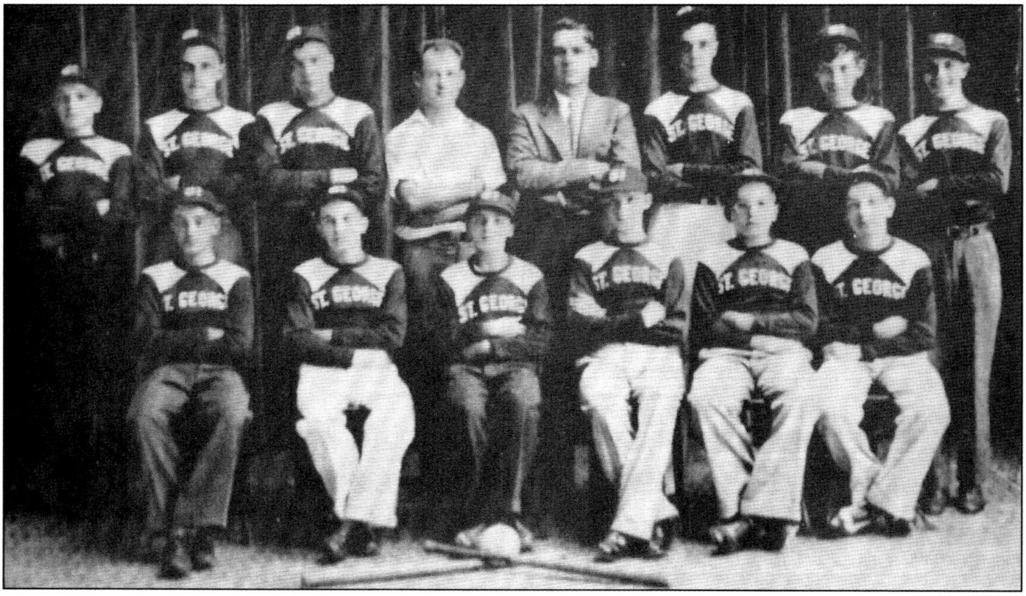

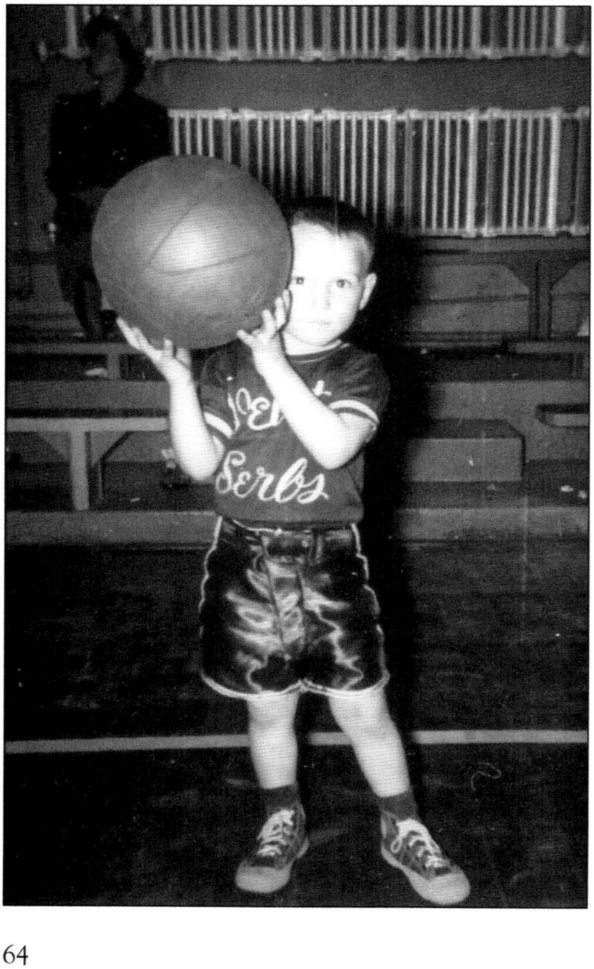

In the early 1900s, Serbs who helped found the Holy Resurrection Serbian Orthodox Cathedral in Chicago, Illinois, also helped form the St. George Lodge—under the Serb National Federation—and the Junior Order of the St. George Lodge. This photograph from April 1943 shows the St. George Lodge Junior Order baseball team. (Courtesy of Holy Resurrection Serbian Orthodox Cathedral, Chicago, Illinois.)

In this undated photograph, likely from the 1940s or 1950s, a young unnamed boy shows off his basketball skills during a tournament. Basketball is especially popular among Serbs. The Serb National Federation held its first basketball tournament in Cleveland, Ohio, in 1936—a tournament that continues today and has been hosted in the Chicagoland area several times. (Courtesy of Dorothy Lalich.)

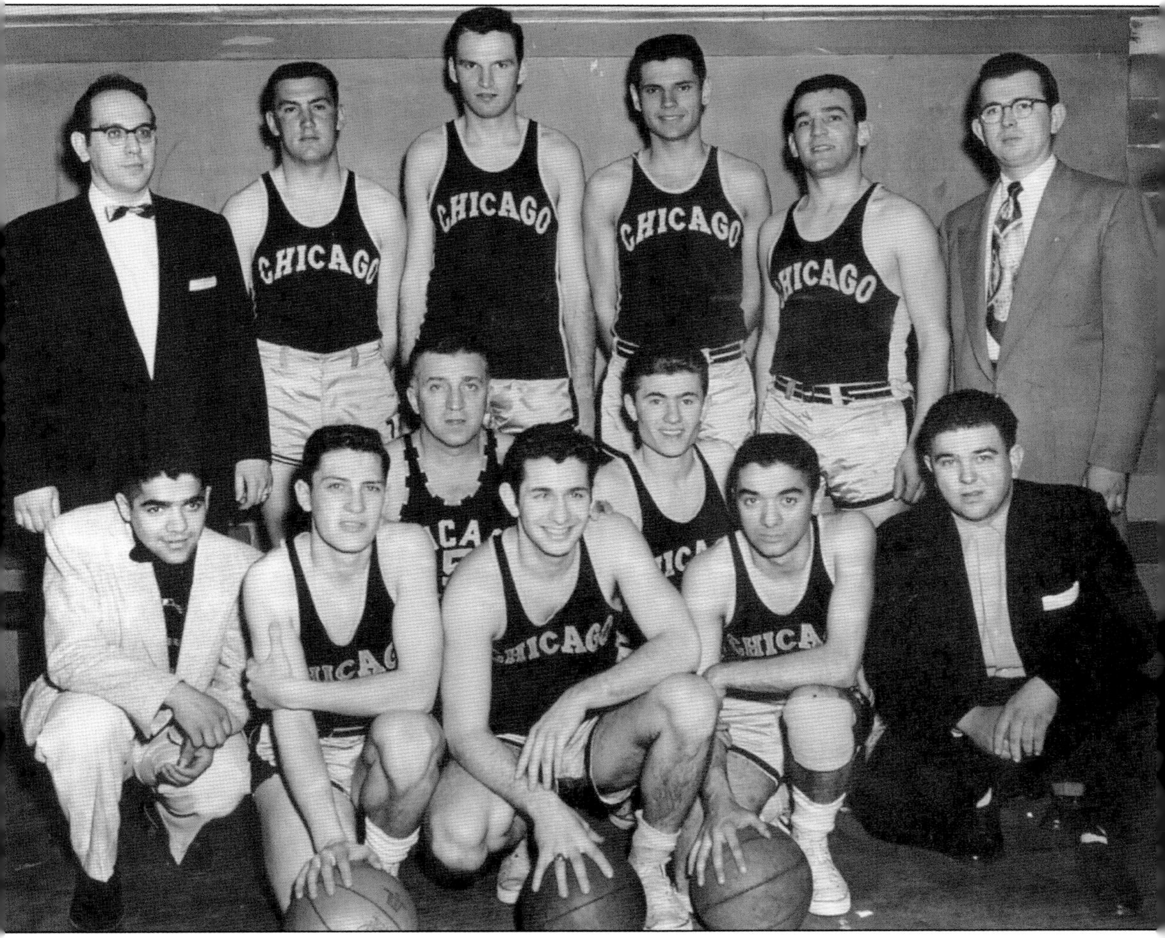

In this photograph, members of the 1957 Chicago Serbs basketball team pose prior to playing in a tournament held by the Serb National Federation. Cleveland, Ohio, hosted the first SNF basketball tournament in March 1936. The basketball tournament has been held every year since then, except for 1943–1945 (due to World War II) and 1962. In 1936, there were 12 teams, and the winning team, Aliquippa, beat South Bend by a score of 49-31. South Chicago produced the first women's basketball team. Throughout its 100-plus year history, the SNF has hosted annual athletic tournaments in a variety of sports and in dozens of cities in the United States and Canada. The tournaments include a lot of sports but are interspersed with Serbian dances (*zabavas*) and the opportunity to catch up with friends from other church parishes and Serbian communities. (Courtesy of Serb National Federation, Pittsburgh, Pennsylvania.)

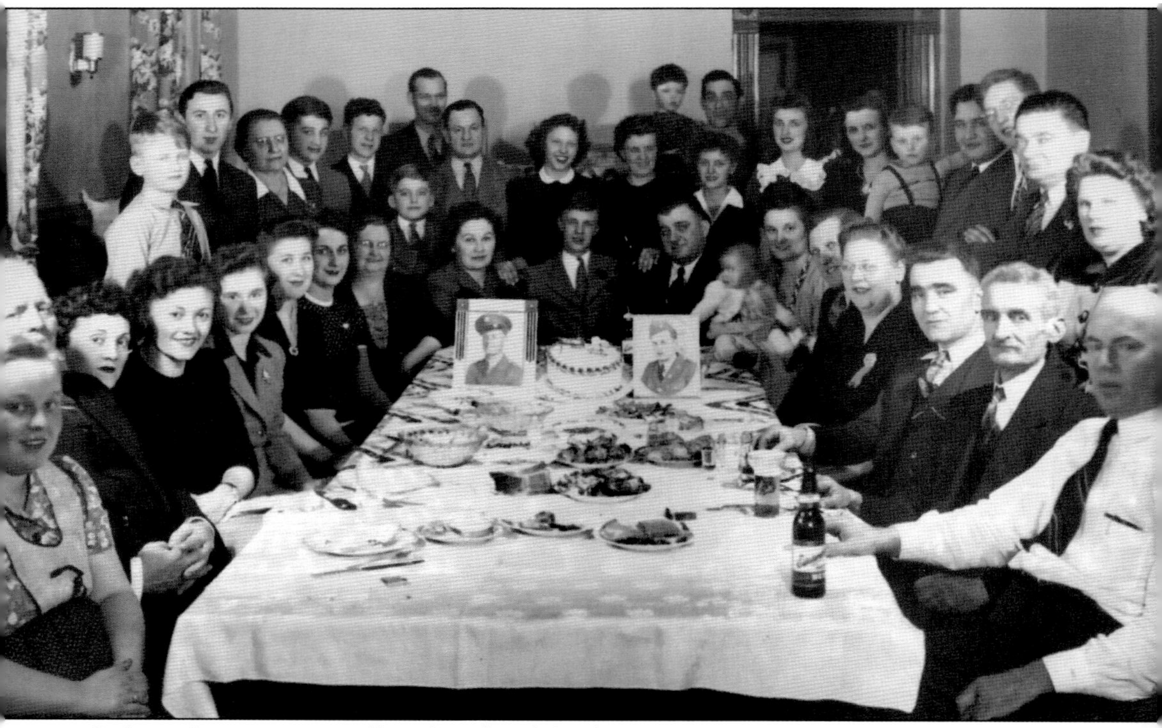

Serbian Americans proudly enlisted and fought in wars as part of the armed forces. Serbian Americans fought in both world wars and also in the conflicts in Korea and Vietnam. The Babich family hosted a gathering for friends and family on January 25, 1943, the eve of Nick Babich's enlistment. Babich is seated at center while his father, Stanko Babich; mother, Milka (Adamovich) Babich; and sister, Dorothy (Babich) Lalich, stand behind him. Families would often host elaborate gatherings in advance of deployments, especially because—once soldiers were deployed—it was difficult to stay in touch with family and friends, and communication was delayed. (Courtesy of Dorothy Lalich.)

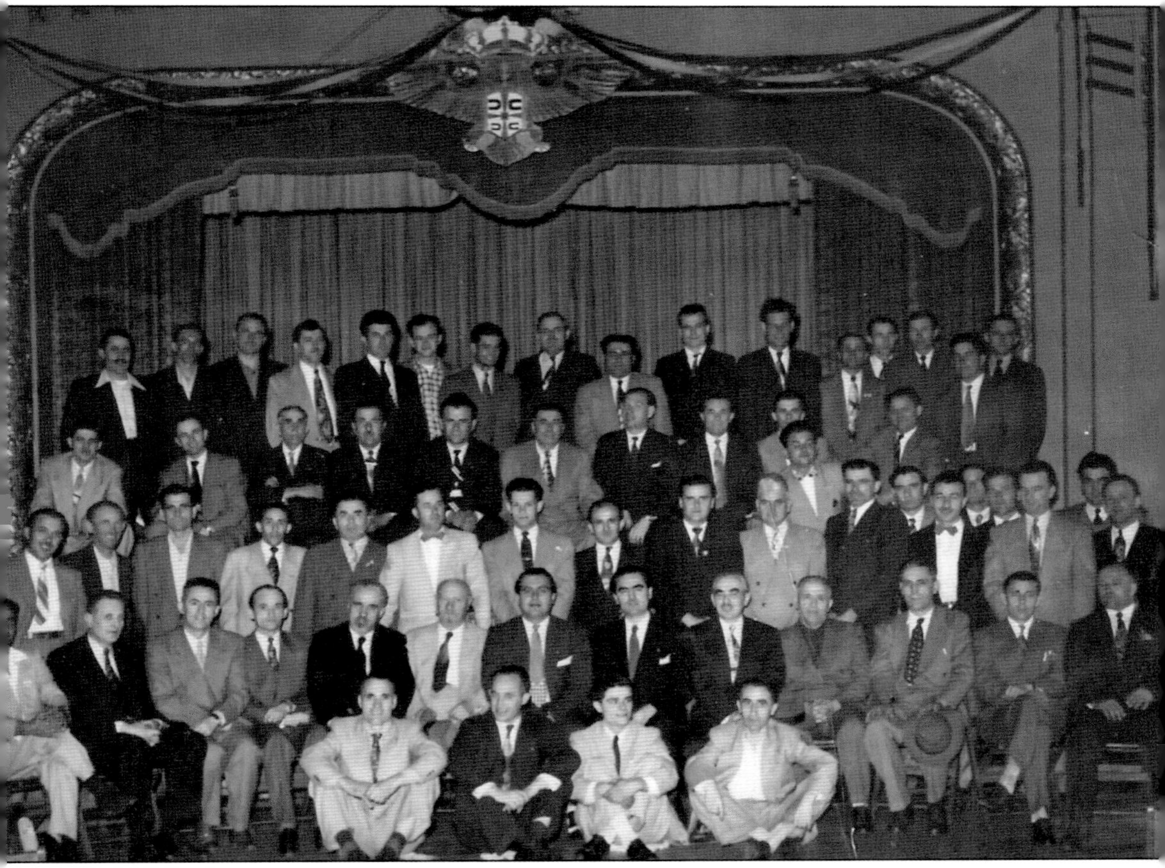

During World War II, two resistance forces developed in Yugoslavia and fought the Axis powers while engaging in a civil war with one another. The Communist Party led the Partizan force, and its leader, Josip Broz Tito, ultimately became president of Yugoslavia. The Četniks were loyal to the monarchy, and their most visible leader during World War II was Draža Mihailović. The Partizans prevailed, and at the end of World War II, Četniks were banned in the new Yugoslavia. Mihailović was captured, tried, and executed in 1946. Many other Četniks were able to escape to avoid being prosecuted, and those who came to the Chicagoland area established a Četnik Hall in Northwest Indiana. Pictured here are some of the earliest Četnik members in the Chicagoland area. (Courtesy of Milan Marich.)

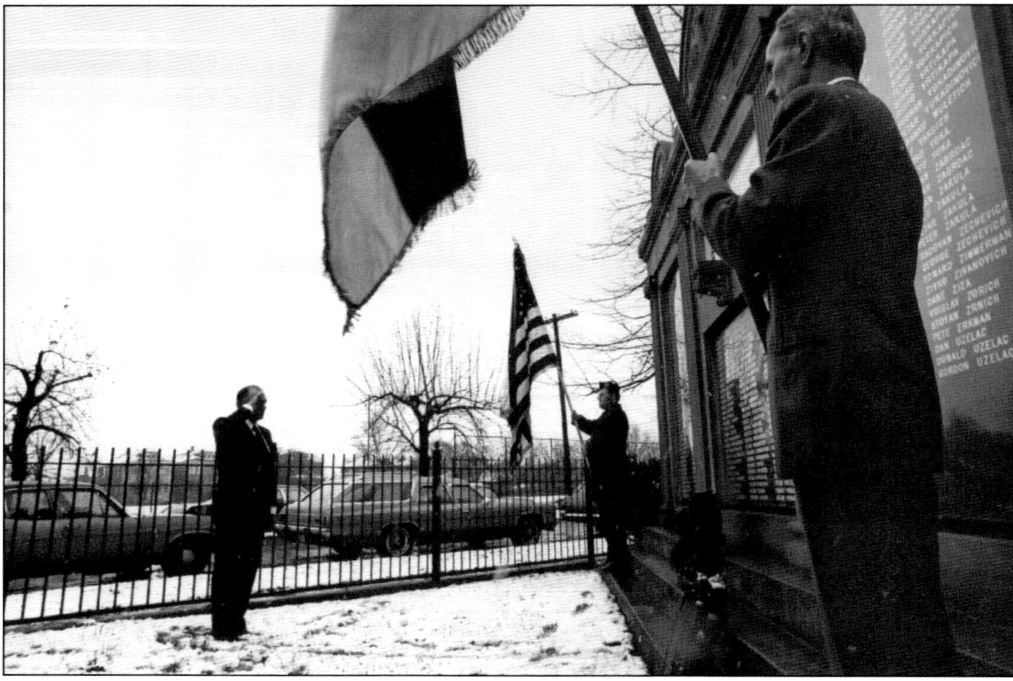

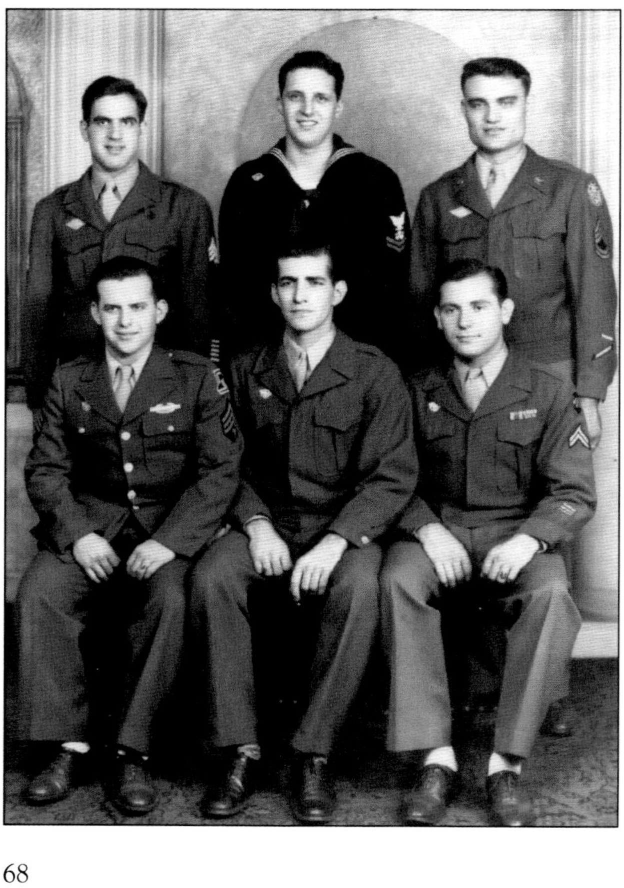

Like many immigrants, Serbian Americans served in all branches of the United States military. The St. Sava Serbian Orthodox Church in Gary, Indiana, commemorates its parishioners who served in World War II by listing their names on a monument that was erected in 1947. Above, Nick Chabraja salutes the monument at the church's second location, at Thirteenth and Connecticut Streets. When a fire destroyed the church, the monument survived and was relocated to the church's new location in Merrillville, Indiana. Among the parishioners who served was a group of friends—pictured at left while on leave at the same time during World War II. From left to right are (first row) Mickey Crnoevich, Steve Barich, and George Milovanovich; (second row) Ray Chelovich, Miles Stepanovich, and Nick Sever. (Courtesy of St. Sava Serbian Orthodox Church, Merrillville, Indiana.)

Five

Our Religion

Once a critical mass of Serbian immigrants settled in the Chicagoland area, it became clear that they would need to establish parishes in order to have a place to worship. Serbs practice Eastern Orthodox Christianity.

Serbs in the Wicker Park neighborhood of Chicago founded Holy Resurrection, while Serbs on the south side of Chicago founded St. Archangel Michael, Serbs in Gary, Indiana, founded St. Sava, and Serbs around Indiana Harbor founded St. George. Each of these parishes is active today—along with others that were built throughout the greater Chicago and northwest Indiana area to serve the growing number of parishioners—although only St. George Serbian Orthodox Church is still located in the same place as when it was established in 1911.

In 1923, Bishop Mardarije founded the St. Sava Serbian Orthodox Monastery in Libertyville, Illinois. The monastery is listed on the National Register of Historic Places and maintains a symbolic importance among Serbs due to its long history in the United States. In 1984, the New Gračanica Monastery was built—a slightly modified replica of old Gračanica of Kosovo, which was built in 1321 and holds historic and cultural significance for Serbs around the world.

Serbian Orthodox churches are immediately recognizable thanks to their Serbo-Byzantine architectural style; many of the churches in the Chicagoland area are replicas of those in southeastern Europe. Initially, immigrants converted houses or other church buildings into a Serbian Orthodox church, but dedicated parishioners raised or donated money to build churches in the traditional stone and brick style.

Inside the churches, the most prominent features are the iconostasis, the wall of icons separating the nave from the sanctuary, and the icons or frescoes that adorn the walls and ceilings inside the building. Similarly, Orthodox Serbs will also hang an icon—usually of the family's patron saint—on their wall at home.

The churches themselves are the focal point for the most sacred Orthodox customs, including christenings, weddings, and funerals. They are also home to Sunday schools where children learn the Serbian language and Eastern Orthodox religion.

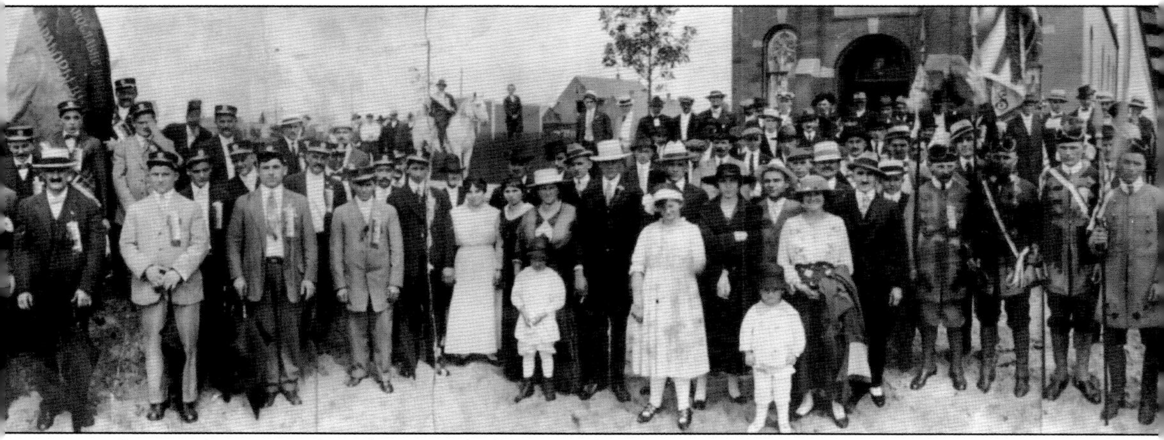

Taken in the 1920s, this photograph depicts a then-typical celebratory gathering of parishioners from the St. George Serbian Orthodox Church in East Chicago, Indiana. Of note are the various flags, along with the ribbons, sashes, and hats worn by the attendees—depicting their affiliation as members of the different fraternal organizations existing in the parish at the time.

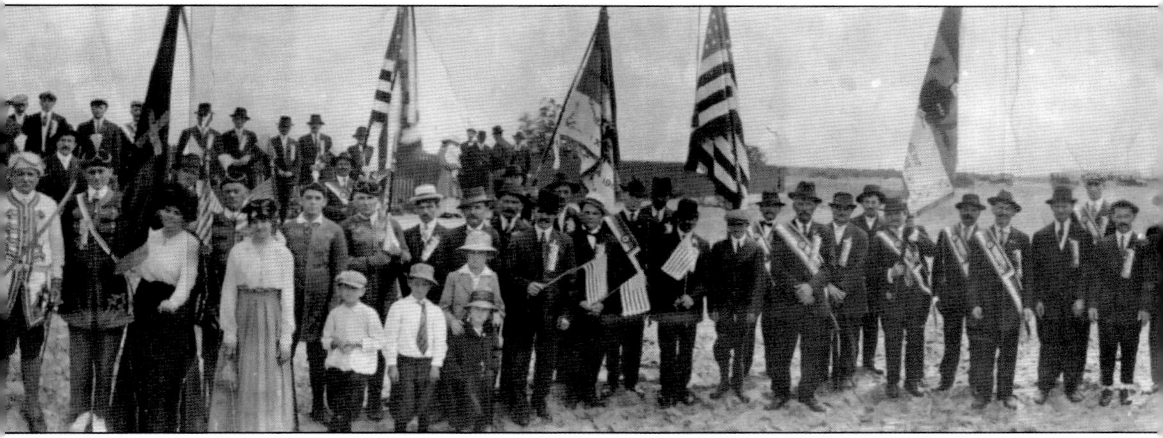

These organizations included the St. George Serbian Benevolent Society, No. 104; the St. Elijah Society Lodge 27; King Peter I; Sloboda; and Radomir Putnik. Many of these are still active today. (Courtesy of St. George Serbian Orthodox Church, East Chicago, Indiana.)

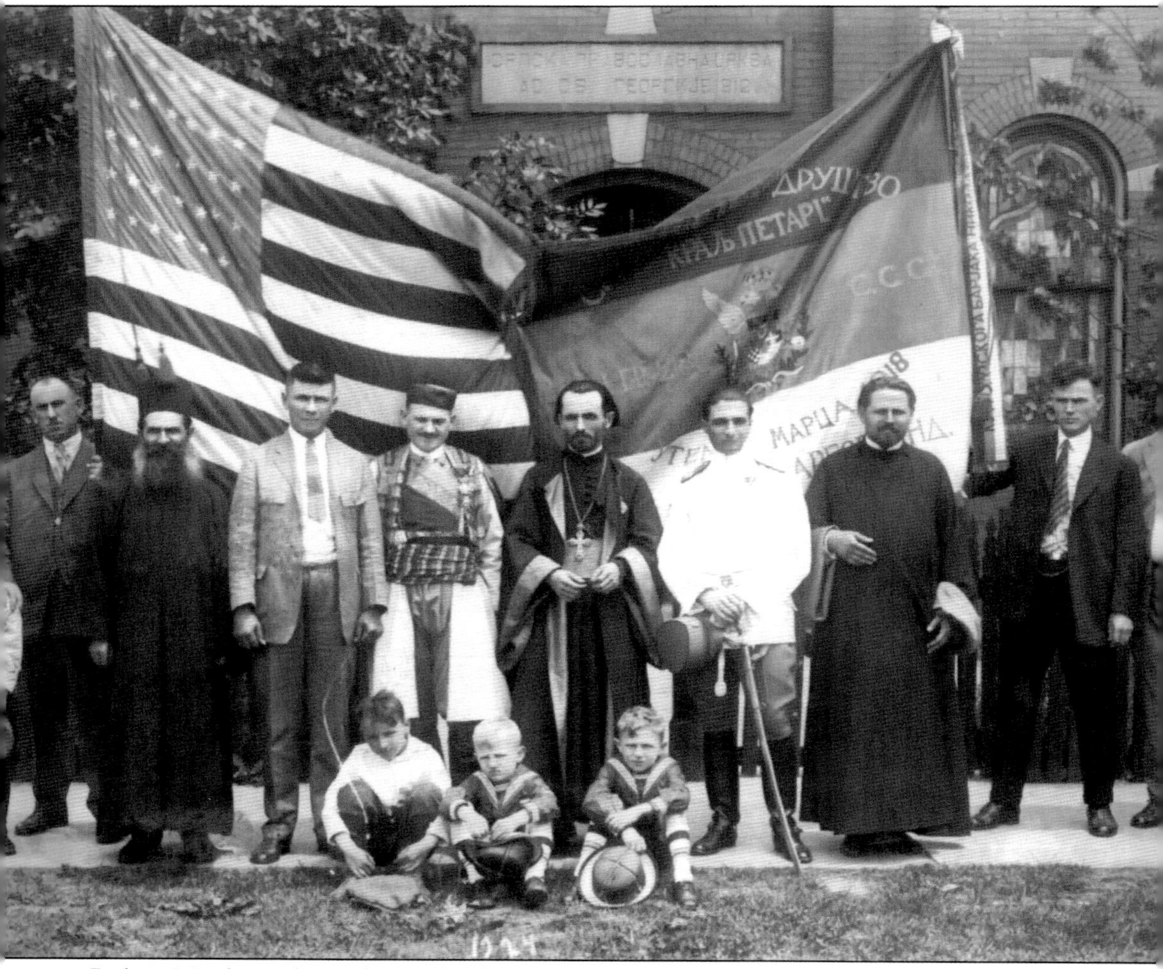

Bishop Mardarije (center) was the first Serbian Bishop of America and Canada for the new American Serbian Diocese, which was recognized in 1921 by the Serbian Orthodox Church in Belgrade. Prior to the formation of the American Serbian Diocese, Serbian Orthodox churches in America were under the jurisdiction of the Russian Orthodox Church. Bishop Mardarije visited St. George Serbian Orthodox Church of East Chicago, Indiana, in 1924. The visit took place about one year after he founded the St. Sava Serbian Orthodox Monastery in Libertyville, Illinois. The St. George Serbian Orthodox Church was consecrated on May 5, 1912, and remains in the same location in East Chicago, Indiana. St. George is the oldest continuously used Serbian Orthodox church building in the Chicagoland area and among the oldest in the United States. (Courtesy of St. George Serbian Orthodox Church, East Chicago, Indiana.)

The construction of the St. Sava Serbian Orthodox Monastery in Libertyville, Illinois, began in the 1930s. Since then, families have been visiting the monastery, cemetery, and the grounds around it. Pictured are the Tesović and Mulin families in 1962. The St. Sava Serbian Orthodox Monastery is listed on the National Register of Historic Places. (Courtesy of St. Sava Serbian Orthodox Church, Merrillville, Indiana.)

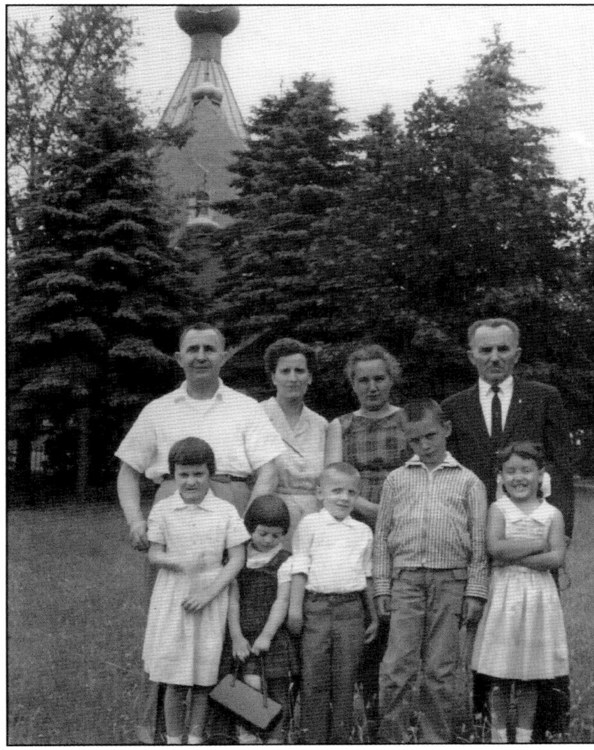

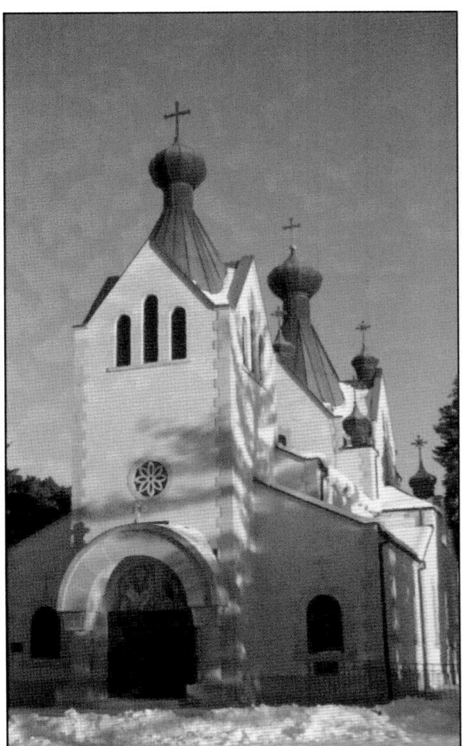

The St. Sava Serbian Orthodox Monastery in Libertyville, Illinois, includes a School of Theology as well as a large Orthodox cemetery. At one time, Peter II Karađorđević, the third and final King of Yugoslavia and last reigning member of the Karageorgevich dynasty, was buried here until he was moved to Serbia for reburial in 2013. (Courtesy of Milena Radjenovich.)

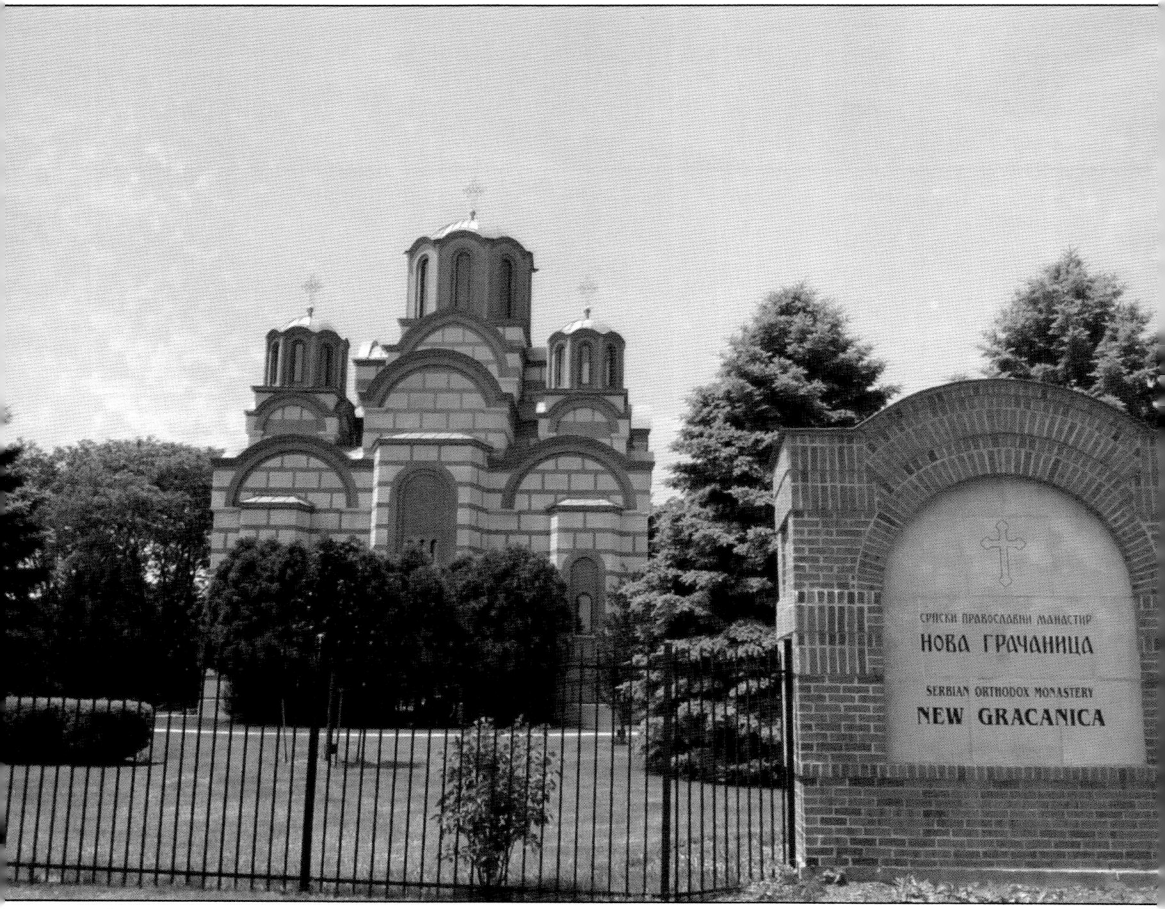

Plans for the New Gračanica Monastery began in 1977, with the church being completed and consecrated in 1984. The building is a slightly larger architectural replica of the original Gračanica in Kosovo, which was built in 1321 under the direction of King Stefan Milutin. New Gračanica's wooden entrance doors include 23 images of monasteries and churches from various regions throughout Serbia. The grounds also include a cemetery and seminary. New Gračanica is the seat of the Diocese of New Gračanica and Midwestern America. Metropolitan Irinej, who was born in 1914 in a small village in Yugoslavia, founded and built the church and complex. He studied theology in England and the United States before entering the St. Sava Serbian Orthodox Monastery in Libertyville, Illinois. He was consecrated bishop in 1962 and was elected metropolitan in 1984. He died in 1999 and is buried at New Gračanica. (Courtesy of Milena Radjenovich.)

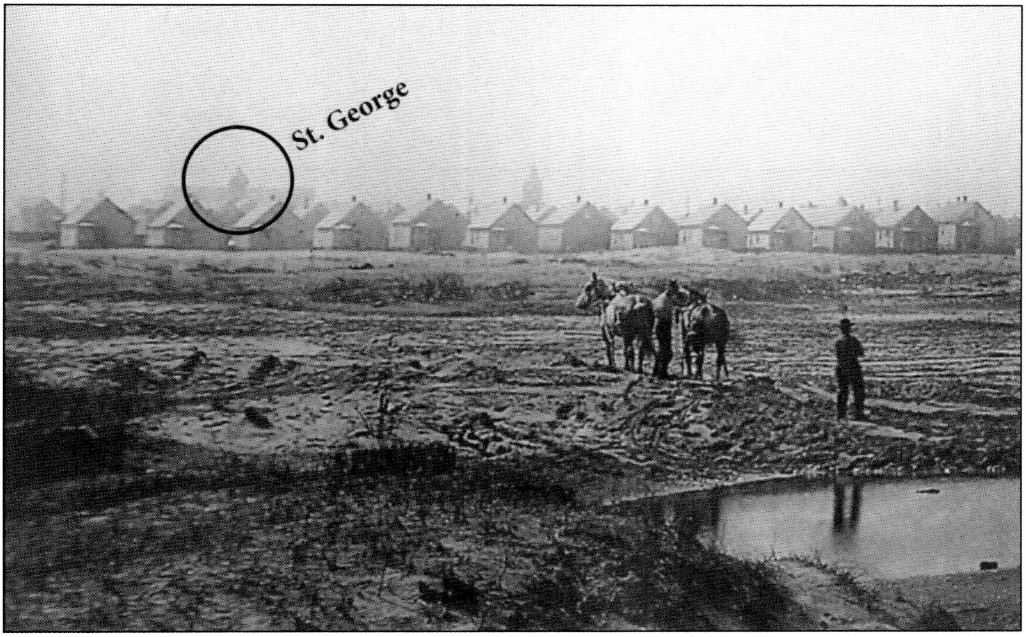

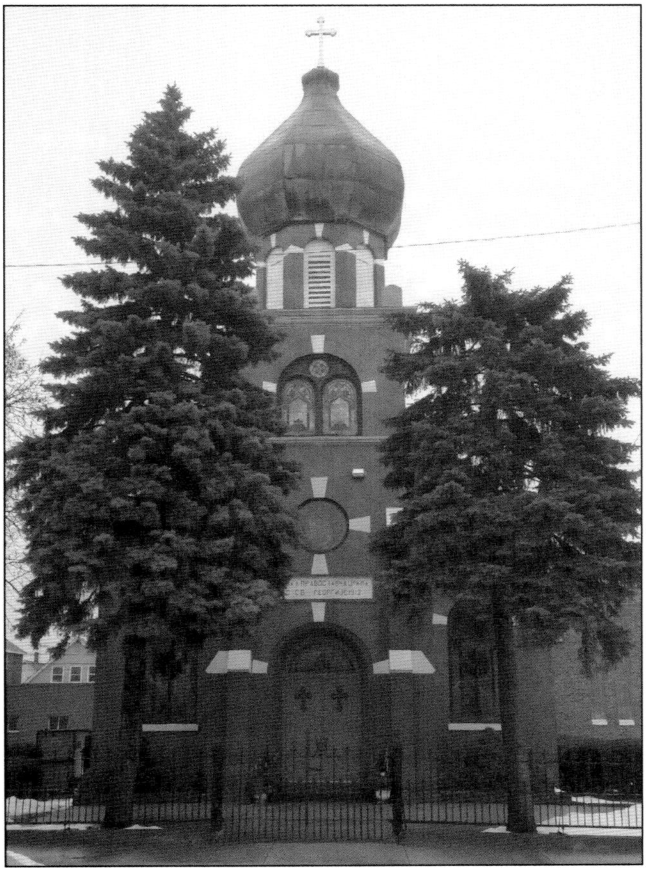

The St. George Serbian Orthodox Church dome can be seen in the top left corner of the above photograph from 1920. Four Serbian fraternal groups established the parish on October 30, 1911, and the church was consecrated on May 5, 1912. Despite a gradual and dramatic shift in the demographics of East Chicago, Indiana, the church has been in the same location since its founding. St. George is the oldest continuously used Serbian Orthodox church building in the Chicagoland area and among the oldest in the United States. The building, pictured at right, underwent a restoration in 1989 but remains largely unchanged from when it was built. St. George's boasts a modest yet dedicated group of parishioners, some of whom are third or fourth generation Serbian immigrants. (Courtesy of St. George Serbian Orthodox Church, East Chicago, Indiana.)

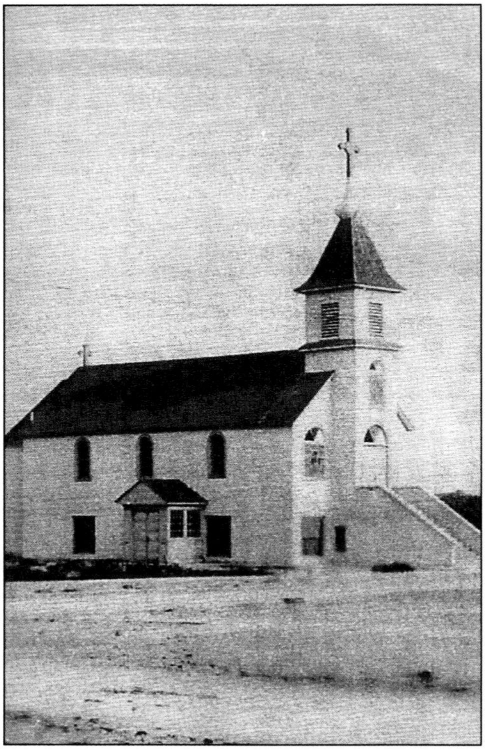

The St. Sava Serbian Orthodox Church in Gary, Indiana, was first consecrated in 1915 and remained in the same spot at Twentieth and Connecticut Streets until 1938, when the parish finally outgrew the location. The second church was consecrated a few blocks away. (Courtesy of St. Sava Serbian Orthodox Church, Merrillville, Indiana.)

Like other immigrants, Serbs built churches where the largest concentration of their parishioners lived. At the turn of the 20th century, many Serbs lived near the steel mills in Gary, Indiana. Pictured here are parishioners from the early 1920s. (Courtesy of St. Sava Serbian Orthodox Church, Merrillville, Indiana.)

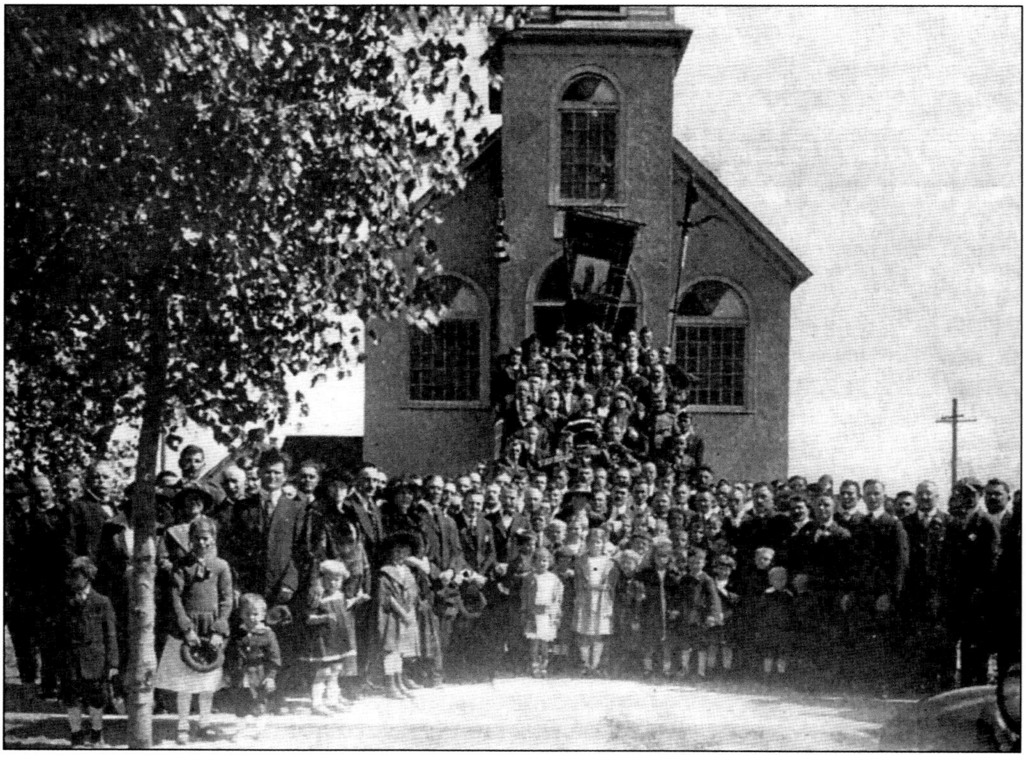

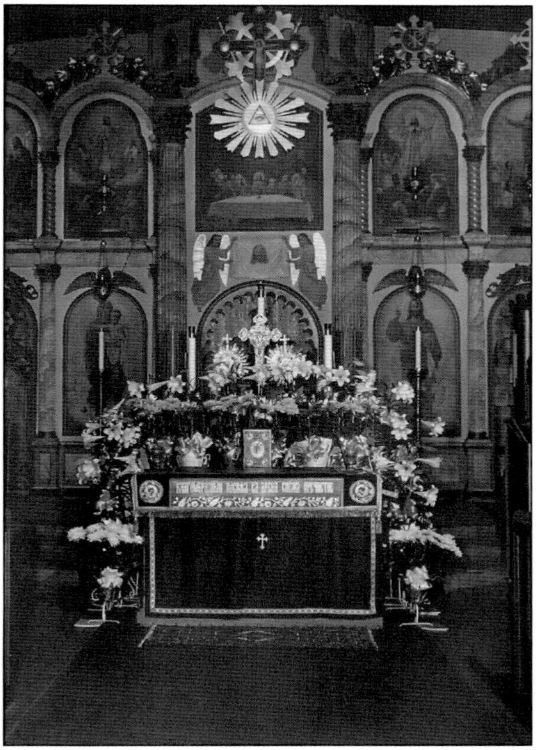

Icons decorate the interiors of Serbian Orthodox churches. Pictured is the interior of the St. Sava Serbian Orthodox Church, at its location at Thirteenth and Connecticut Streets in Gary, Indiana. The church was destroyed in a fire and only a few items survived, including a church bell, a time capsule, and a cloth from the altar. (Courtesy of St. Sava Serbian Orthodox Church, Merrillville, Indiana.)

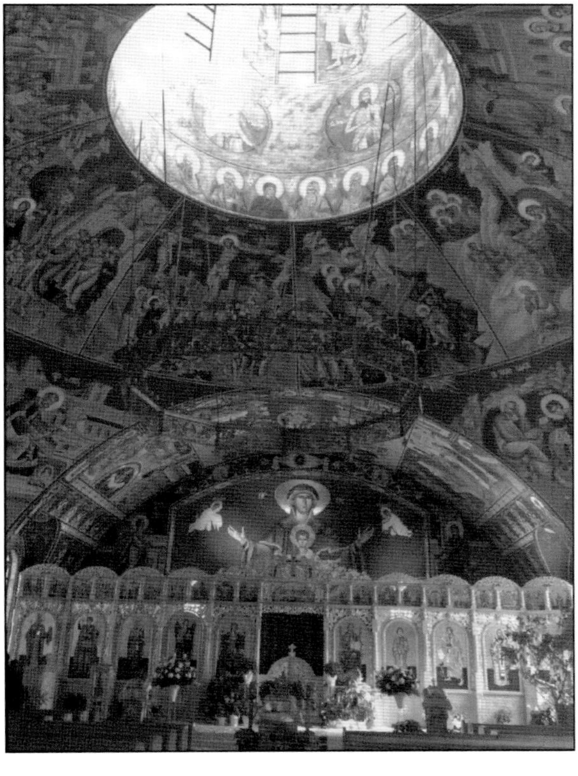

The interiors of Serbian Orthodox churches include an iconostasis—separating the nave from the sanctuary—and are typically decorated with frescoes or murals. The St. Archangel Michael Serbian Orthodox Church of Lansing, Illinois, completed its fresco project in 2014, after nearly a decade. Iconographer Filip Subotić, who studied at the St. Sava School of Theology, painted the frescoes. (Courtesy of Milena Radjenovich.)

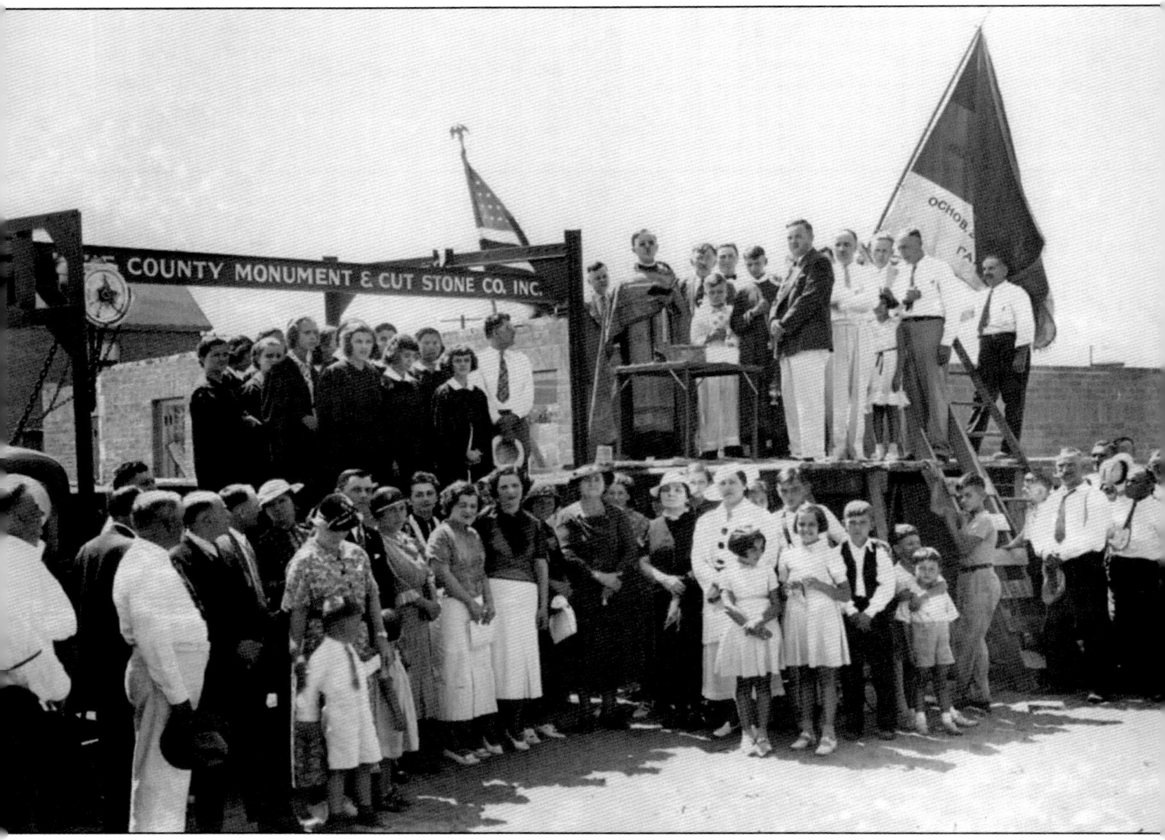

The St. Sava Serbian Orthodox Church was founded in Gary, Indiana, in 1914 at the corner of Twentieth and Connecticut Streets. In response to the rapid growth of church membership, a second location was built a few blocks away, at Thirteenth and Connecticut Streets. The first Serbian Bishop of America and Canada, Bishop Mardarije blessed the ground of the second site in 1929. Here, parishioners from the St. Sava Serbian Orthodox Church gather around the construction site for the new church. Bishop Irinej, who became Metropolitan Irinej, blessed the cornerstone of the new church in 1937, when construction began. The church was completed in 1938. The famous Serbian inventor Nikola Tesla served as the godfather (*kum*) of the event; he was unable to attend but sent a representative to read a letter he had written to the parish. The church remained at Thirteenth and Connecticut Streets until 1991, when a new church was consecrated in nearby Merrillville. (Courtesy of St. Sava Serbian Orthodox Church, Merrillville, Indiana.)

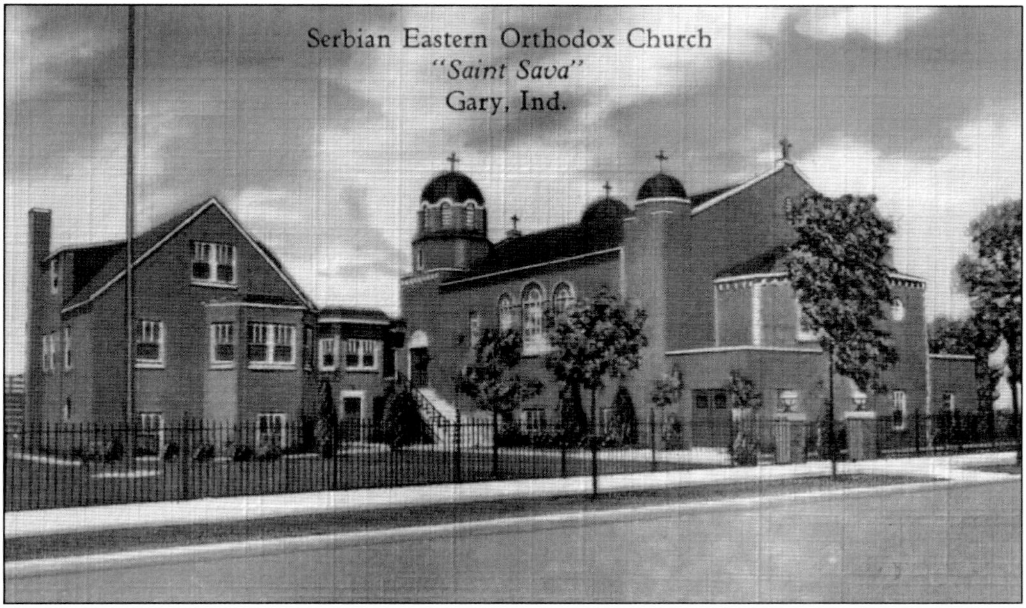

After the St. Sava Serbian Orthodox Church outgrew its original location in fewer than 25 years, the parish built a new church at Thirteenth and Connecticut Streets. The new church included a hall and a parish house for the priest and his family. (Courtesy of St. Sava Serbian Orthodox Church, Merrillville, Indiana.)

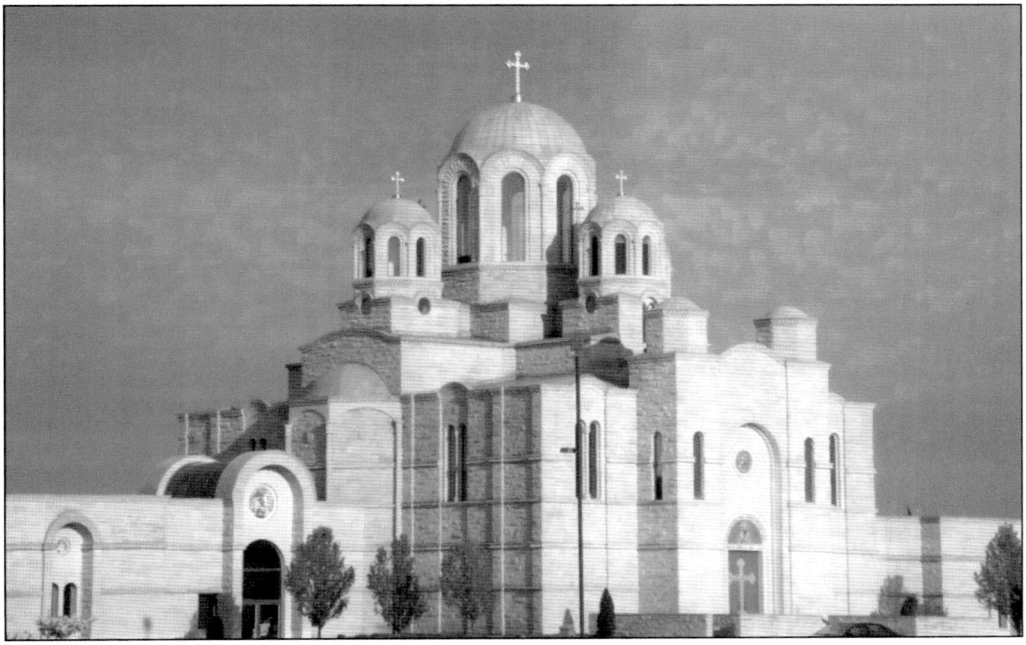

Having outgrown its second location, the St. Sava Serbian Orthodox Church built a larger church to accommodate its growing parish in Merrillville, Indiana. The parish recently celebrated its 100th anniversary. In that time, one of its altar boys—Vojislav Nastić—became the first American-born Serbian to be proclaimed an Orthodox saint. He is now known as St. Varnava. (Courtesy of Dorothy Paunovich.)

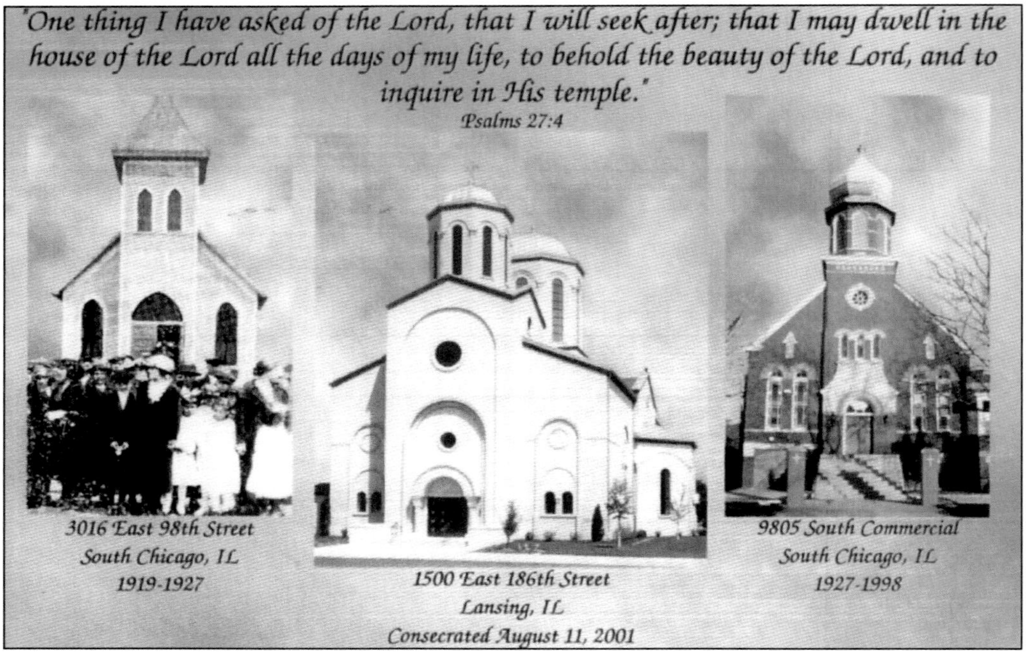

During the last 100 years, Serbian Orthodox churches have had to address the changing demographics of their neighborhoods. In 1919, the St. Archangel Michael Serbian Orthodox Church was originally located in South Chicago, where many Serbs worked and lived. It moved to its second, larger location around the corner in 1927 and is now located in Lansing, Illinois—about 15 miles south. (Courtesy of Ljiljana Dobrosavljević.)

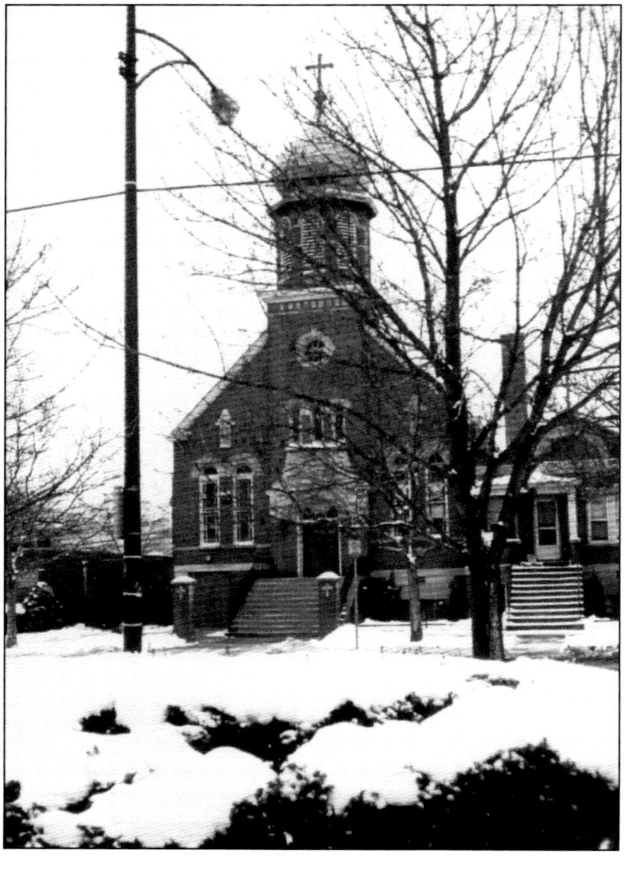

For more than 70 years, the St. Archangel Michael Church in South Chicago was located on Commercial Avenue. Its onion-shaped dome was visible to the many Serbs who lived in the area. The property also included a parish house and picnic grounds where the church would hold weekly picnics with Serbian music and food. (Courtesy of Ljubi Ostoich Hayden.)

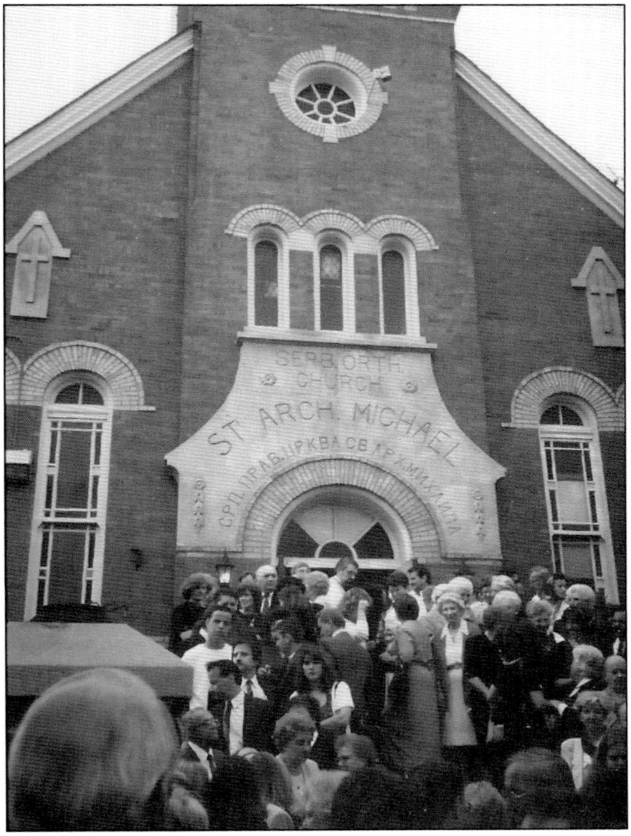

In 1998, parishioners of the St. Archangel Michael Serbian Orthodox Church came together for one final service at the church's South Chicago location. They gathered outside on the church's steps to take a photograph commemorating the occasion. A new church was built in Lansing, Illinois, a southern suburb of Chicago. (Courtesy of Ljiljana Dobrosavljević.)

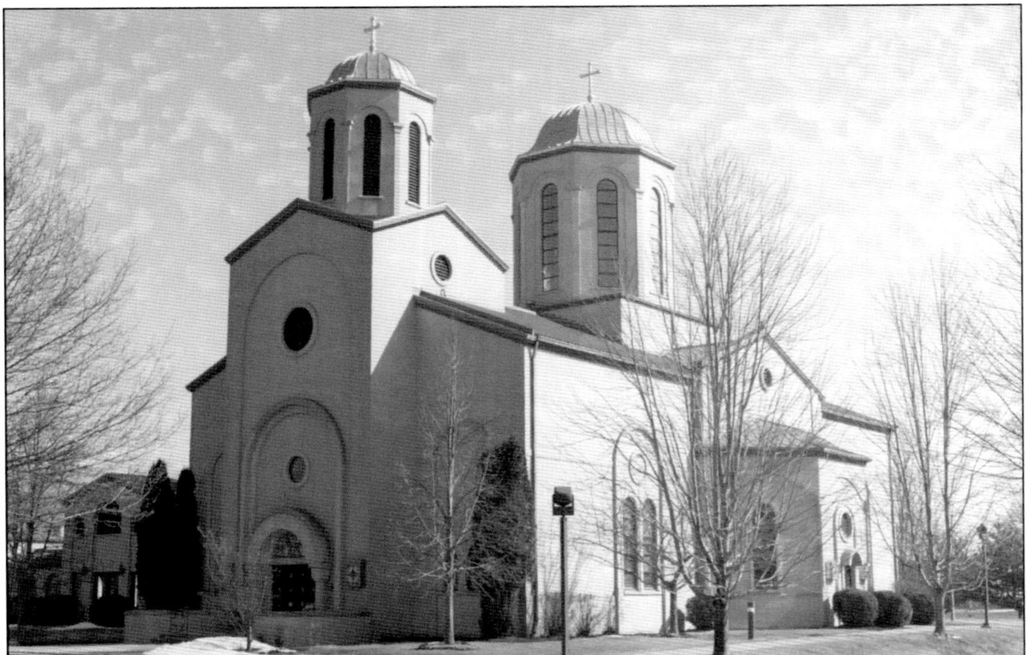

The St. Archangel Michael Serbian Orthodox Church in Lansing, Illinois, was consecrated in 2001. Services were held for nearly three years in the church's social center, which is located on the same property, until the church was built. (Courtesy of Marina Marich.)

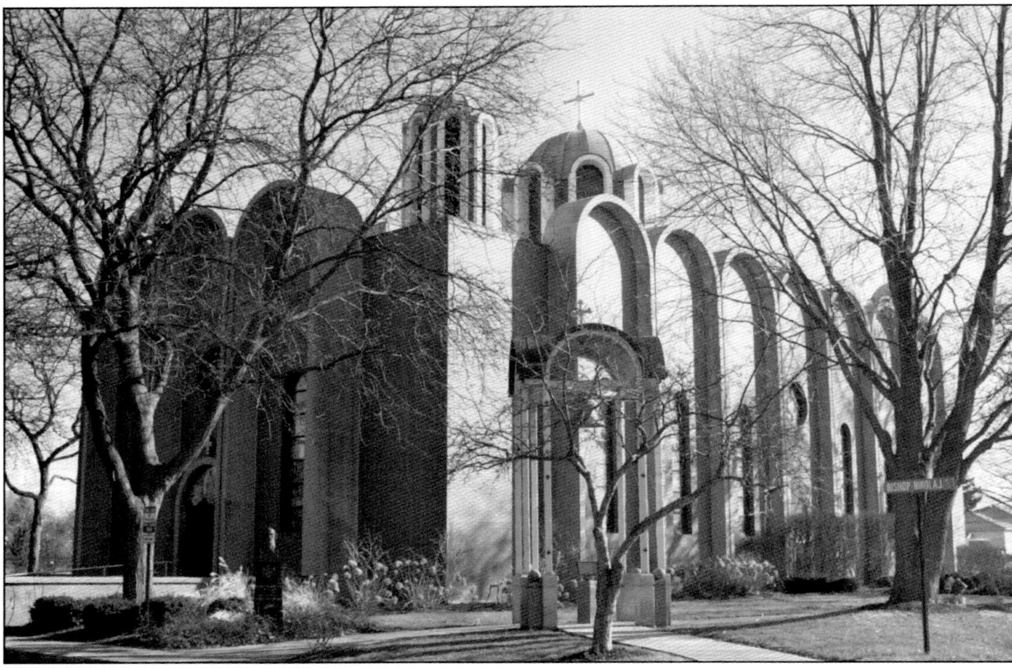

The Holy Resurrection Serbian Orthodox Cathedral's history dates back to 1905, when its first chapel was consecrated. Outgrowing the building, the parish built a new church and hall on the same site, on Schiller Street in Chicago. The parish remained there until 1975, when the cathedral was built at the intersection of Redwood Drive and Serbian Road. (Courtesy of Marina Marich.)

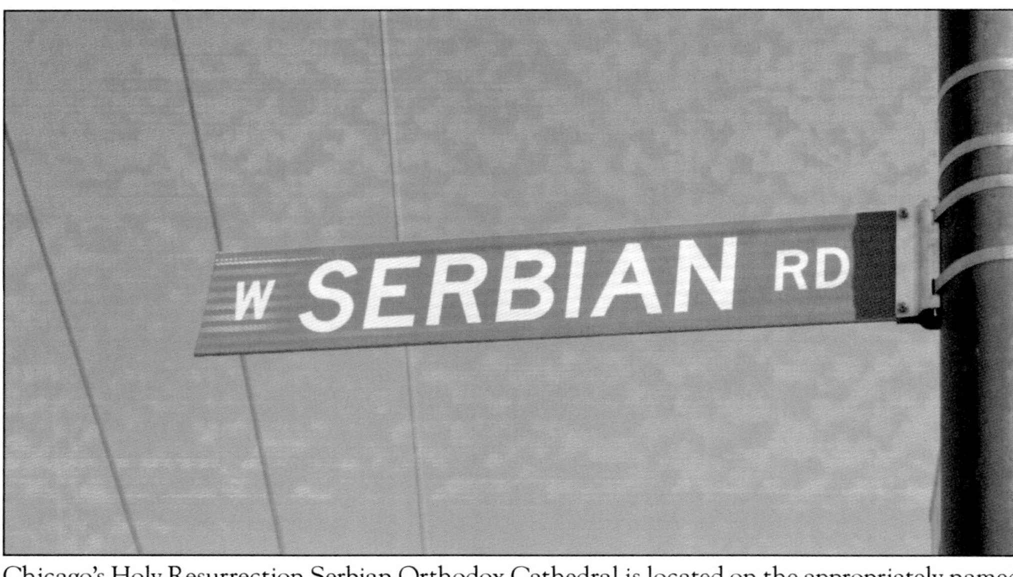

Chicago's Holy Resurrection Serbian Orthodox Cathedral is located on the appropriately named Serbian Road. In 1975, the Chicago City Council changed the name of the street to Serbian Road in recognition of the contributions that the Serbian community made to the city. It was reported that this was the first street in Chicago to be named after an ethnic group. (Courtesy of Marina Marich.)

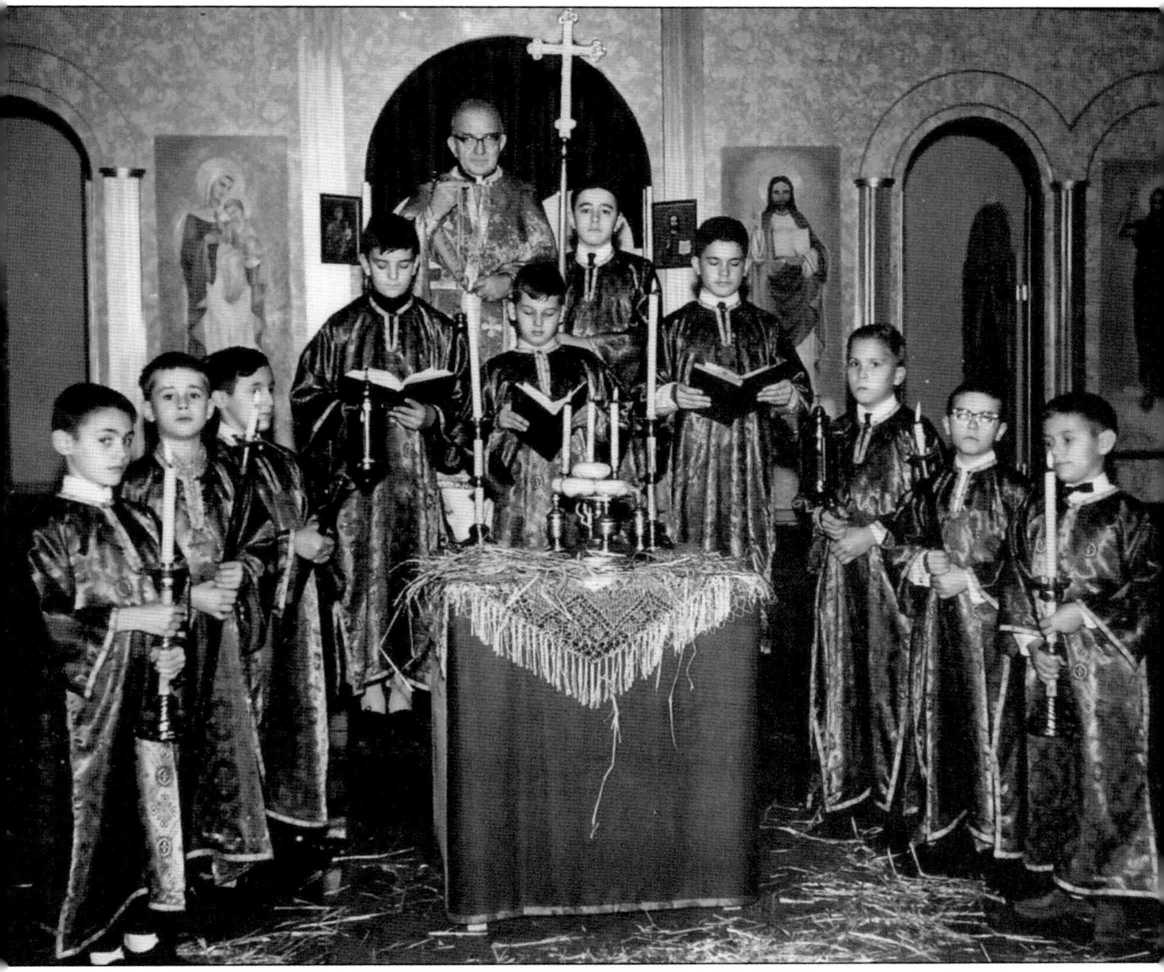

Altar boys assist the higher clergy during services by carrying candles or a cross, loading incense in the censer, and helping prepare antidoron for Holy Communion. This allows the higher clergy to focus on the service. Altar boys wear special liturgical vestments that are blessed by the priest before they wear them. Although the minimum age of altar boys may vary, altar boys must be mature enough to carry out their duties without disrupting the service. This photograph was taken during Christmas Eve services in 1967, at St. Elijah Serbian Orthodox Church on Forty-first and Adams Streets in Gary, Indiana. The priest is Rev. Dušan Shoukletovich. (Courtesy of St. Sava Serbian Orthodox Church, Merrillville, Indiana.)

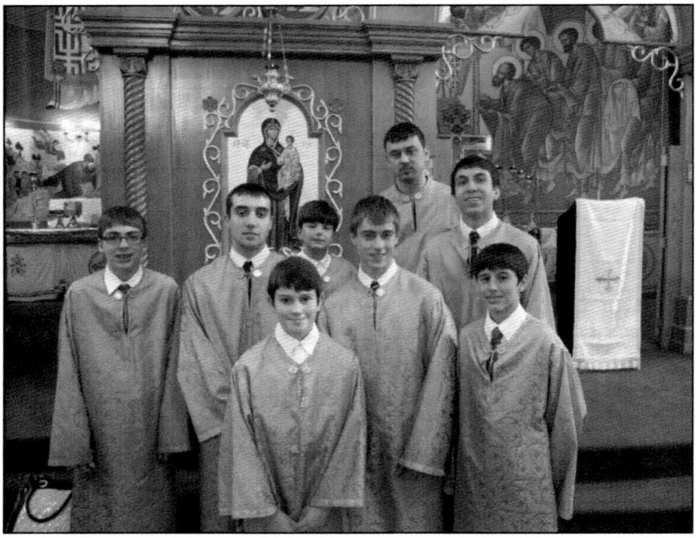

Serbian Orthodox churches continue the tradition of having altar boys take part in, and assist with, weekly services. Pictured from left to right are (first row) Dušan Matić; (second row) Danilo Orlich, Dejan Stefanovich, Nikola Jeftić, and Christopher Orlich; (third row) Nikola Djukić and Marko Ivanović; and (back row) Nikola Ajder—head altar boy. (Courtesy of St. Sava Serbian Orthodox Church, Merrillville, Indiana.)

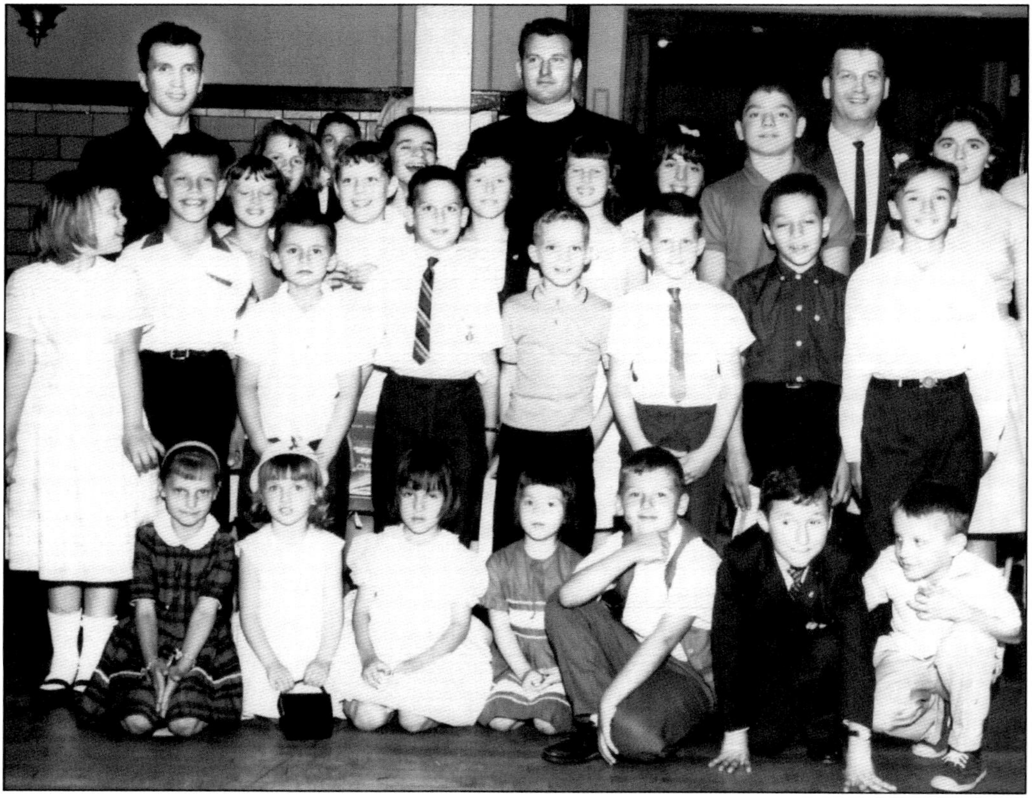

Serbian Orthodox churches hold weekly Sunday school classes to teach children about the history, culture, and spiritual values of the Orthodox Christian faith, as well as the Serbian language. Dušan Bunjevich (back, left) led the St. Sava Sunday School in the 1960s and later became a priest. Gordon Gerbick (back, right) was the school board president. Also pictured is Rev. Velimir Petakovich (back, center). (Courtesy of St. Sava Serbian Orthodox Church, Merrillville, Indiana.)

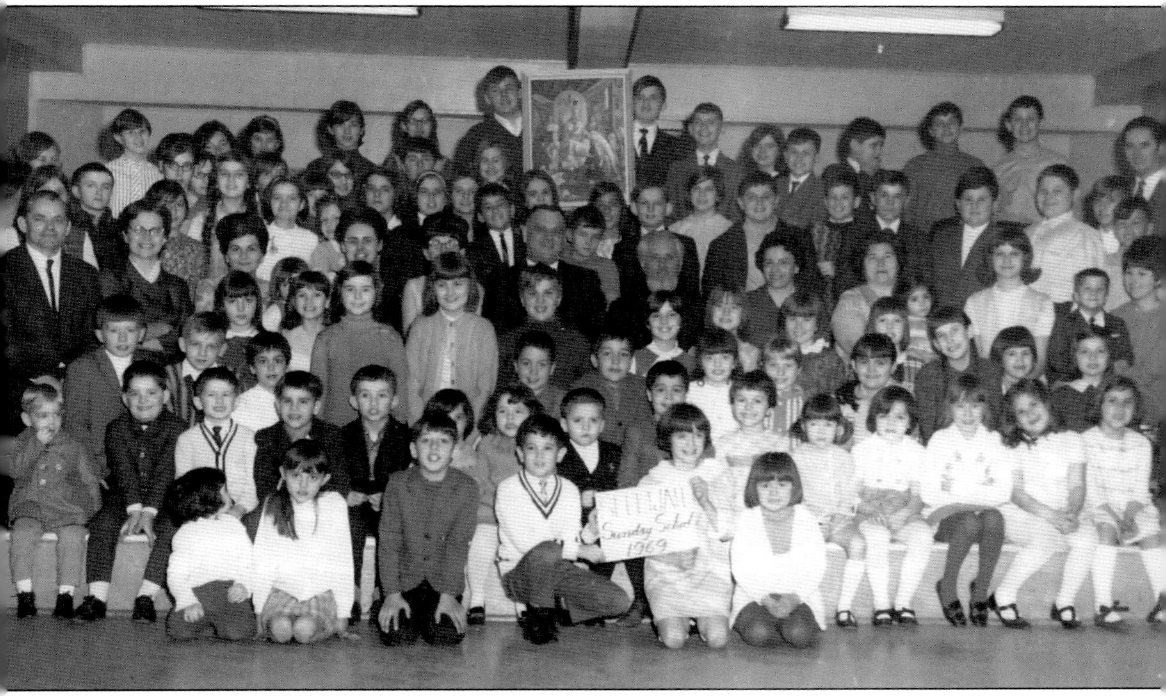

Northwest Indiana witnessed a surge of new parishioners who came to the area after World War II. Many were in search of good jobs and a sense of community with fellow Serbian immigrants. Gary, Indiana, just outside Chicago, was a popular city among Serbs. The St. Elijah Serbian Orthodox Church was originally located in Gary before it moved to nearby Merrillville in the 1960s, to accommodate a growing congregation. Pictured is a Sunday school class at the St. Elijah Serbian Orthodox Church in Merrillville in 1969. Sunday school classes were typically held in church halls while parents attended weekly services. There, children would learn the Serbian language and Eastern Orthodox religion. This became increasingly important as a way to maintain culture and traditions for multigenerational families. (Courtesy of Milan Marich.)

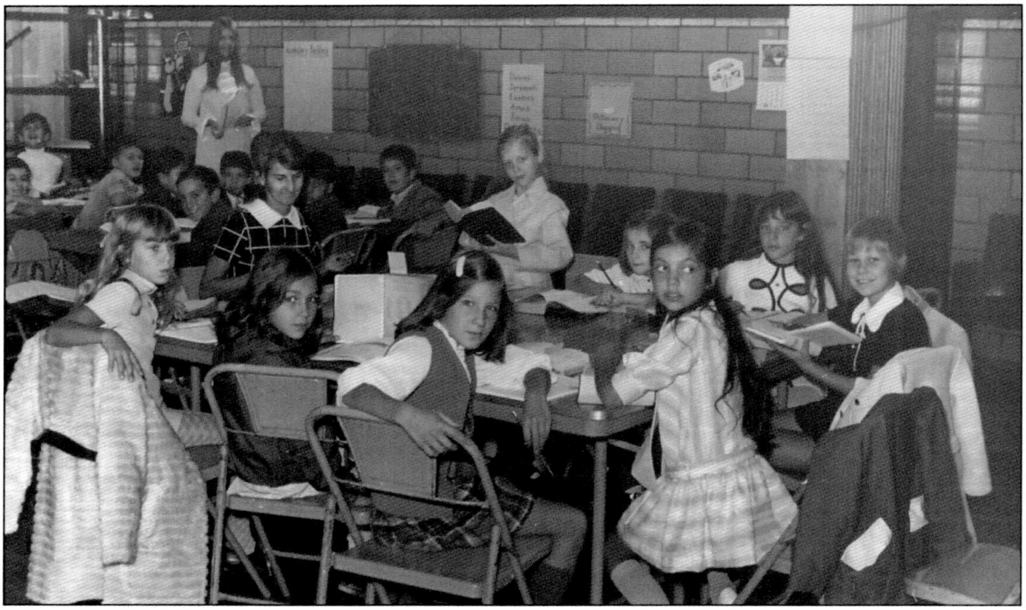

Sunday school students from the 1960s prepare to learn at the St. Sava Serbian Orthodox Church, when it was located at Thirteenth and Connecticut Streets in Gary, Indiana. The classes were held in the church hall basement while parents attended services. The two teachers pictured are (sitting) Donna Erceg and (standing) her assistant, Joanne (Milanovich) Samardzija. (Courtesy of St. Sava Serbian Orthodox Church, Merrillville, Indiana.)

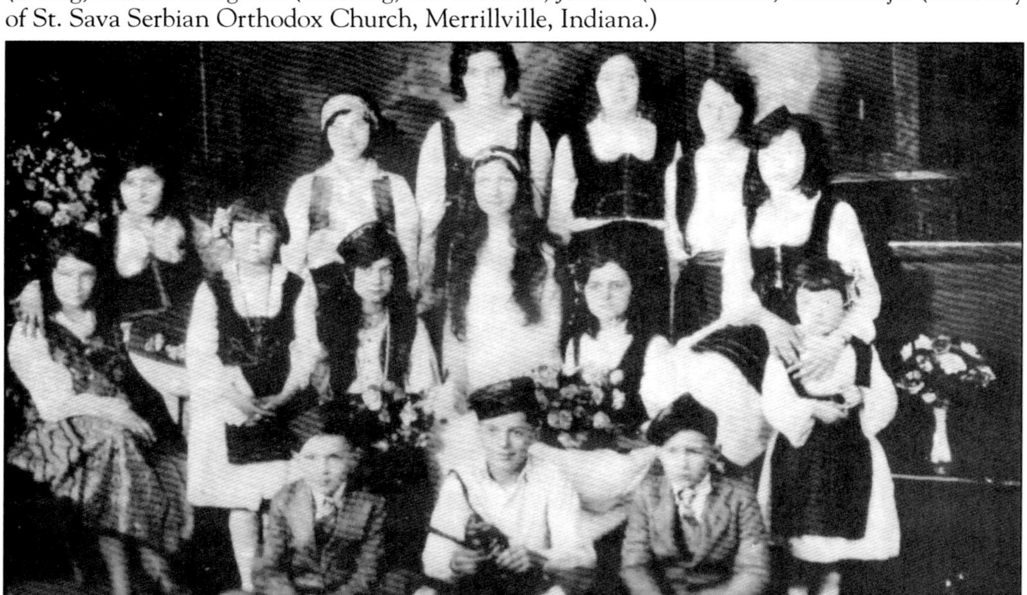

In 1930, children in Serbian school at the Holy Resurrection Serbian Orthodox Cathedral performed a play called *Srbijanka Bila*, which roughly translated to "*Serbia Was*." Like other Serbian churches, Holy Resurrection holds Serbian school every Sunday. Holy Resurrection is the first church in North America, however, to have a dual-language Serbian Orthodox parochial school for students from pre-school through the eighth grade. (Courtesy of Holy Resurrection Serbian Orthodox Cathedral, Chicago, Illinois.)

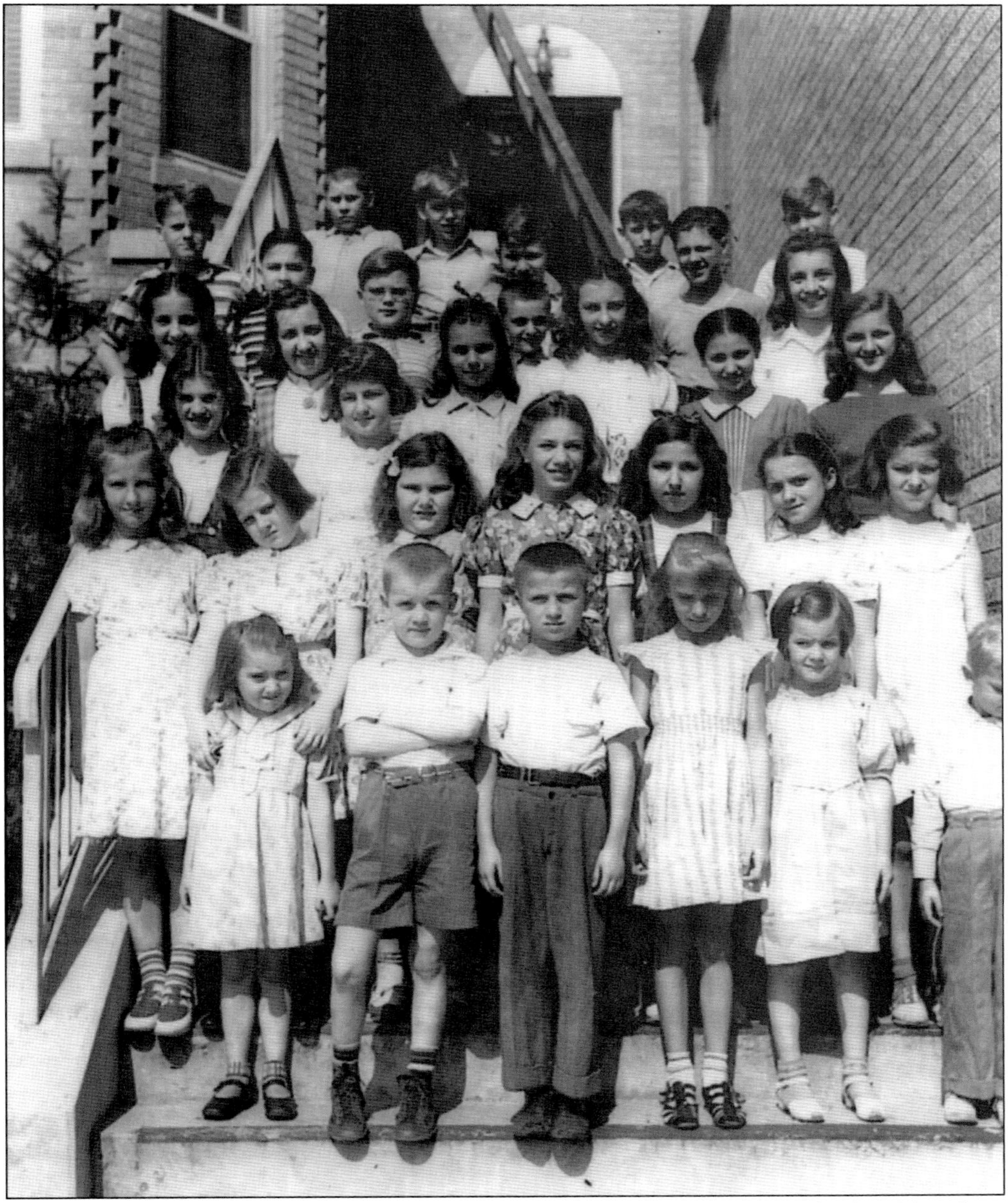

Sunday school students pose on the steps outside of St. Sava Serbian Orthodox Church in the early 1940s, when it was located at Thirteenth and Connecticut Streets in Gary, Indiana. Many of the children's families immigrated to Gary, where there was a robust Serbian American community that regularly participated in church activities and helped to maintain the parish. Bishop Mardarije, the first Serbian Bishop of America and Canada, blessed these grounds in 1929, and Bishop Irinej, who became Metropolitan Irinej, blessed the cornerstone of the new church at Twentieth and Connecticut Streets in 1937, when construction began there. The church was completed in 1938. The church remained at Thirteenth and Connecticut Streets until 1991, when a new church was consecrated in Merrillville, Indiana. (Courtesy of St. Sava Serbian Orthodox Church, Merrillville, Indiana.)

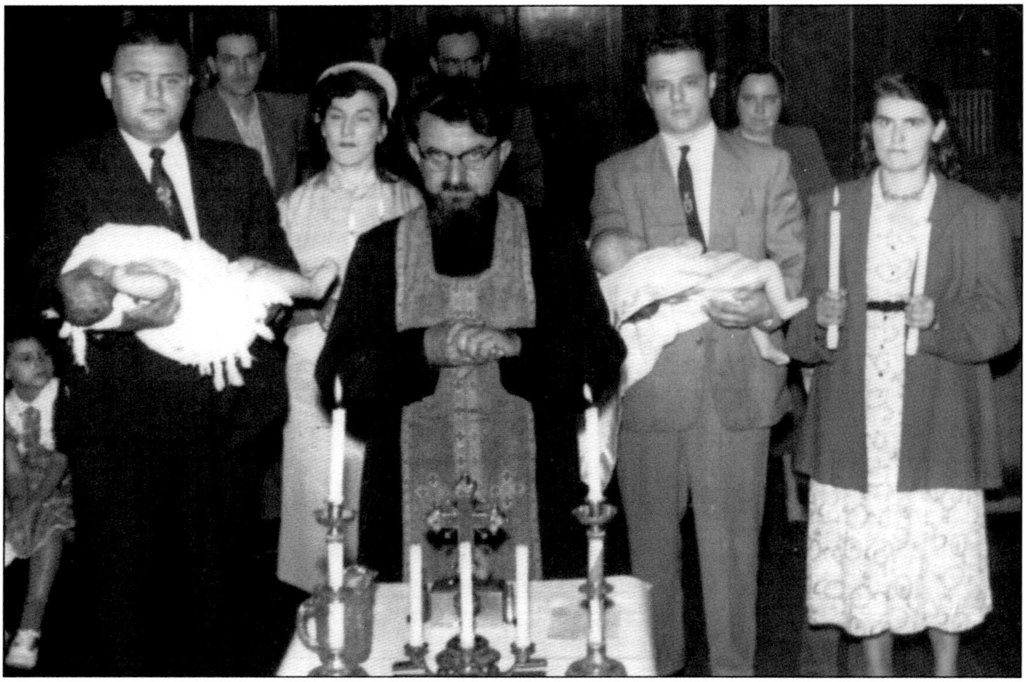

Rev. Svetozar Radovanovich presided over two simultaneous christenings in the early 1950s, at the St. Sava Serbian Orthodox Church location at Thirteenth and Connecticut Streets. The kumovi hold the child during this religious ceremony and their role is to educate the child in the ways of the religion. (Courtesy of St. Sava Serbian Orthodox Church, Merrillville, Indiana.)

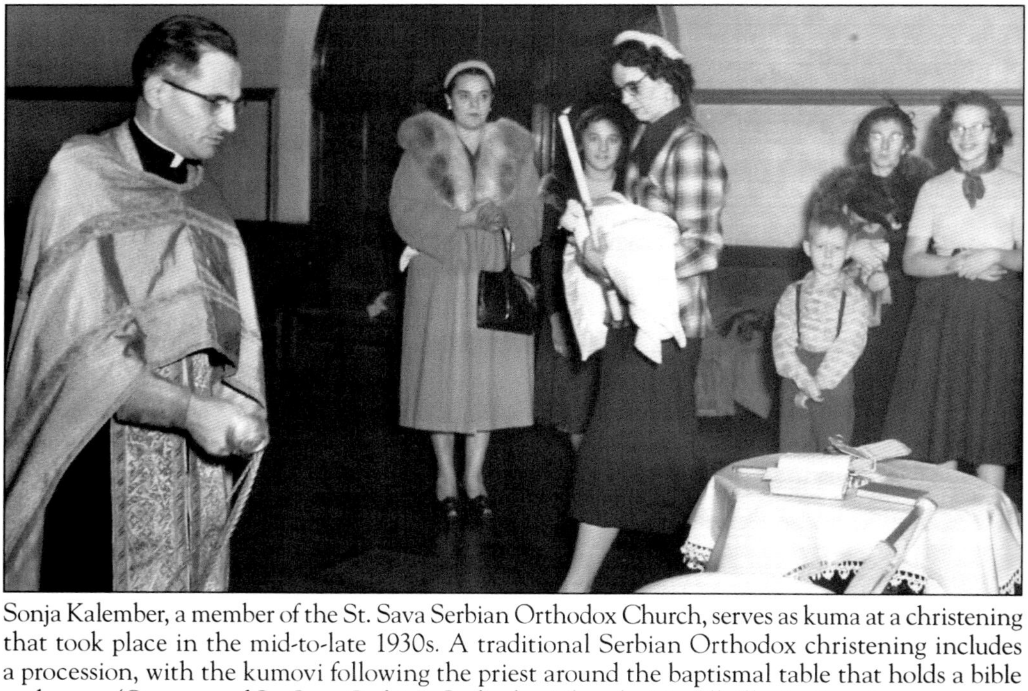

Sonja Kalember, a member of the St. Sava Serbian Orthodox Church, serves as kuma at a christening that took place in the mid-to-late 1930s. A traditional Serbian Orthodox christening includes a procession, with the kumovi following the priest around the baptismal table that holds a bible and cross. (Courtesy of St. Sava Serbian Orthodox Church, Merrillville, Indiana.)

Rev. Peter Bankerovich begins the procession for a christening that took place in 1963, at the St. Sava Serbian Orthodox Church's Thirteenth and Connecticut Streets location. The baby is immersed in baptismal water, and the godparents walk around the table with the baby wrapped in a blanket. (Courtesy of Milan Marich.)

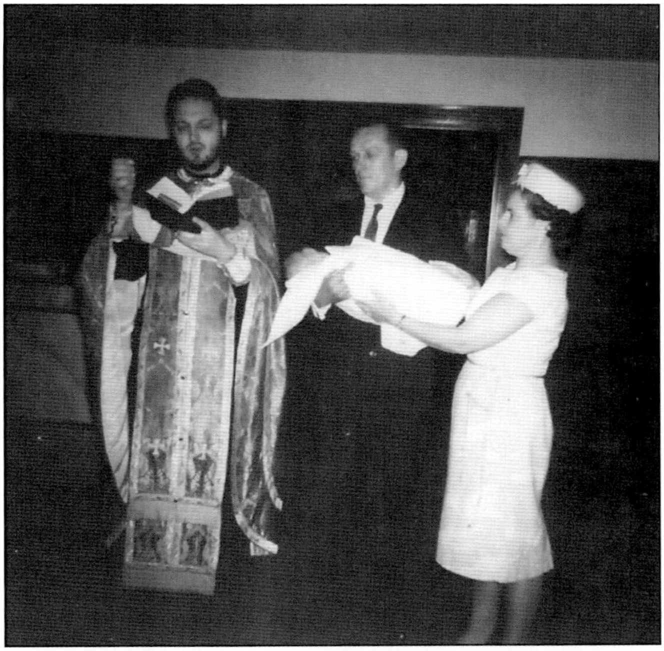

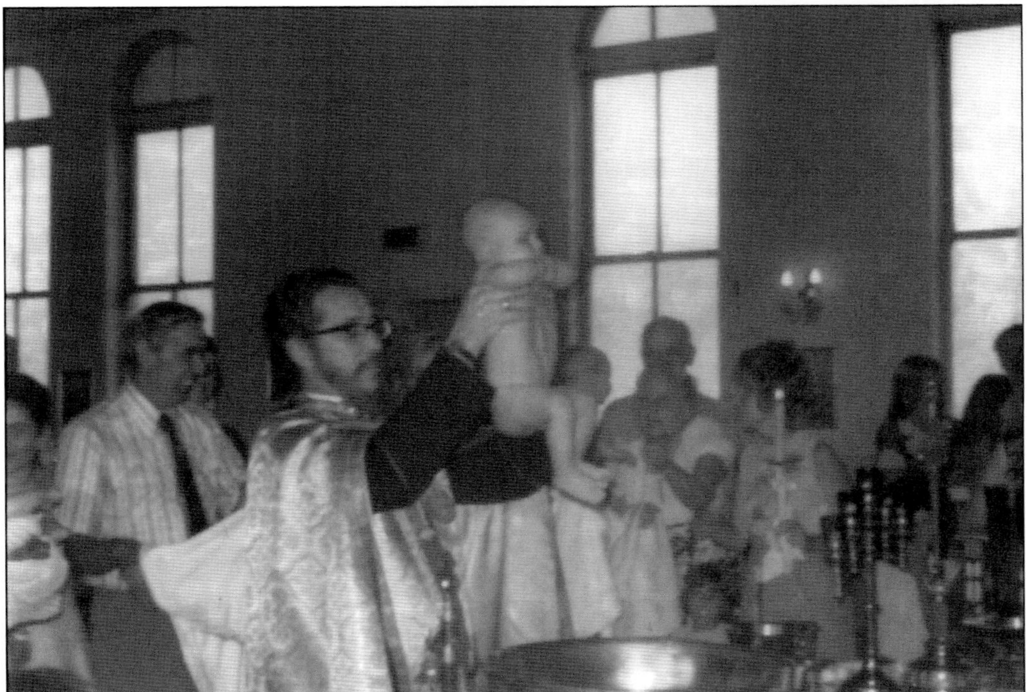

Today's Serbian Orthodox christenings are similar to those done years ago. In this photograph from the early 1970s, Rev. Velimir Kovacevich immerses an unidentified baby during his christening at the St. Archangel Michael Serbian Orthodox Church in South Chicago. Kovacevich was elevated to Metropolitan Christopher, becoming the first American-born bishop to serve a diocese of the Serbian Orthodox Church in America. (Courtesy of Dorothy Lalich.)

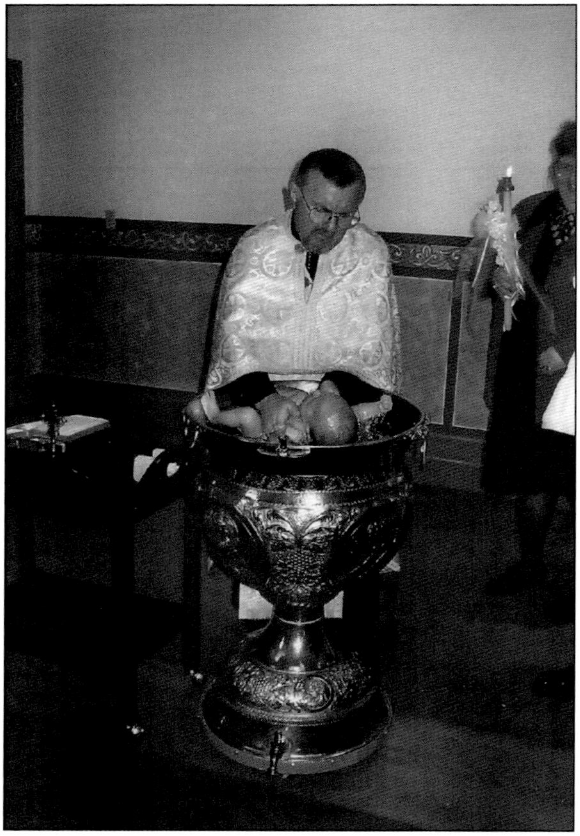

In this 2002 photograph, Rev. Jovan "John" Todorovich, from the St. Sava Serbian Orthodox Church, blesses baby Lauren Ivankovich by immersing her in baptismal water. (Courtesy of St. Sava Serbian Orthodox Church, Merrillville, Indiana.)

As part of the Orthodox christening, the priest anoints parts of the baptized infant with a special substance made of olive oil and perfumes. The ritual, still done today, signifies when the one being baptized is made a Christian. Pictured is Fenna Liese Paunovich, at her christening on May 17, 2014, at St. Sava Serbian Orthodox Church in Merrillville, Indiana. (Courtesy of Jelena (Kurtes) Mulin.)

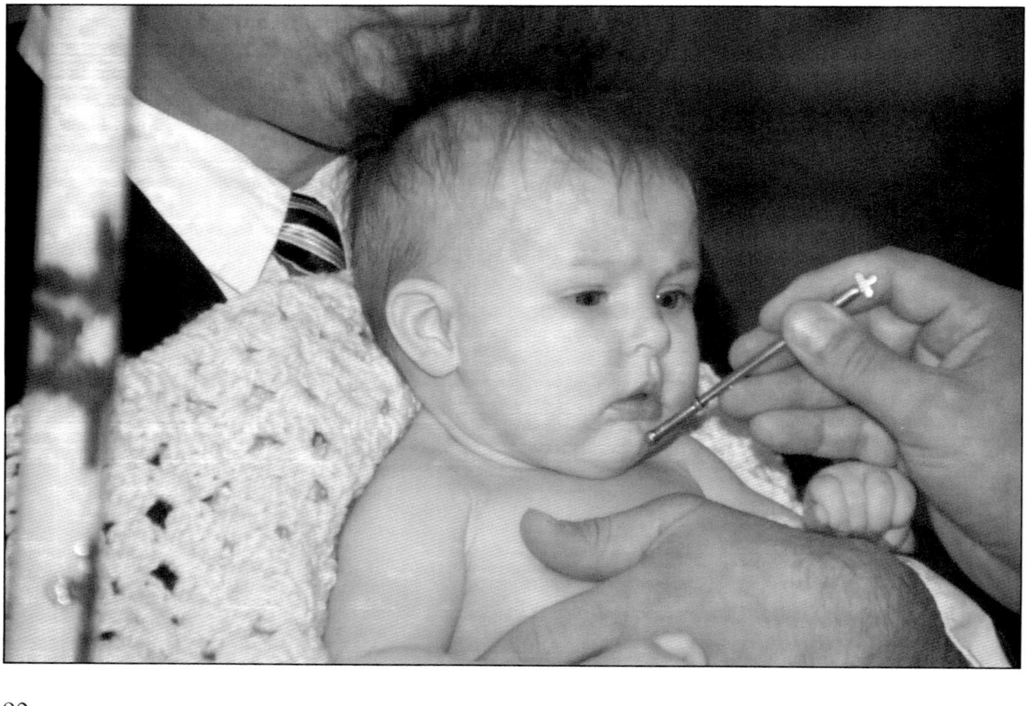

Six

Our Holidays

There is no better time of the year to honor customs and traditions than during the holidays. For Serbs, one particular holiday that is unique to their culture and holds a special place is Slava, or a family's patron saint day.

Every Serbian Orthodox family celebrates a patron saint. Tradition holds that families were assigned patron saints whose birthdays were closest to the day when the families converted from paganism to Christianity. While there are some variations in traditions based on Serbian regions, the celebration typically includes several items to symbolize Christianity: an icon of the patron saint, a candle, bread (*kolač*), a wheat pudding (*žito*), and red wine.

The candle remains lit all day. A priest blesses the bread, cuts it crosswise, and pours red wine on it. The bread is then broken into four parts and shared with guests. There is traditionally a feast at the home of those celebrating Slava. There, friends and guests drink wine, eat, and give well wishes to the family.

Slava is passed down from generation to generation through families. In November 2014, Slava was added to the United Nations Education, Scientific, and Cultural Organization's (UNESCO) Intangible Cultural Heritage of Humanity list.

In addition to honoring the unique traditions of Slava, Serbs also maintain distinct customs for Christmas. The Serbian Orthodox Church follows the Julian calendar, with Christmas (Božić) taking place each year on January 7. On Christmas Eve (Badnje Veče), families prepare meals that follow the rules of fasting (no meat or dairy) and bring a log (*badnjak*), straw, and walnuts into their homes for health and good fortune in the coming year. Typically, Serbian Americans in the Chicagoland area will attend Christmas Eve services at a church, where a badnjak will be burned on behalf of all parishioners. Each family takes home a piece of the badnjak to celebrate Christmas. In Serbia, many families continue to cut down their own badnjak to bless and decorate in their homes.

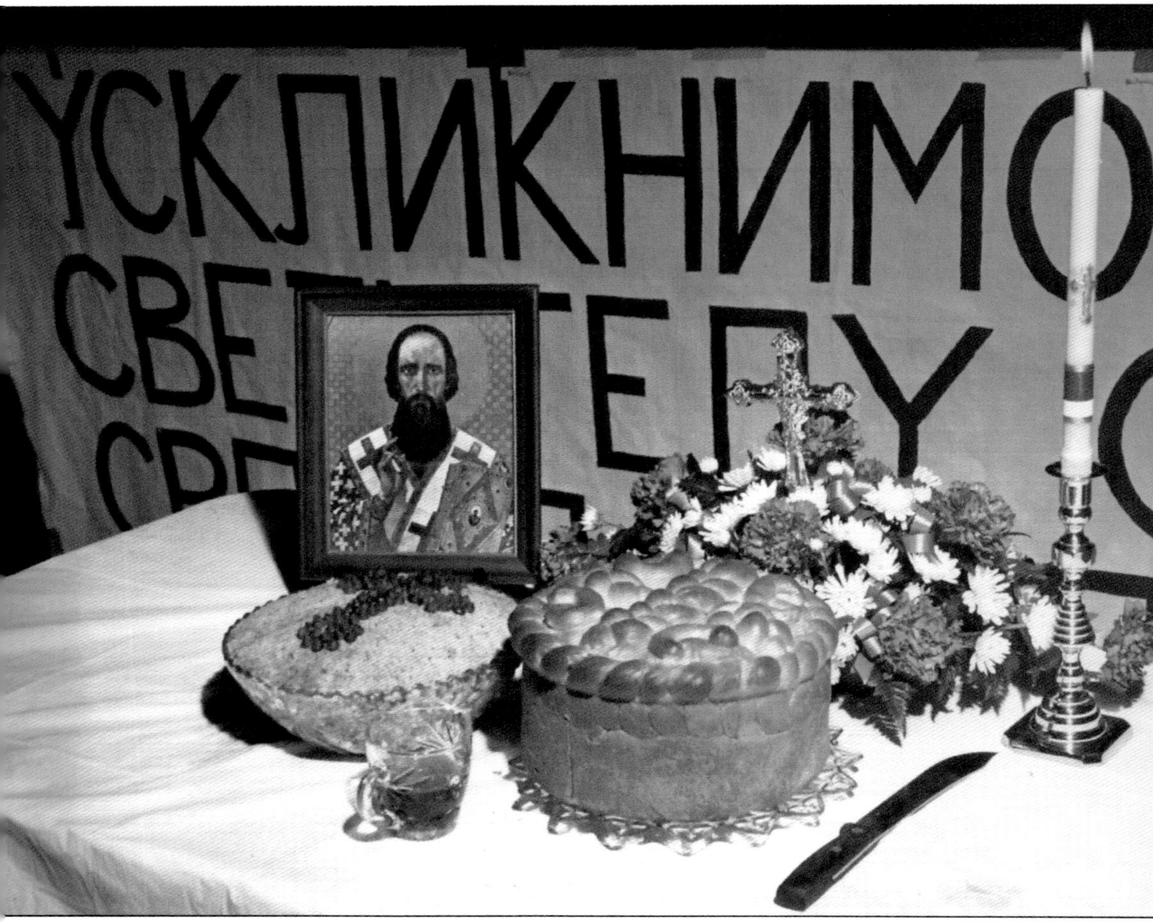

Every Serbian Orthodox family celebrates a patron saint through a holiday called Slava. Slava is a uniquely Serbian holiday and tradition that has been recognized and added to the United Nations Education, Scientific, and Cultural Organization (UNESCO) Intangible Cultural Heritage of Humanity list. Slava is passed down from generation to generation through families. While there are some variations in traditions based on Serbian regions, the celebration typically includes several items to symbolize Christianity. The photograph was taken at St. Sava Serbian Orthodox Church in the early 1970s as part of St. Sava Day, an annual Slava that celebrates and honors children and church schools. In addition to displaying an icon, the celebration also includes a candle, kolač, žito, and red wine. The candle remains lit all day, and a priest blesses the bread. (Courtesy of St. Sava Serbian Orthodox Church, Merrillville, Indiana.)

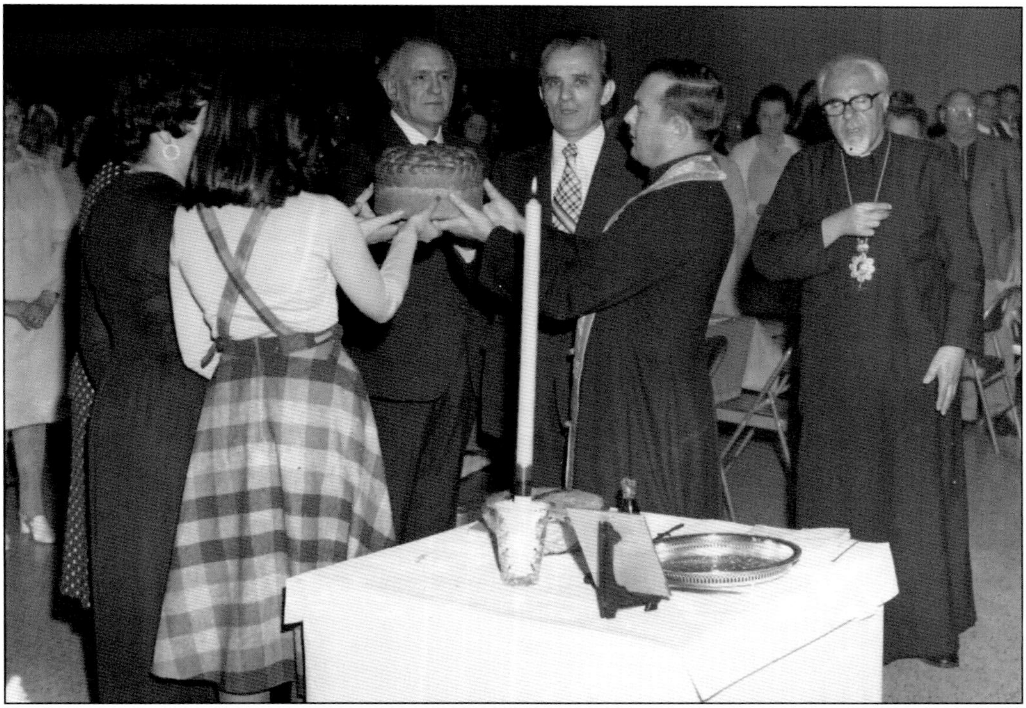

Nick Chabraja (left)—past president of the St. Sava Serbian Orthodox Church—and Zivojin Cokić (center) celebrate St. Sava Day in the early 1970s. As part of the blessing, Rev. Jovan "John" Todorovich (right) rotates the bread, gives thanks to the patron saint, and says prayers for prosperity. Bishop Irinej is seen crossing himself at far right. (Courtesy of St. Sava Serbian Orthodox Church, Merrillville, Indiana.)

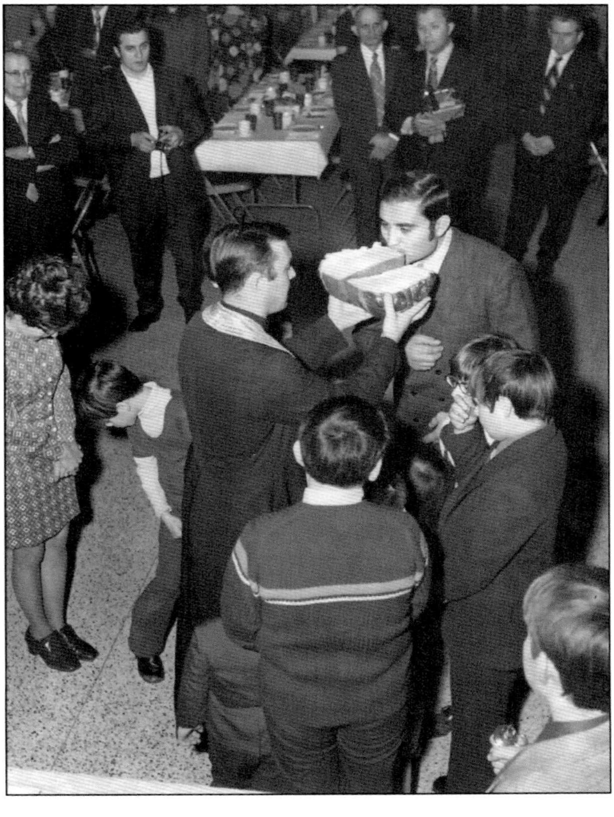

Joe Sever, Sunday school president at the St. Sava Serbian Orthodox Church, kisses the kolač to celebrate St. Sava Day in the early 1970s. Pictured with Joe are children from each class at the Sunday school. Rev. Jovan "John" Todorovich blessed the bread before pouring red wine onto it and breaking it into four pieces. (Courtesy of St. Sava Serbian Orthodox Church, Merrillville, Indiana.)

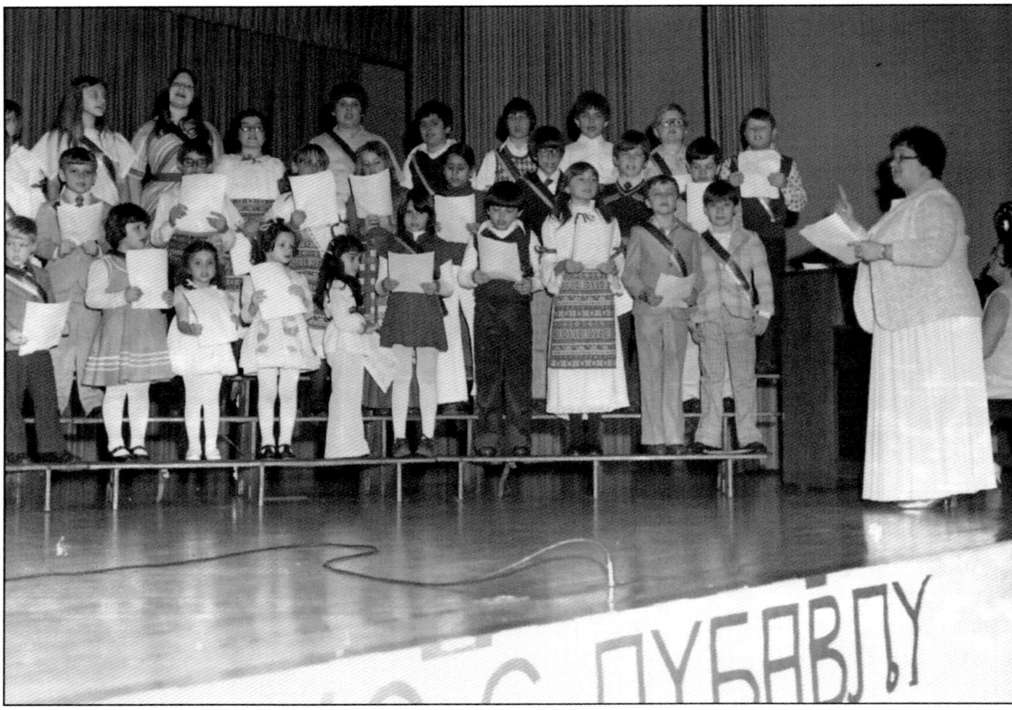

Kids from the St. Sava Serbian Orthodox Church perform as part of the St. Sava Day celebrations that took place at the church's site at Thirteenth and Connecticut Streets. The children present a poem, sing a song, or issue a declamation in Serbian. The teacher pictured is Violet Golub. (Courtesy of St. Sava Serbian Orthodox Church, Merrillville, Indiana.)

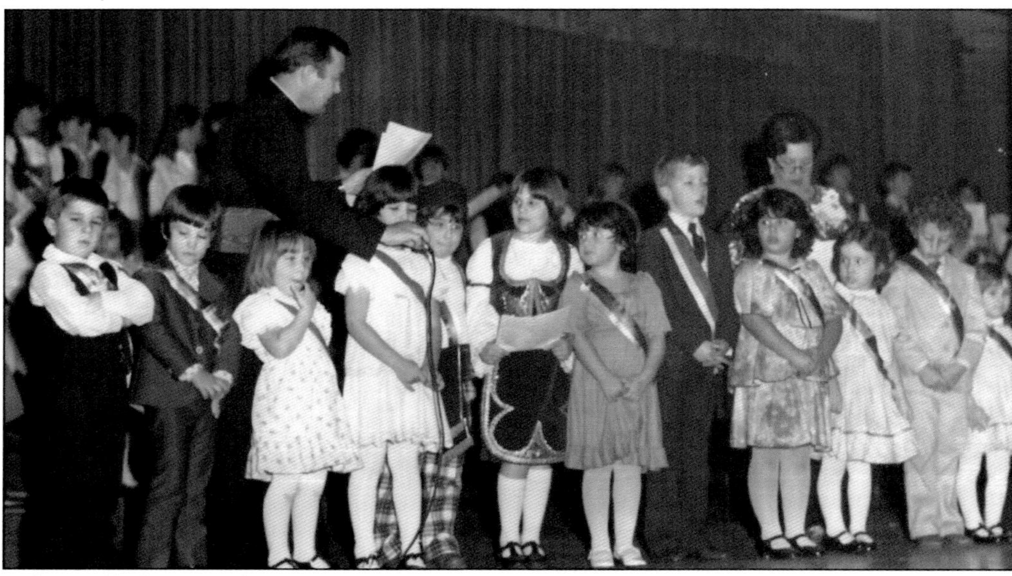

Kids stand before attendees at a St. Sava Day celebration in the early 1970s, reciting their declamation in Serbian. In this photograph, some children are wearing a traditional nošnja, while others are wearing sashes (*trobojke*) with the colors of the Serbian flag: red, blue, and white. (Courtesy of St. Sava Serbian Orthodox Church, Merrillville, Indiana.)

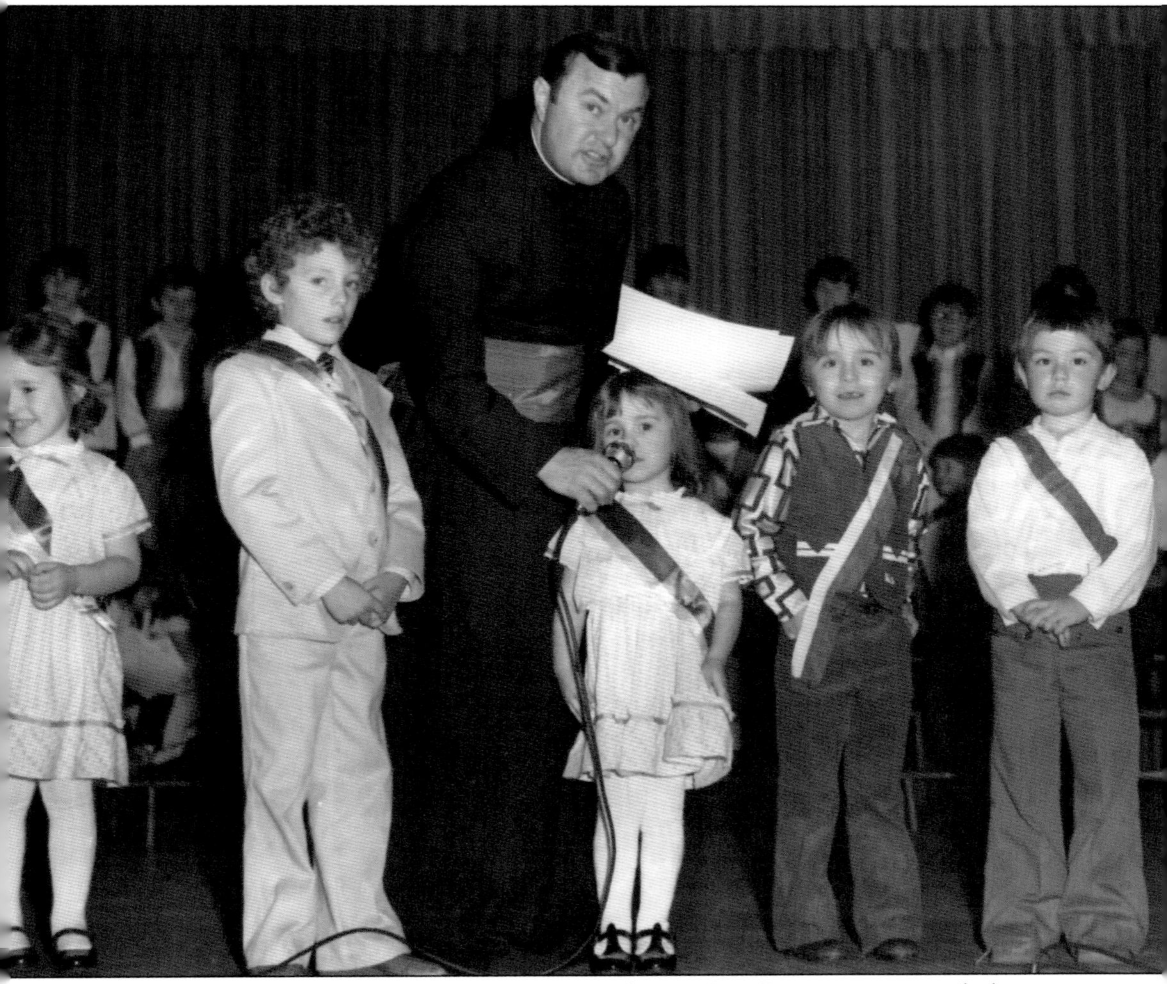

Even at a very young age, kids were expected to present their St. Sava Day poem, song, or declamation in Serbian—which helped them learn the language. Rev. Jovan "John" Todorovich is pictured helping a younger child with her presentation. As more generations were born in the United States, fewer and fewer Americans of Serbian descent spoke Serbian. By insisting that children presented in Serbian, the church helped establish a linguistic tie between the children and their heritage. The kids pictured here are also wearing trobojka in the colors of the Serbian flag. While these sashes are very popular at Serbian Orthodox weddings, they are also used for a variety of other celebrations. (Courtesy of St. Sava Serbian Orthodox Church, Merrillville, Indiana.)

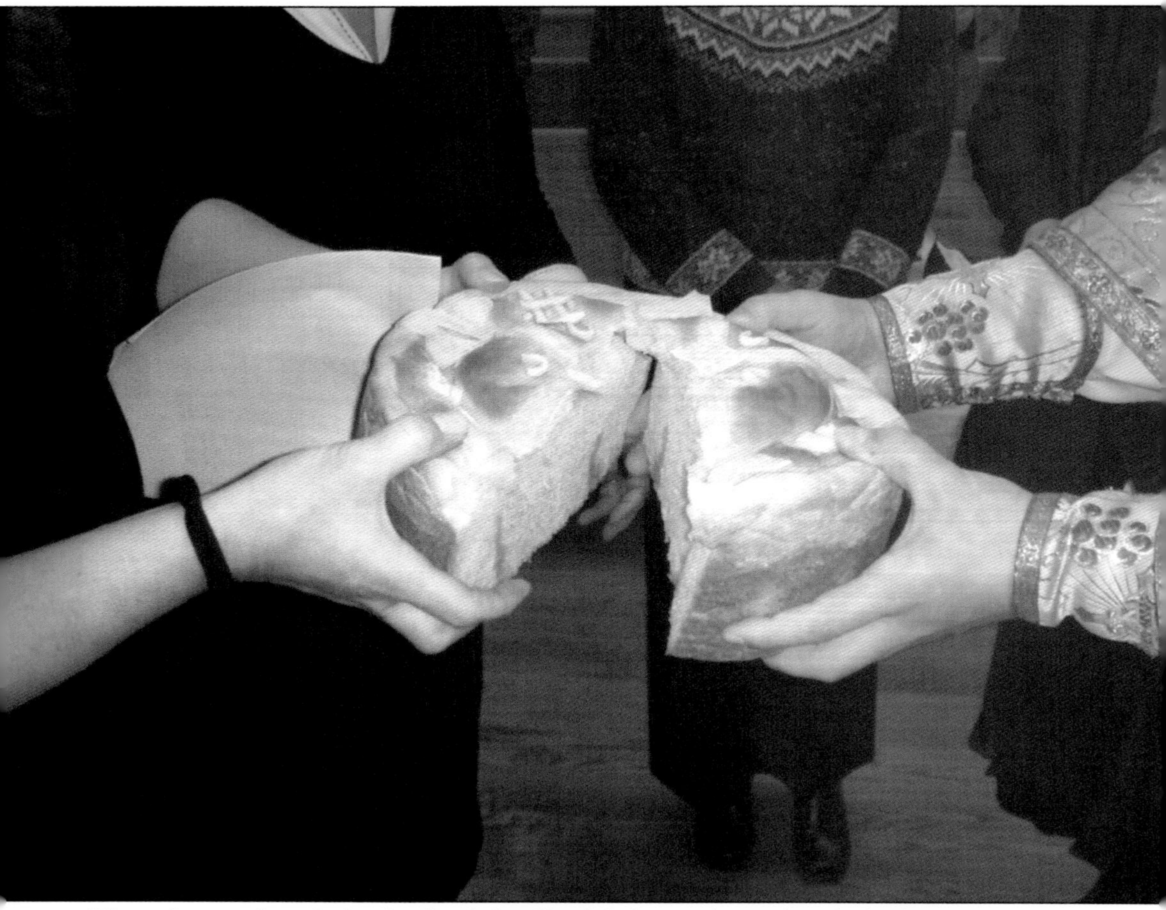

The wife or mother of a family often bakes *Slavski kolač*, or Slava cake. The loaf of bread is typically decorated with Christian symbols, or images of food and prosperity. A priest blesses the bread, cuts it crosswise, and pours red wine on it. The bread is broken into four parts and shared with guests. The Slavski kolač is often placed in the center of the table at the family's home. Slava is an exclusively Serbian holiday, and Serbs do not celebrate saint's feast days as an individual but collectively, as a family. Commonly, if a person is born close to a patron saint holiday, he or she may often be given the first name of the saint. (Courtesy of St. Sava Serbian Orthodox Church, Merrillville, Indiana.)

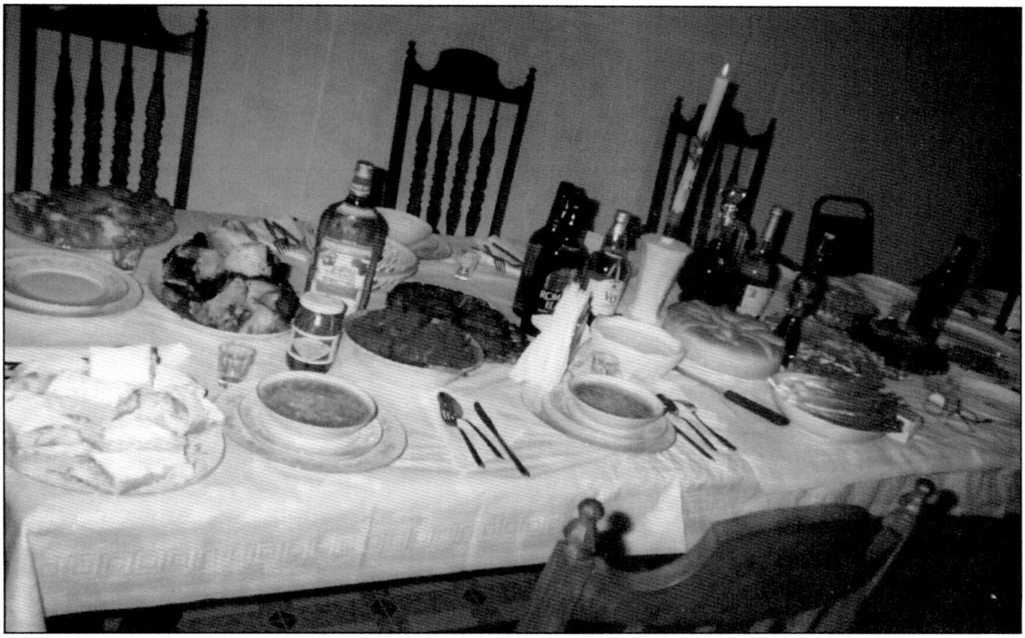

A Slava celebration would not be complete without a feast. Food that is typically served includes soup, stuffed cabbage rolls (sarma), roasted pig or lamb (pečenje), cheese strudel (pita) and desserts. Guests drink red wine and fruit brandy (rakija). Those celebrating Slava invite family and friends to help them honor their patron saint. (Courtesy of Milan Marich.)

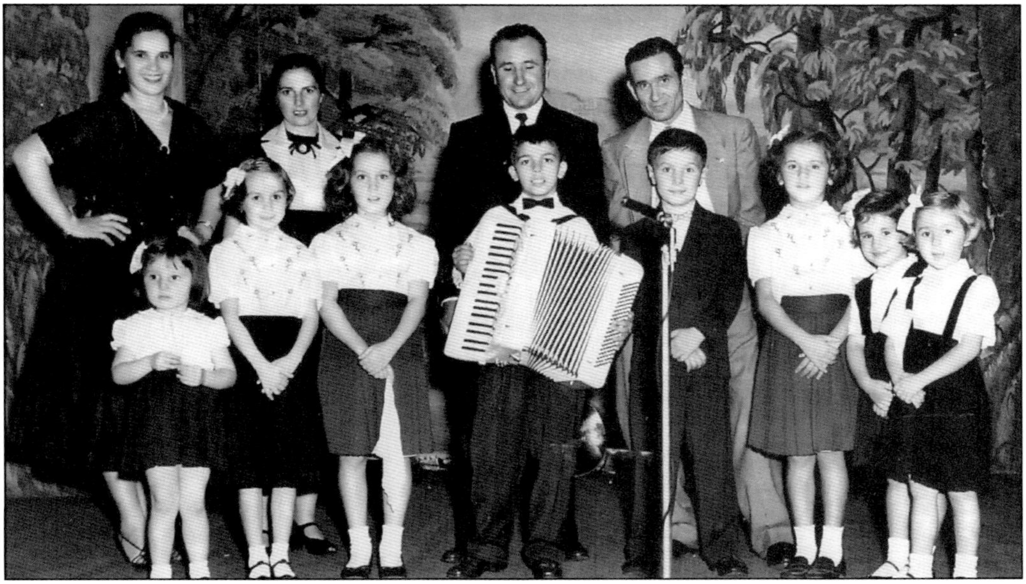

The Galić and Dragić families performed Serbian songs and instruments at events such as this one—the 1955 St. Sava Day. Pictured from left to right are (first row) Millie (Samardzija) Maddocks, Smilka (Dragić) Parker, Zora (Galić) Gros, George Dragić, Milan Samardzija, Mary (Galić) Cucuz, Liba (Galić) Jacobs, and Dorothy (Dragić) Mokry; and (second row) Dragica Galić, Sofia Dragić, Djordje Stojanović, and Blagoje "Blazo" Dragić. (Courtesy of St. Sava Serbian Orthodox Church, Merrillville, Indiana.)

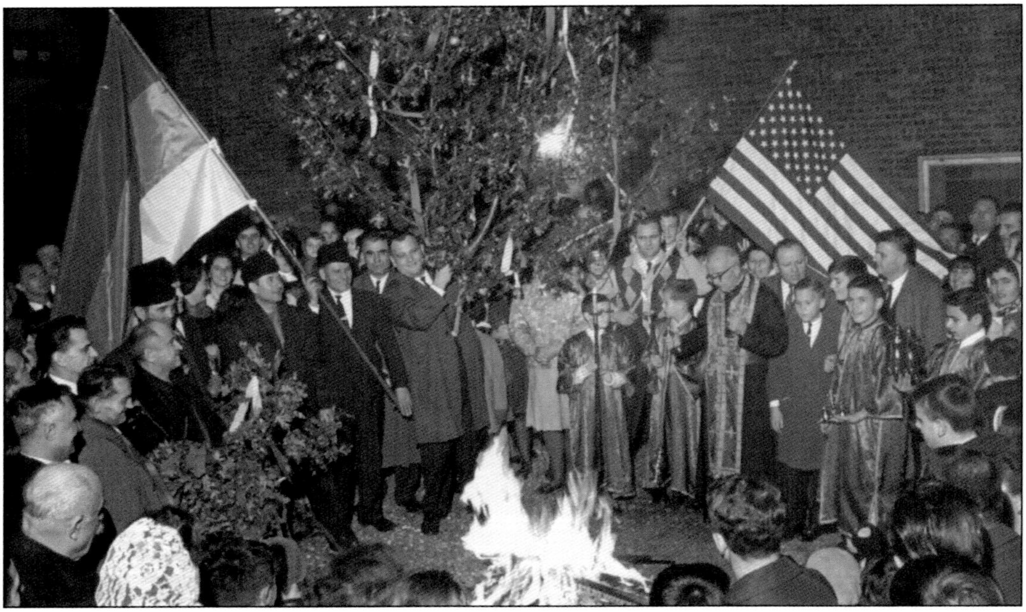

Christmas Eve—or Badnje Veče—services include the burning of a *badnjak* at the church. St. Elijah Serbian Orthodox Church president Branko Tarailo holds the badnjak. Father Dušan Shoukletovich blesses it in this 1960s photograph—from when the church was located at Forty-first and Adams Streets in Gary, Indiana. (Courtesy of St. Sava Serbian Orthodox Church, Merrillville, Indiana.)

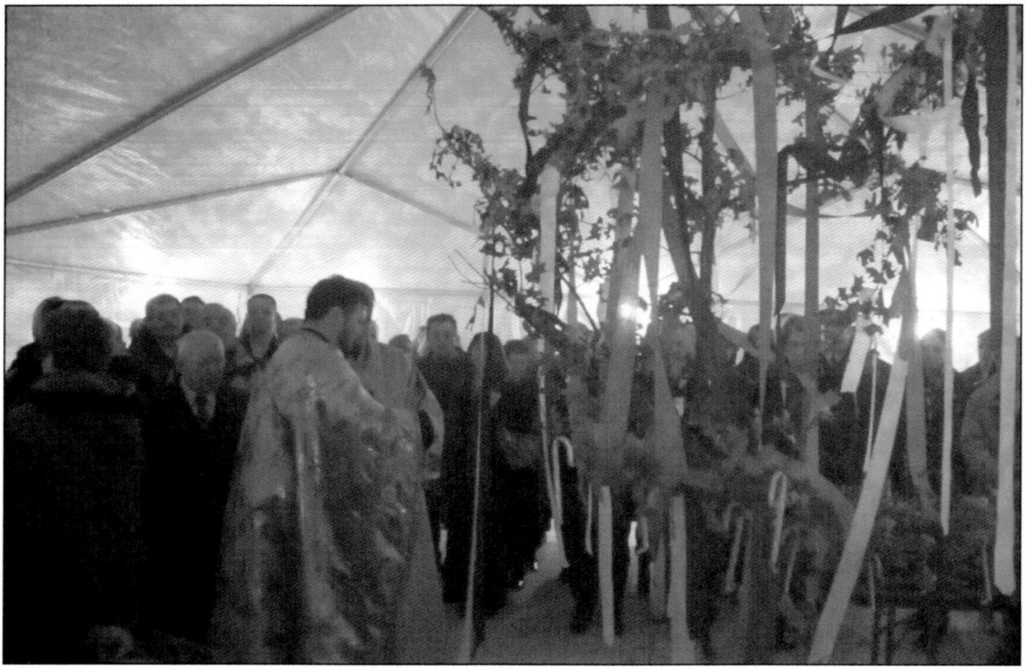

Rev. Marko Matić blesses the badnjak before it is burned as part of Badnje Veče celebrations at the St. Sava Serbian Orthodox Church. Parishioners join the priest for the blessing before going outside to observe the burning. (Courtesy of St. Sava Serbian Orthodox Church, Merrillville, Indiana.)

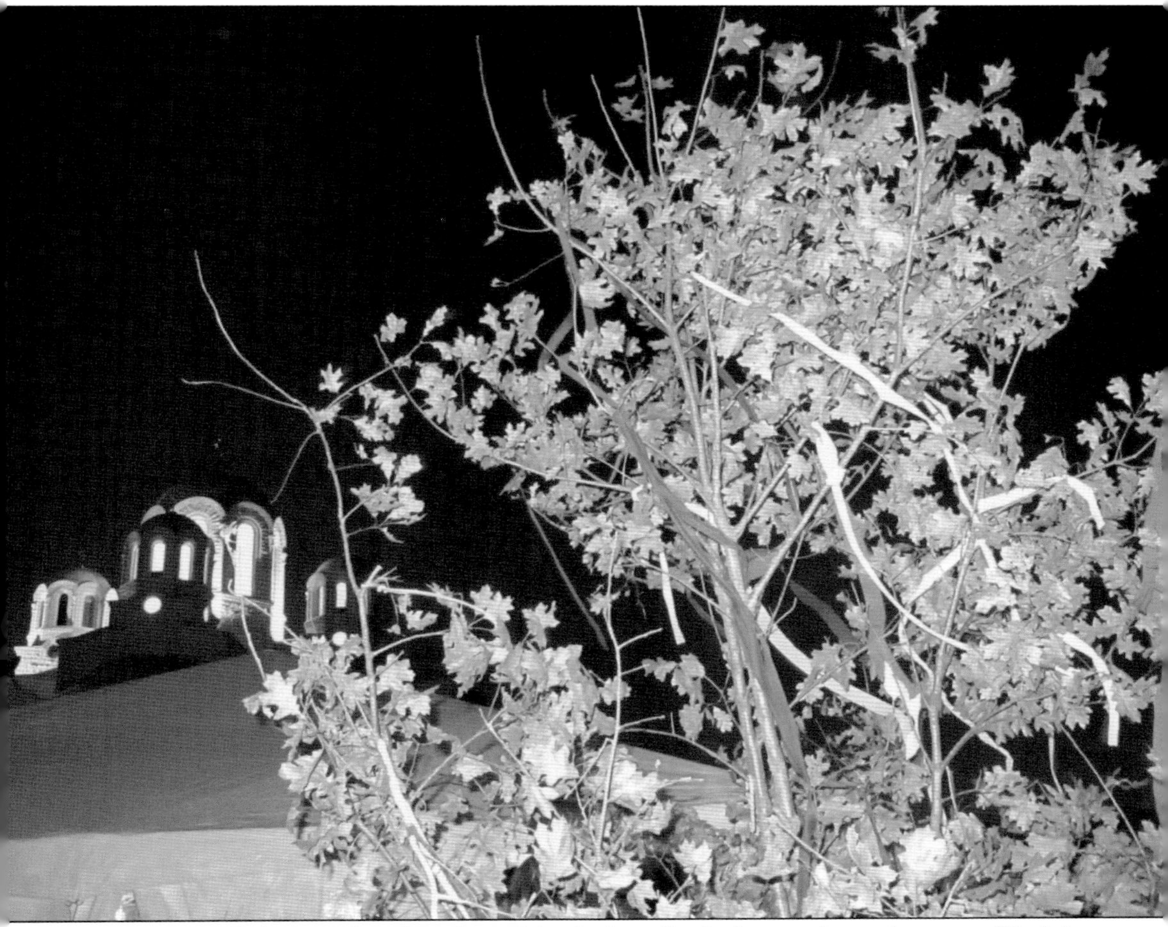

A badnjak stands decorated in the colors of the Serbian flag before it is burned as part of Badnje Veče festivities at the St. Sava Serbian Orthodox Church. (Courtesy of St. Sava Serbian Orthodox Church, Merrillville, Indiana.)

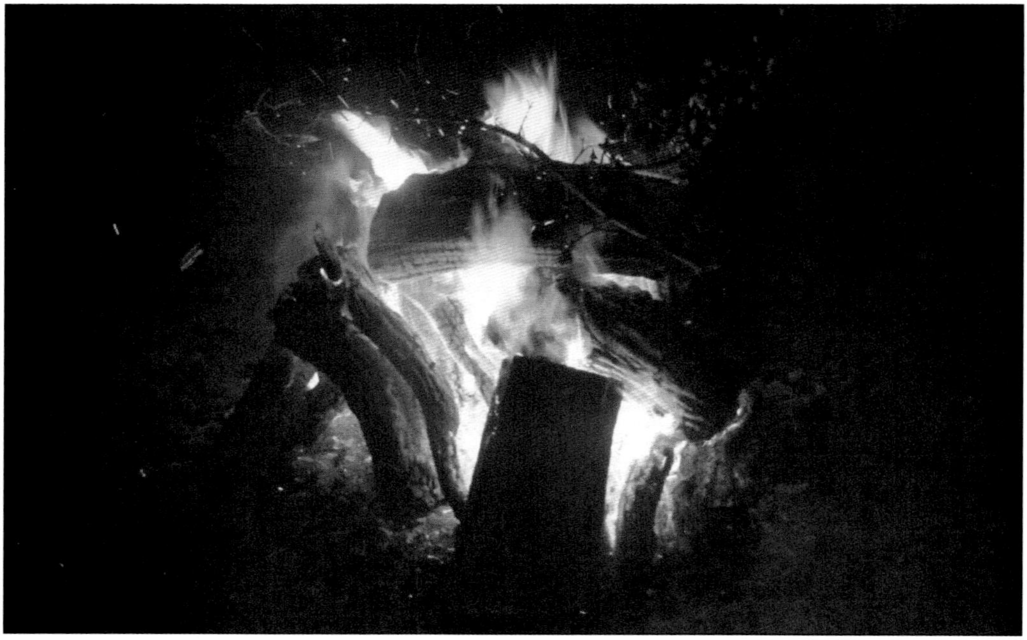

A badnjak burns outside as the culmination of the Badnje Veče ceremony. Parishioners gather around the burning badnjak until it is extinguished. Traditionally, the churches will host a dinner that follows fasting customs at the hall or social center. (Courtesy of St. Sava Serbian Orthodox Church, Merrillville, Indiana.)

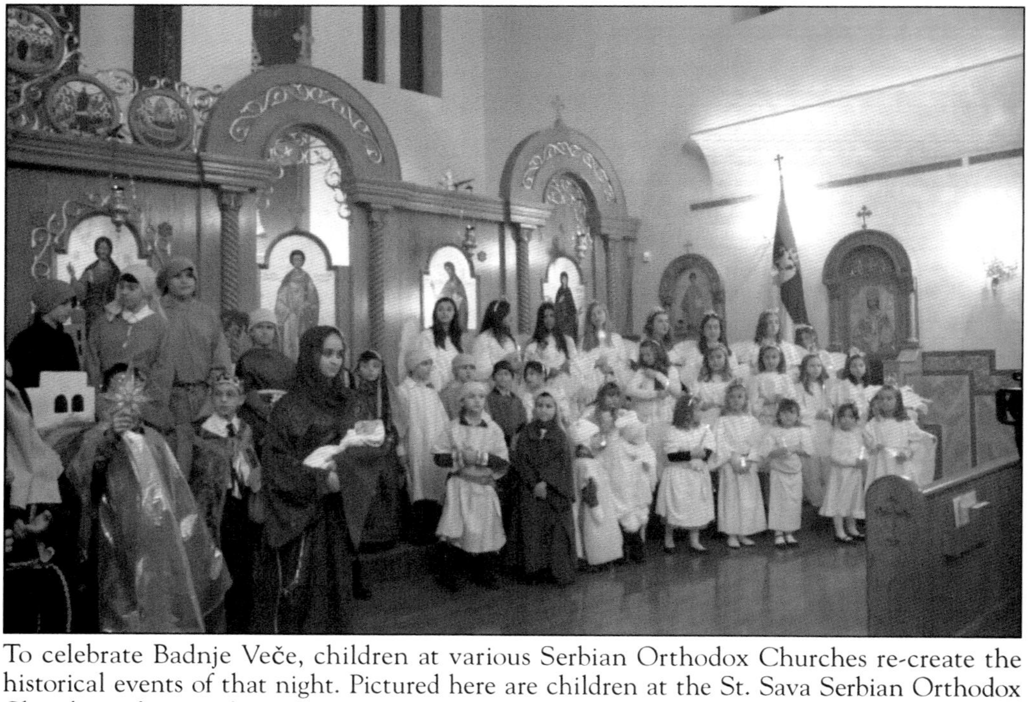

To celebrate Badnje Veče, children at various Serbian Orthodox Churches re-create the historical events of that night. Pictured here are children at the St. Sava Serbian Orthodox Church, performing for parishioners in 2010. (Courtesy of St. Sava Serbian Orthodox Church, Merrillville, Indiana.)

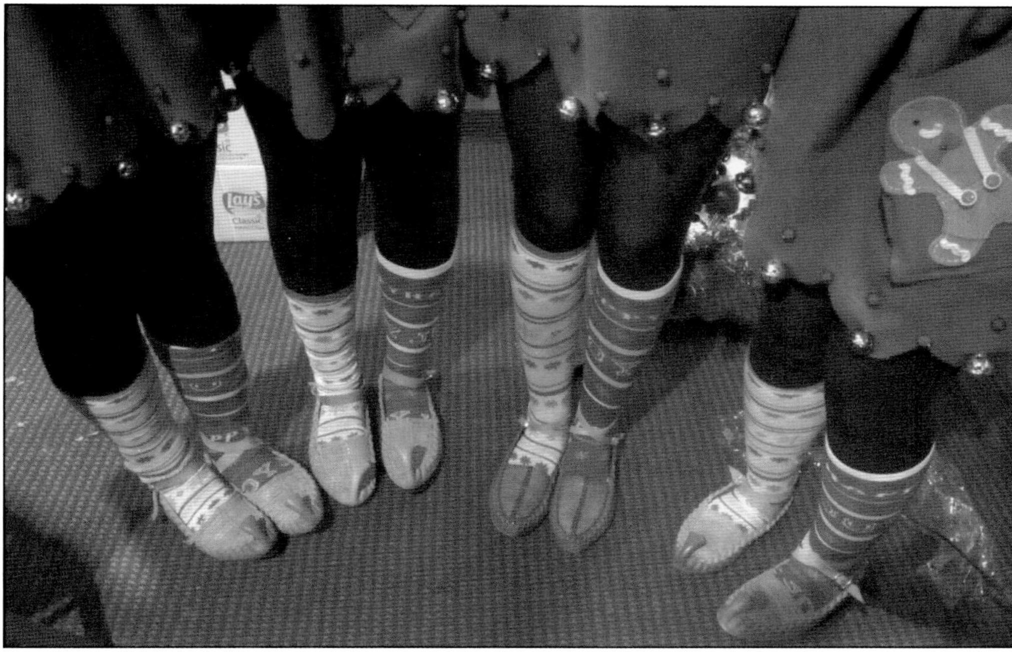

With multiple generations of Serbian Americans living in the Chicagoland area, the traditions and customs of Serbs and Americans start to blend. Pictured here are Serbian kolo dancers, dressed as elves while wearing traditional Serbian opanke. (Courtesy of St. Sava Serbian Orthodox Church, Merrillville, Indiana.)

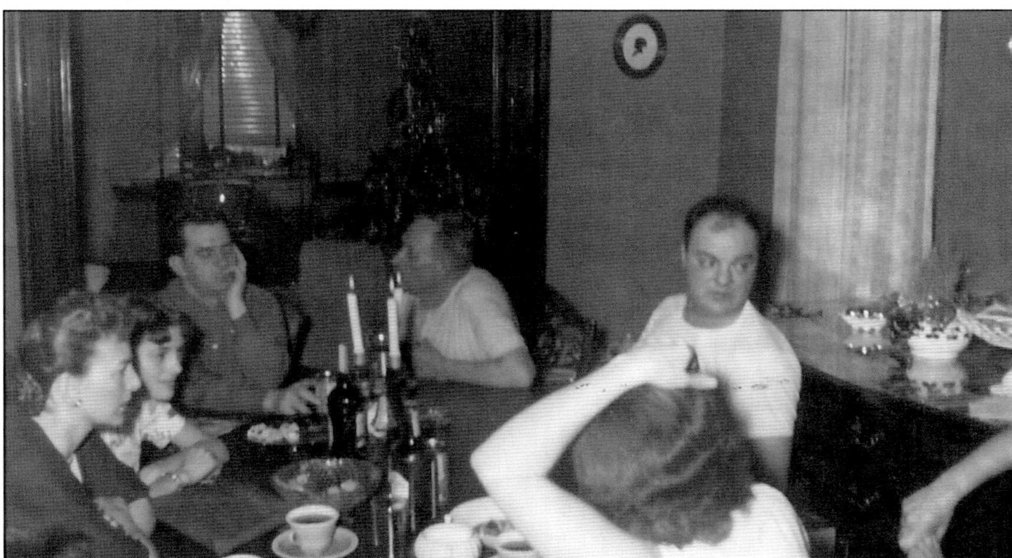

Badnje Veče brings together families to celebrate. The Popovich-Ostoich family gathers on January 6, 1953, at the home of Nikola Popovich and Milan and Sophie (Popovich) Ostoich in South Chicago. Pictured from left to right are Vietta (Popovich) Fuller, Helen (Drobac) Popovich, Marko Popovich, Nikola Popovich, Milan Ostoich, and Sophie (Popovich) Ostoich. (Courtesy of Ljubi Ostoich Hayden.)

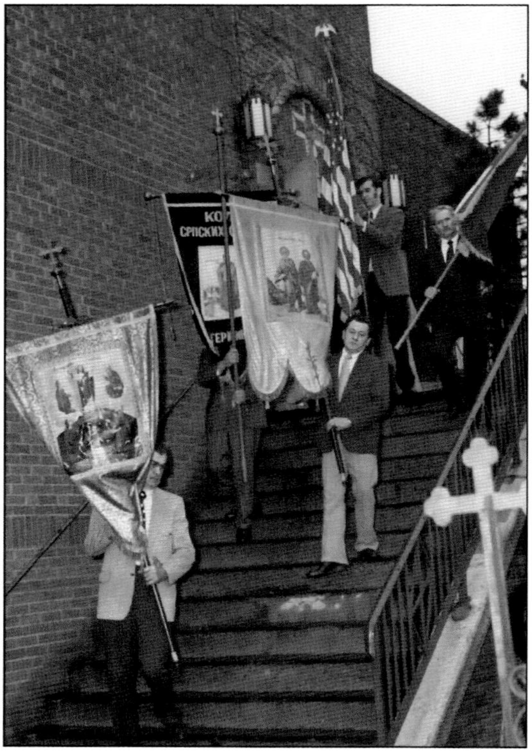

During holidays or special church services, parishioners form a procession outside the church. Pictured here are parishioners from the St. Sava Serbian Orthodox Church, preparing to walk outside in the early 1970s—when the church was located at Thirteenth and Connecticut Streets in Gary, Indiana. (Courtesy of St. Sava Serbian Orthodox Church, Merrillville, Indiana.)

For Easter, Serbians greet each other with the expression "*Hristos Voskrese*" (Christ Is Risen) and the reply "*Vaistinu Voskrese*" (Indeed He Is Risen). Serbian families also celebrate Easter by playing an egg tapping game. Everyone picks an egg to tap, and the last person with an unbroken egg becomes the winner. (Courtesy of St. Sava Serbian Orthodox Church, Merrillville, Indiana.)

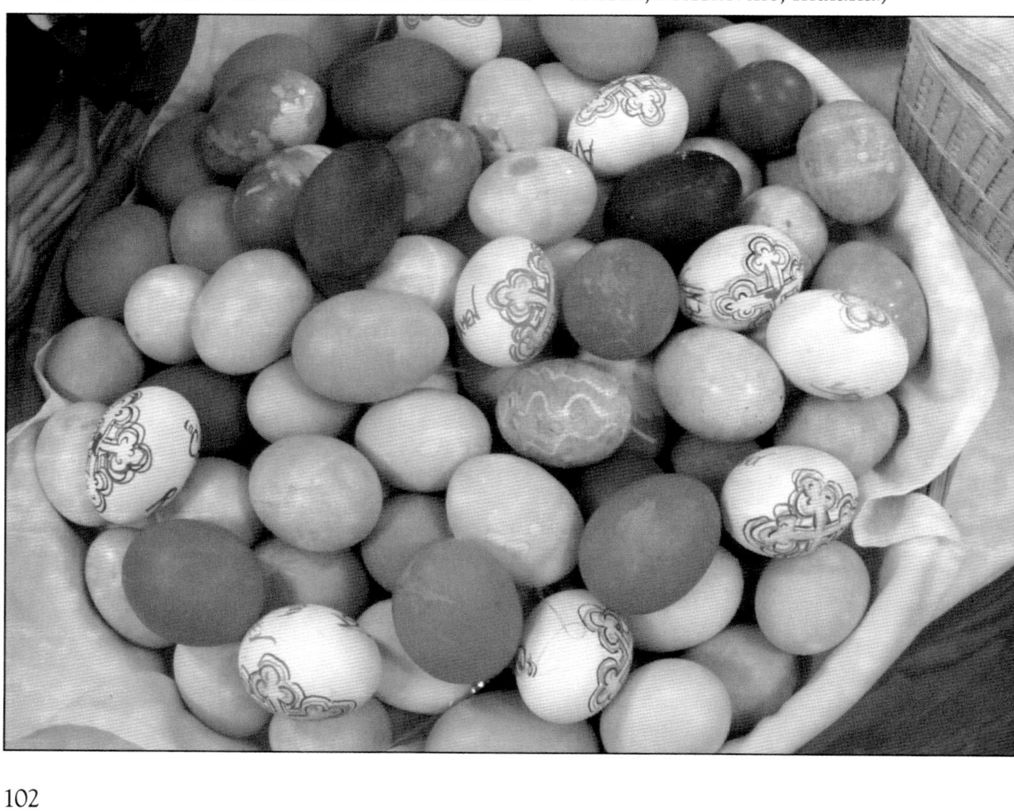

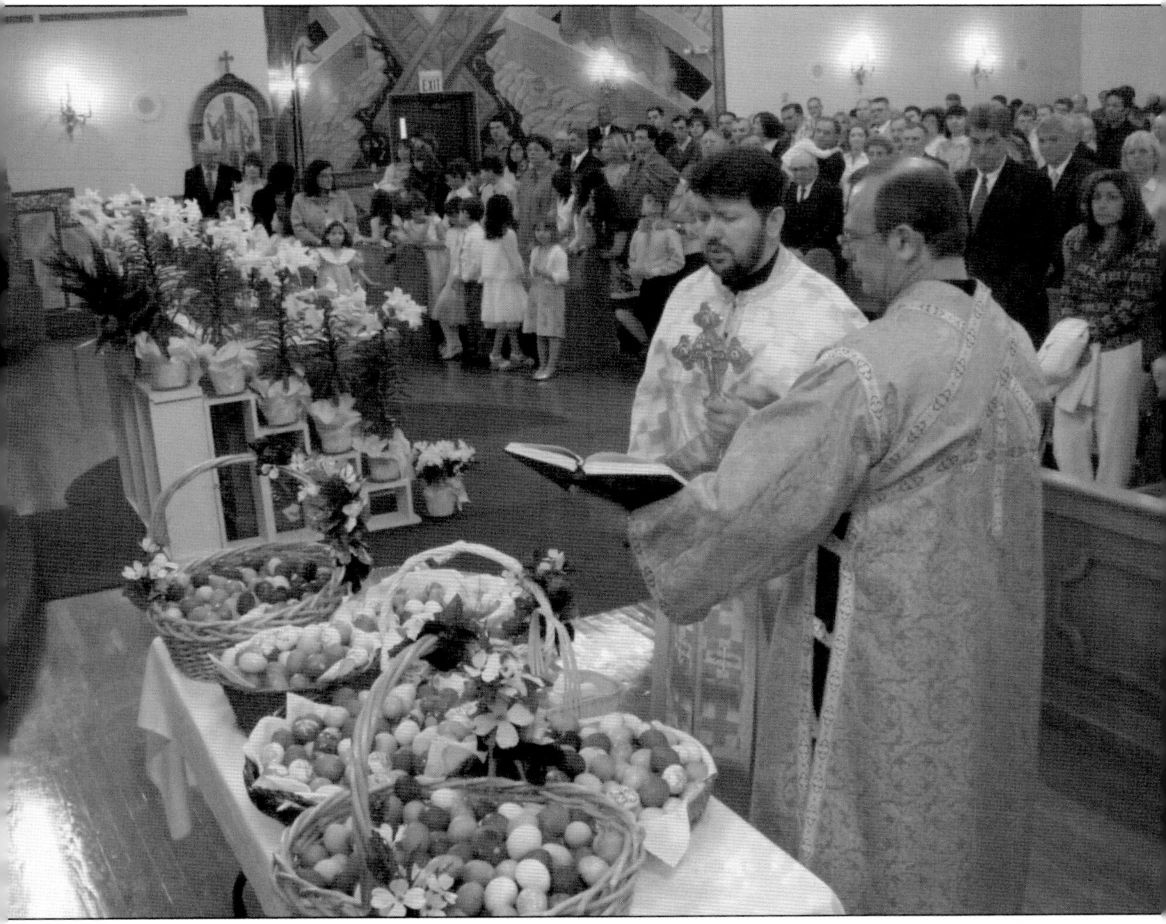

Easter is considered the holiest day of the year for Orthodox Christians. Leading up to Easter, those Serbs who adhere to the Lenten period abstain from certain foods for 40 days. For Eastern Orthodox Christians, that includes abstaining from meat, dairy, and eggs. Easter is an opportunity to break the fast. At church, the Easter service concludes with the priest blessing baskets of colored eggs prepared by families. These eggs are taken home and are part of a typical Easter meal that includes smoked meats, cheeses, and a roasted red pepper spread (ajvar) for appetizers, along with soup, sarma, and pečenje. Pictured is Rev. Marko Matić (left), blessing Easter eggs with the help of John Derado. While the eggs can be colorful, many are red to symbolize happiness and joy. (Courtesy of St. Sava Serbian Orthodox Church, Merrillville, Indiana.)

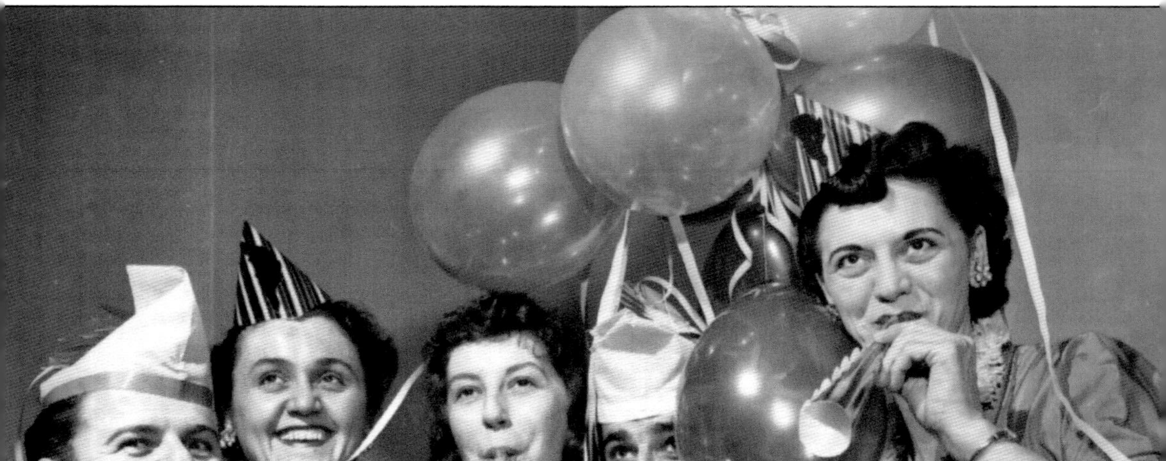

The Karageorge (Karađorđ) singing society from the St. Sava Serbian Orthodox Church always hosted a New Year's Eve party at the church hall. It was an opportunity for Serbs and non-Serbs alike to gather for music, dancing, and food. The singing society also performed at its church functions and for other public appearances. From the time that Serbs first settled in the Chicagoland area, they have maintained a close tie to Serbian music—both in terms of performing and listening to it. Pictured from left to right are Živan Petković, Sofia (Radanovich) Djujich, Dorothy (Nestorovich) Medich, Steve Majstorovich, and Sonja Kalember. Kalember was a publicist and often worked with the local media to advertise the church's activities to the broader Gary community. This photograph from the mid-1950s appeared in the *Gary Post Tribune*. (Courtesy of St. Sava Serbian Orthodox Church, Merrillville, Indiana.)

Seven

Our Weddings

For Serbs living in the United States, Serbian Orthodox weddings present an opportunity to highlight traditional Serbian customs while also incorporating some American elements.

This multiday celebration typically includes several guest gatherings (*skup svatova*). On the morning of the wedding, guests meet at either the bride or groom's house for a pre-ceremony celebration that includes live music and traditional Serbian food and drinks. Historically, the groom and his guests would walk to the bride's home and barter for her hand. Today, there is a modified version of this custom. In Serbia, the bride and groom enter the church together, while in the United States, many Serbian brides choose to have their fathers walk them down the aisle—with the groom seeing his bride in the church for the first time.

A Serbian Orthodox wedding ceremony includes several important and traditional elements. One is that the bride and groom's hands are joined—to symbolize the "oneness" of the couple—and remain joined throughout the service. Another is that the bride and groom wear crowns that represent the creation of a new household—a "kingdom" that the couple must rule.

Two individuals play an important role in Serbian Orthodox wedding ceremonies: the godfather (kum), and an uncle or male relative serving as a witness (*stari svat*). A godmother (kuma) is often present as well. These individuals remain an important part in the lives of the couple and any future children. Many Serbs who marry in the United States today have also adopted the custom of having an extended bridal party that includes groomsmen, bridesmaids, flower girls, and ring bearers.

Finally, while wedding styles have changed over the years—matching the clothing of the times—one textile element has remained consistent in Serbian weddings. The kum and stari svat wear a wedding sash (trobojka) that is either white or the colors of the Serbian flag.

All of these traditional wedding elements form a beautiful wedding celebration, as seen on the following pages, and also serve as a reminder of the ongoing commitment Serbs in Chicagoland have to furthering their culture.

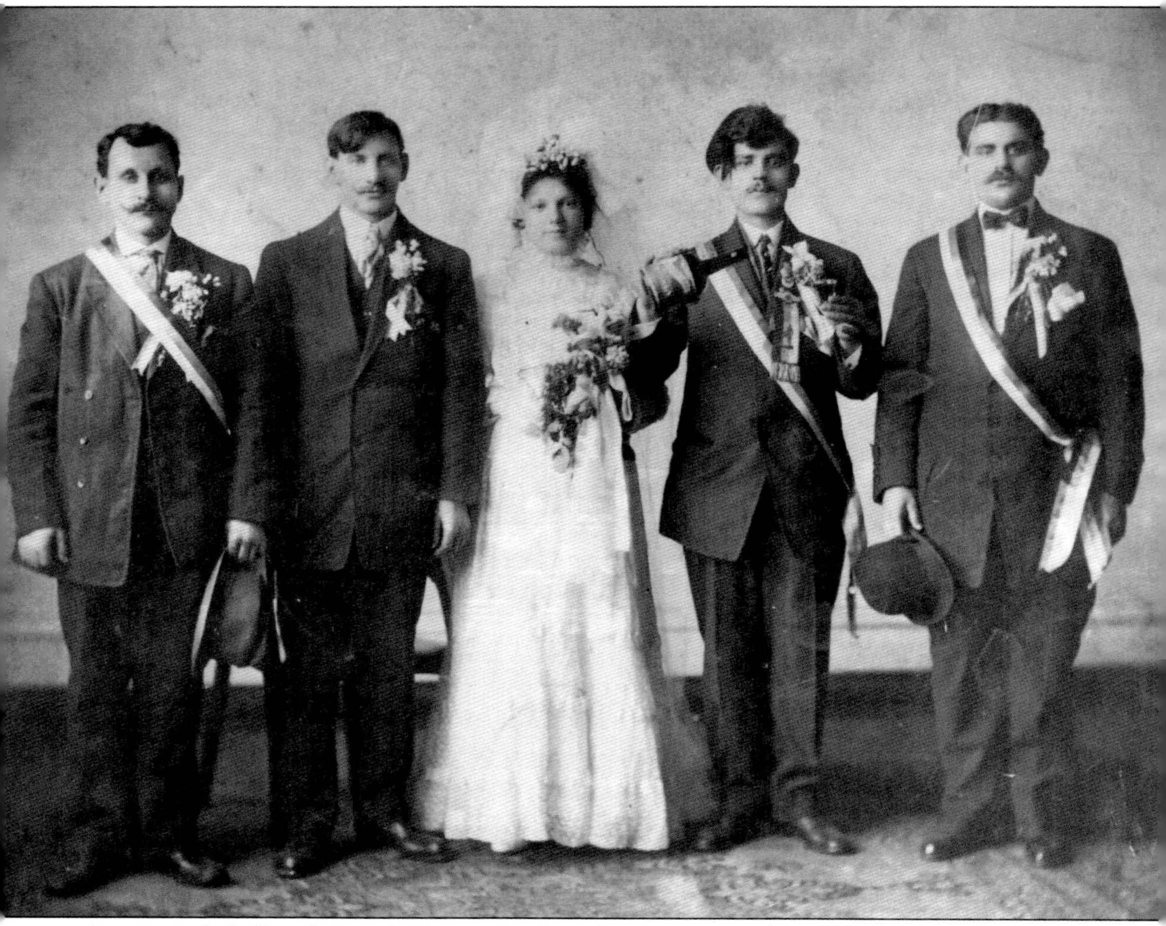

Bozidar Lalich (fourth from left) served as kum for the 1900 wedding of this unidentified couple from the St. Archangel Michael Serbian Orthodox Church. As kum, Lalich was responsible for carrying a bottle of fruit brandy (rakija) and pouring it for guests. For this photograph, Lalich is pretending to pour the rakija as a nod to the wedding custom. Rakija is considered the national drink of Serbs and remains a tradition at Serbian events, especially weddings. This image also depicts another Serbian wedding custom—the kum and the two stari svatovi wear trobojke in the colors of the Serbian flag. Trobojke are still worn in today's Serbian weddings, and can also be white. Serbian weddings are festive occasions and typically consist of multiple days of celebration, culminating in a reception with plenty of Serbian food, drink, music, and dancing. (Courtesy of Dorothy Lalich.)

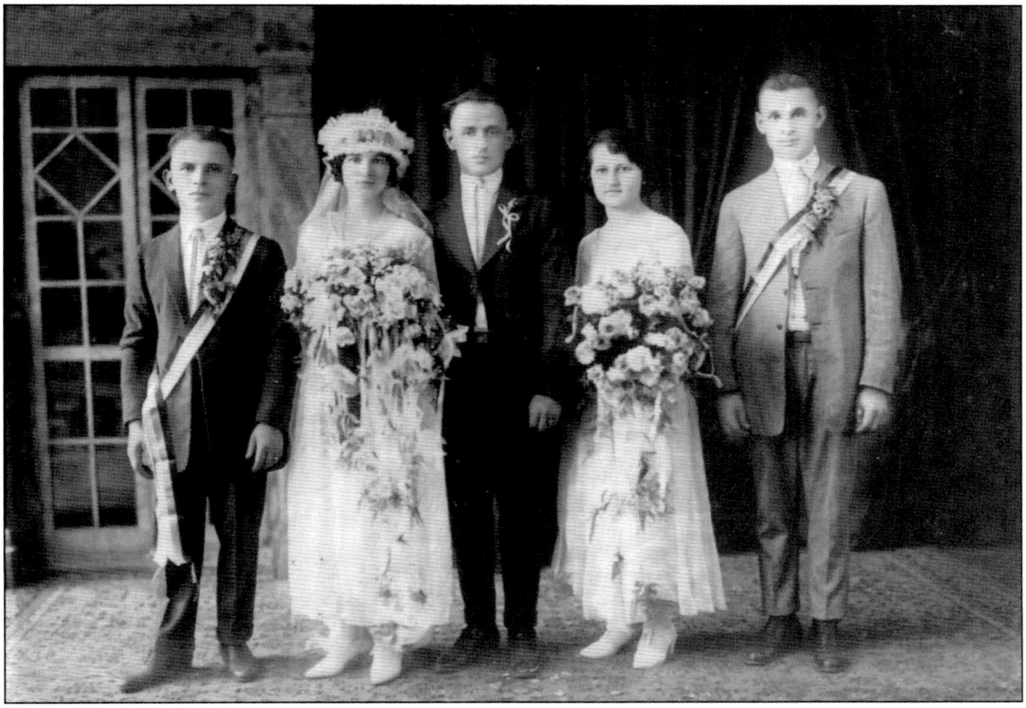

This photograph was taken at the July 1923 wedding of Milka (Raich) Kuruzovich and Dragan "Dan" Kuruzovich, who married at the St. George Serbian Orthodox Church in East Chicago, Indiana. St. George is the oldest Serbian church in the Chicagoland area that is still located at its original address. (Courtesy of St. Sava Serbian Orthodox Church, Merrillville, Indiana.)

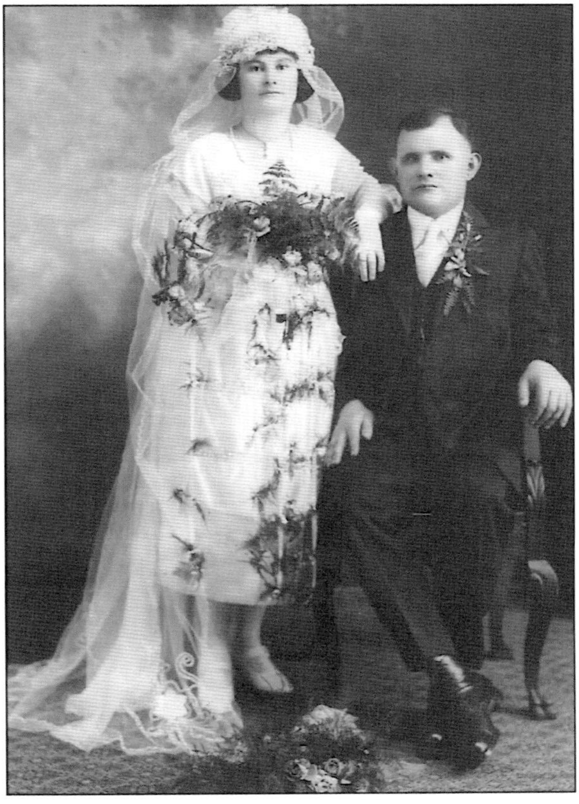

Nikola Tarailo and Mara (Gluhović) Tarailo are pictured here on their wedding day, in 1919 or 1920. Like many immigrants, Tarailo and Gluhović had family in the Chicagoland area and moved here from their homeland before meeting and marrying. In the mid-1960s, the Tarailo family opened the popular Bronko's restaurant in Northwest Indiana. (Courtesy of Nick Tarailo.)

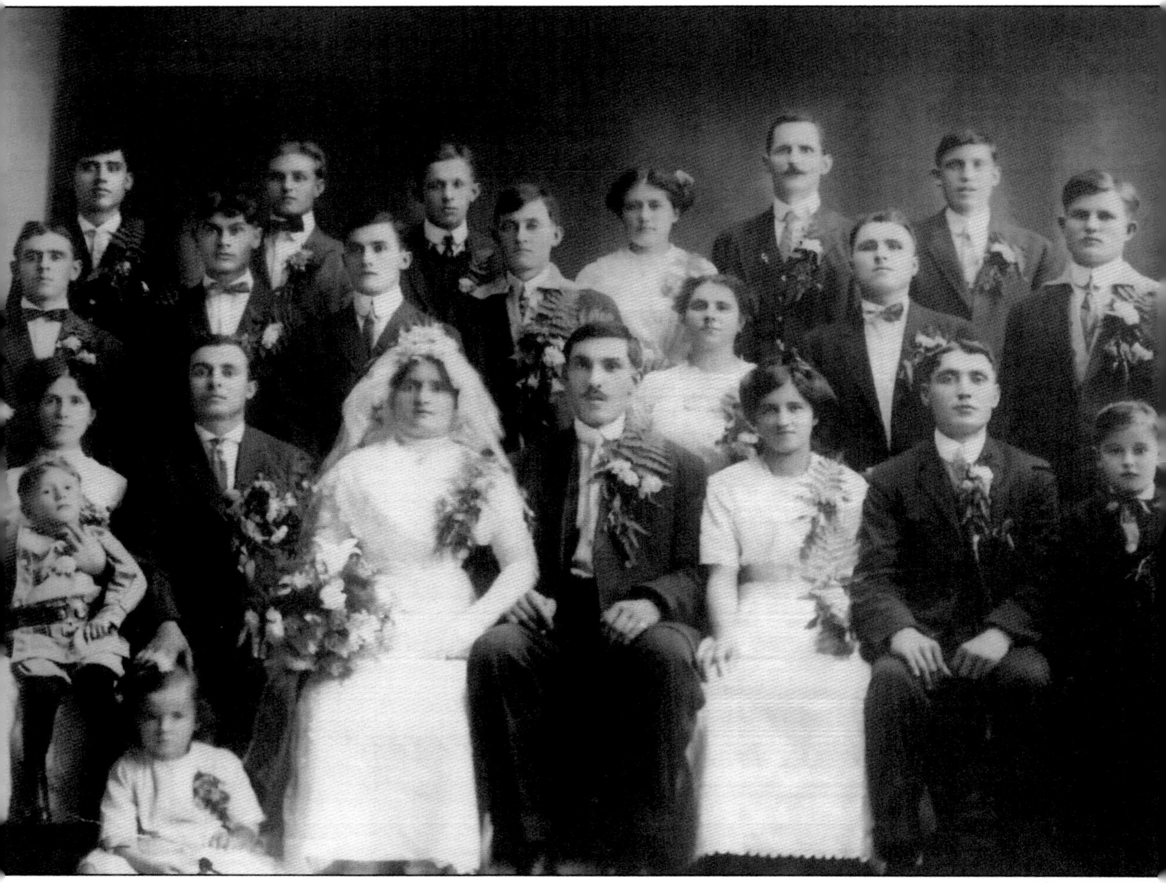

Taken in 1919 or 1920, this photograph shows an unidentified couple who married at the original St. Sava Serbian Orthodox Church, at Twentieth and Connecticut Streets. All of the guests are decorated with a flower. In Serbian weddings, a young woman is designated to decorate each guest and welcome them to the celebration. (Courtesy of St. Sava Serbian Orthodox Church, Merrillville, Indiana.)

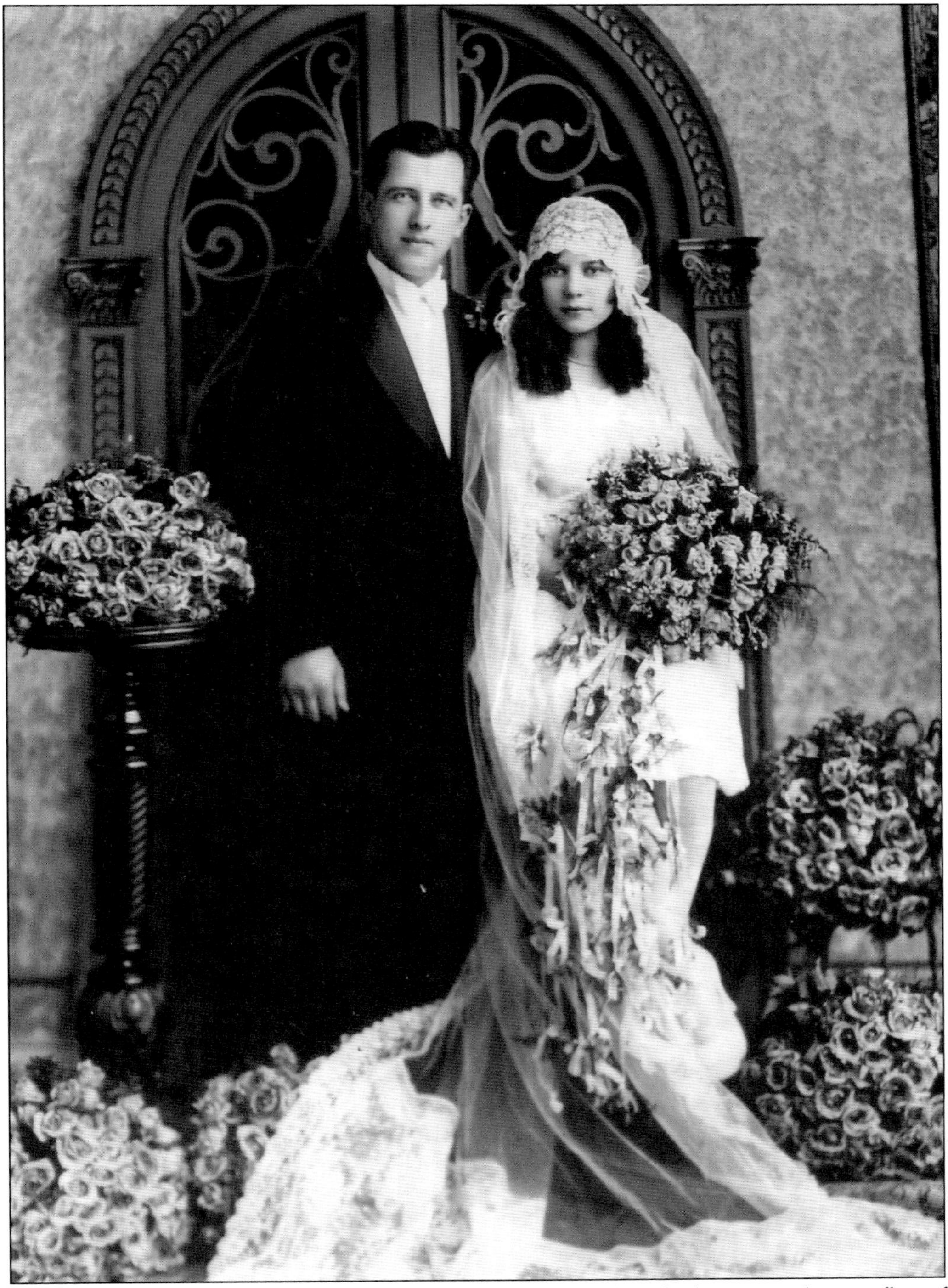

Chris and Anna Mitrovich married in Chicago in 1928. Although there was a large influx of Serbs arriving to the Chicagoland area after World War II, and again after the Balkan wars of the 1990s, Serbs started arriving in the region as early as the late 1800s. (Courtesy of St. Sava Serbian Orthodox Church, Merrillville, Indiana.)

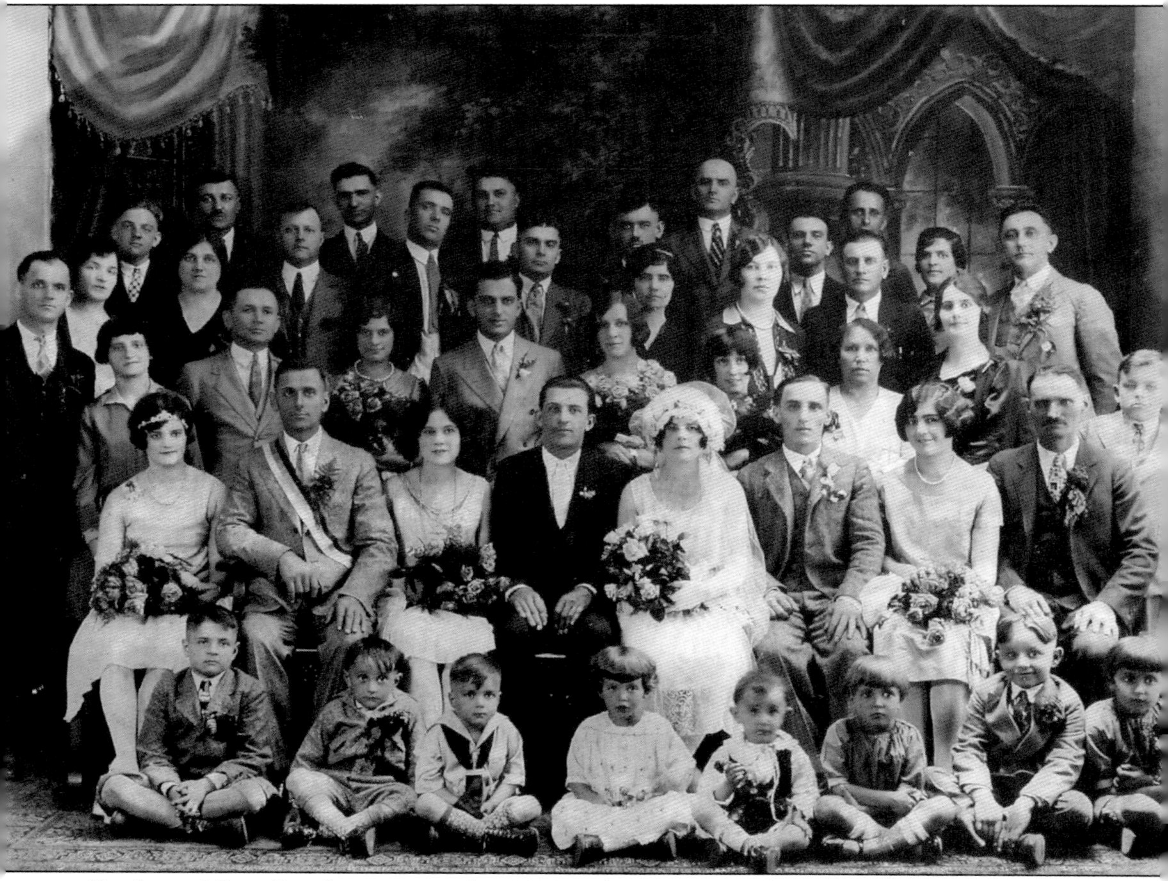

Ranko and Zora Djurdjević married in 1928 at the St. Sava Serbian Orthodox Church in Gary, Indiana. Among the many guests is Mladen Sekulovich (Karl Malden), who is standing in the last row, first on the left. His father, Peter Sekulovich, is in the third row, at far left, and his mother, Minnie Sekulovich, is second from the left in the fourth row. (Courtesy of St. Sava Serbian Orthodox Church, Merrillville, Indiana.)

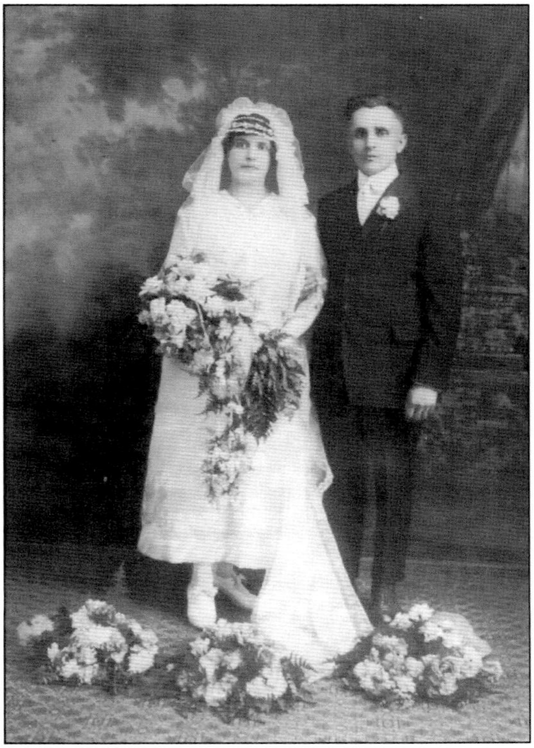

This undated photograph of an unidentified Chicagoland Serbian couple was likely taken at the turn of the 20th century. The style of the photography and clothing is typical of the era. (Courtesy of St. Sava Serbian Orthodox Church, Merrillville, Indiana.)

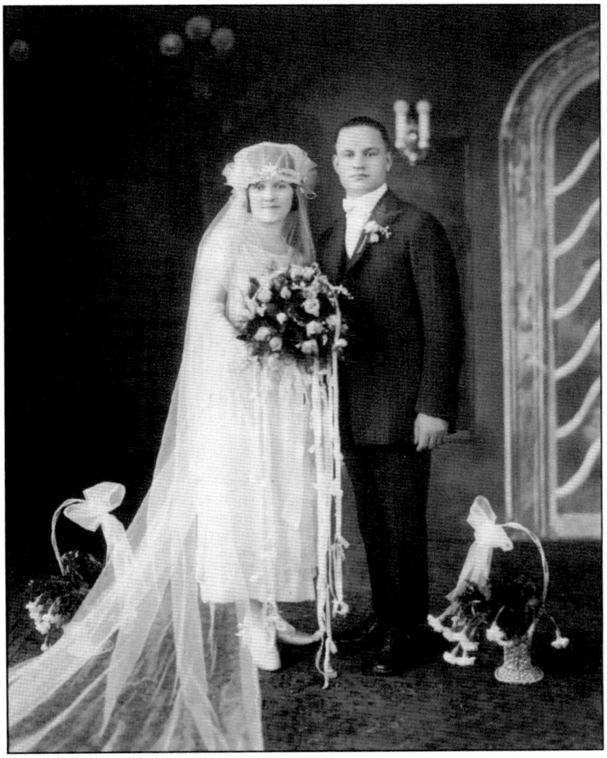

This photograph shows Stanko "Sam" Babich and Milka (Adamovich) Babich on their wedding day in 1924. The Babich and Adamovich families immigrated to the Chicagoland area in the late 1800s and became early members of the St. Archangel Serbian Orthodox Church in South Chicago, Illinois. (Courtesy of Dorothy Lalich.)

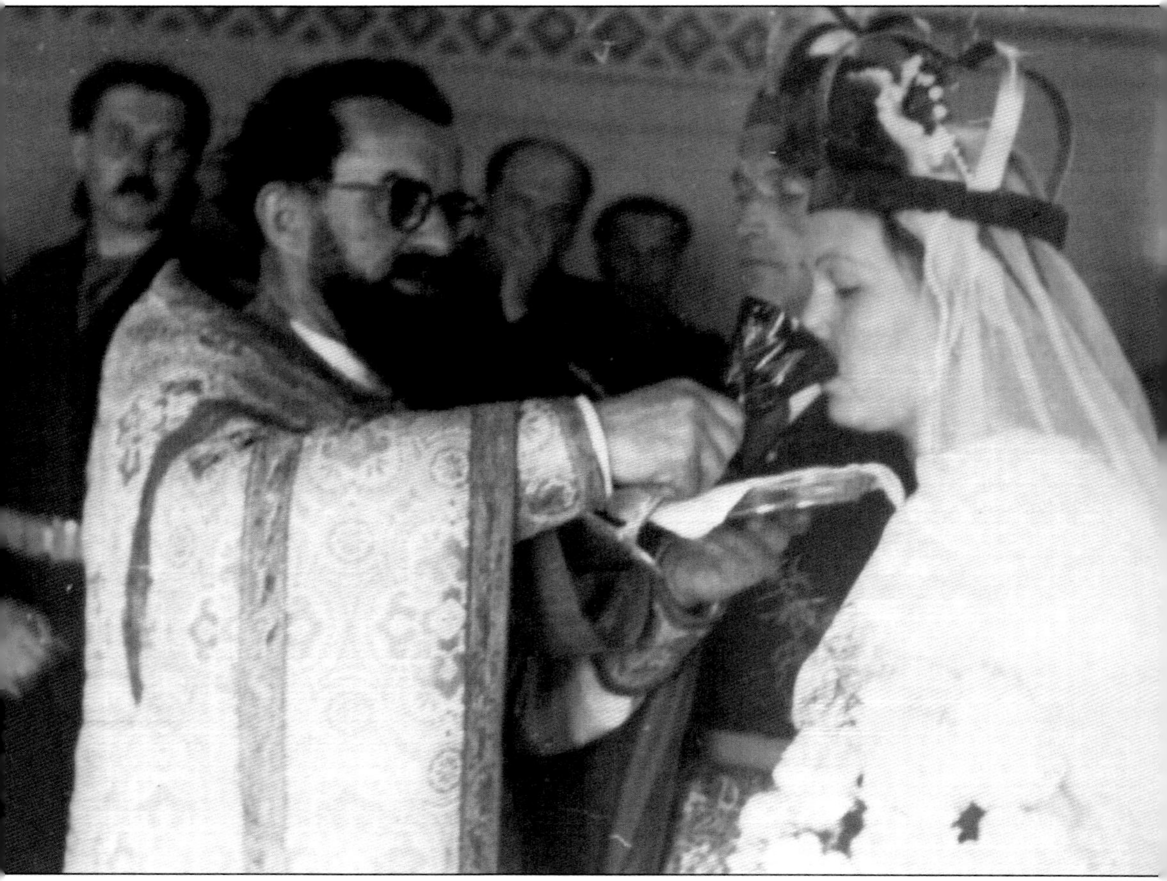

Desimir and Danica Beslich take their vows on June 11, 1949, in a military chapel at a displacement camp in Germany. Despite not having jeweled crowns, the couple used makeshift cardboard crowns to observe traditional Serbian wedding customs. Rev. Svetozar Radovanovich, who married the couple, became the priest at the St. Sava Serbian Orthodox Church in Gary, Indiana, in 1951. (Courtesy of St. Sava Serbian Orthodox Church, Merrillville, Indiana.)

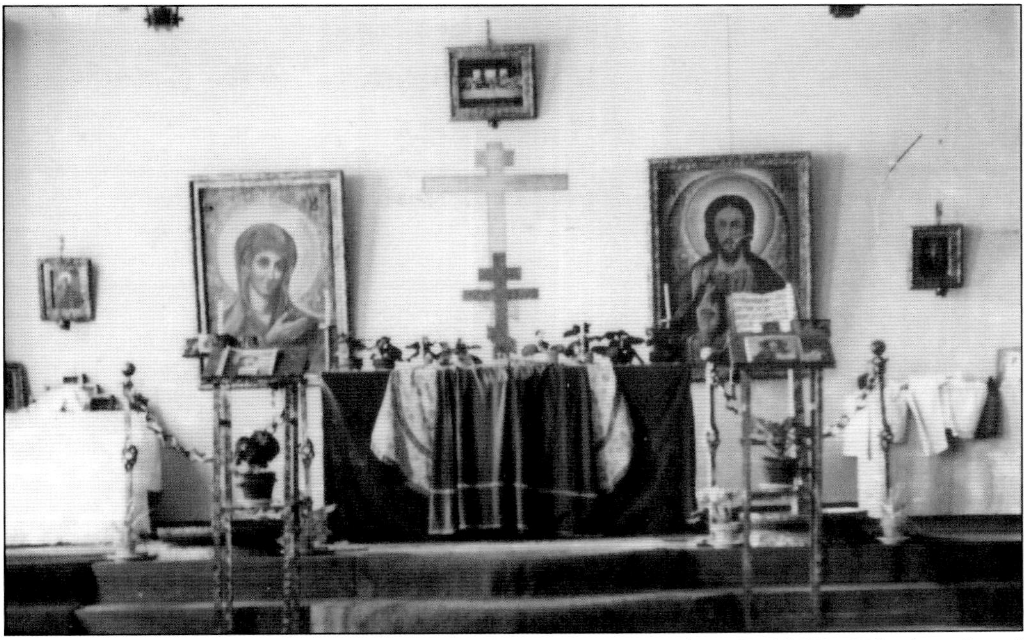

A Serbian community living in German displacement camps after World War II built a chapel in order to hold religious ceremonies. This allowed those staying there to observe customs and traditions while they waited to be moved to a new, permanent home. (Courtesy of St. Sava Serbian Orthodox Church, Merrillville, Indiana.)

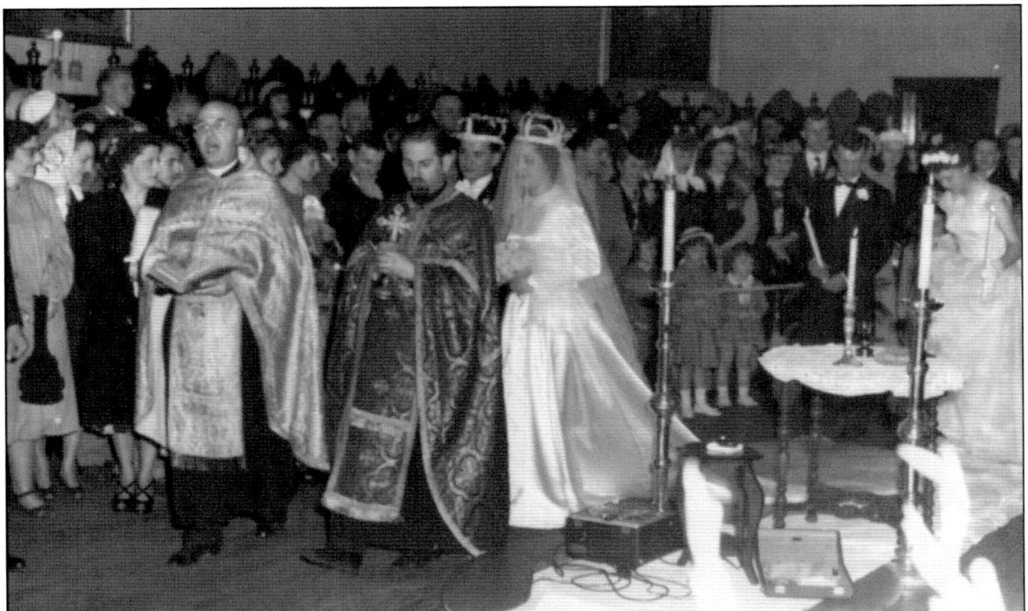

This is the wedding of Babe (Marcetich) and Mitch Solaja, likely held in 1947 or 1948. Dorothy (Babich) Lalich and her brother Nick Babich were kuma and kum for the wedding, which took place at the St. Archangel Michael Serbian Orthodox Church in South Chicago and was officiated by Rev. Andrija Popovich (left). (Courtesy of Dorothy Lalich.)

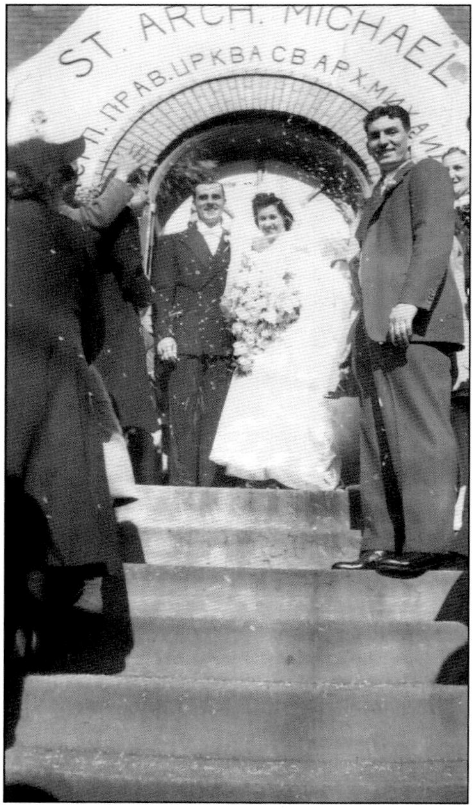

Mike and Jenny (Mistovich) Lalich pose on the front steps of the St. Archangel Michael Serbian Orthodox Church on their wedding day, May 11, 1941. As is still tradition today, the bride and groom emerge from the church after the ceremony to greet their guests for the first time as a married couple. The bride was the sister of Pete Mistovich, who played with the Popovich Brothers tambura group. Also pictured is Bob Glumac, the groom's brother-in-law. (Courtesy of Dorothy Lalich.)

The tight-knit Serbian community often invites many guests to weddings, with receptions typically held in a church hall. This photograph was taken in February 1948, at the wedding reception of Milan and Sophie (Popovich) Ostoich. They wed at the St. Archangel Michael Serbian Orthodox Church in South Chicago, Illinois, and held their reception at the St. Sava Serbian Orthodox Church's hall in Gary, Indiana. (Courtesy of Ljubi Ostoich Hayden.)

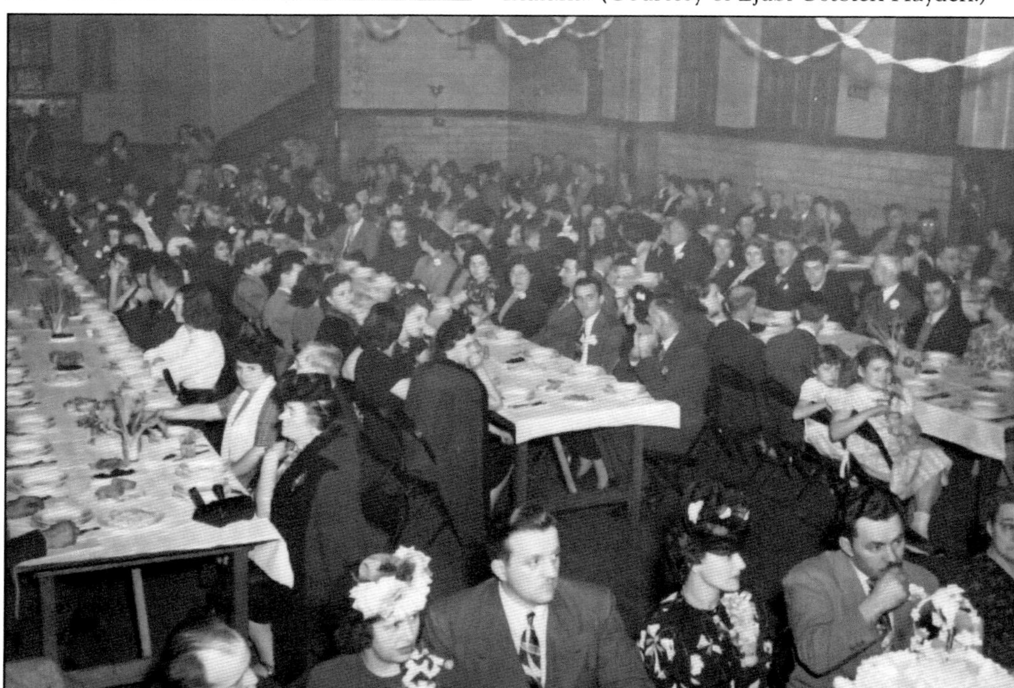

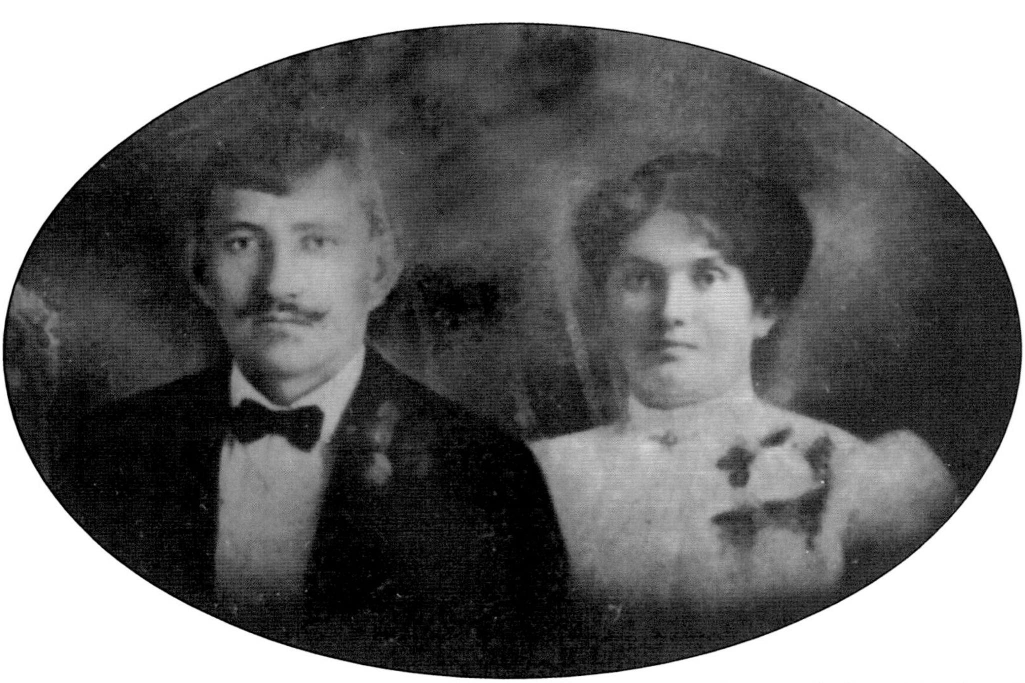

Serbs started immigrating to Chicago in the late 1800s. This 1906 photograph shows Nikola and Ljubica (Lalich) Popovich in a formal portrait taken in Chicago. The Popovich family formed a famous and award-winning tambura band, which played at Serbian weddings all across the Chicagoland region for decades. (Courtesy of Ljubi Ostoich Hayden.)

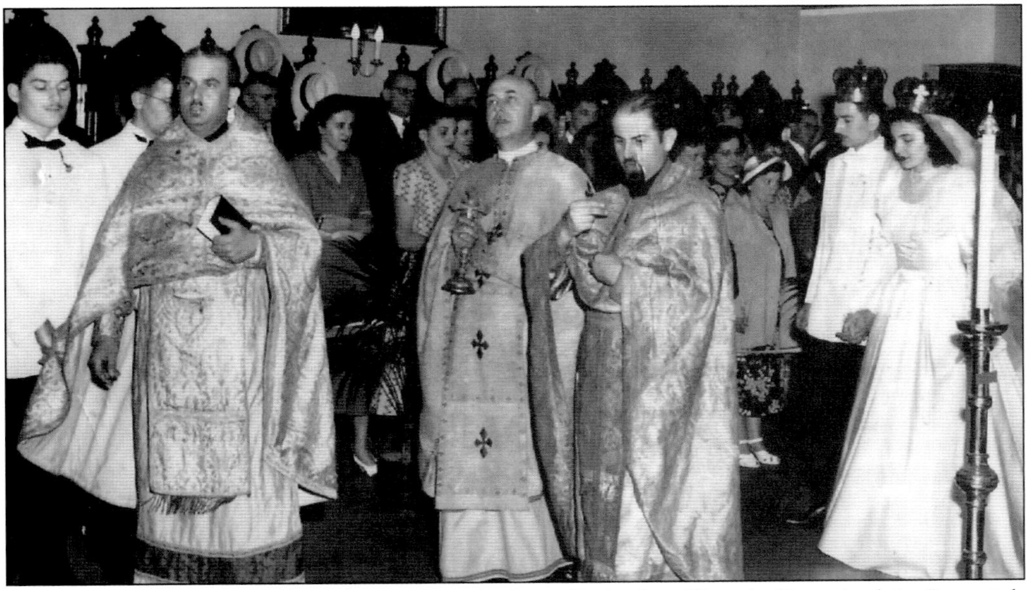

Rev. Nikola Sekulich (left) of the St. Sava Serbian Orthodox Church, Rev. Andrija Popovich (center) of the St. Archangel Michael Serbian Orthodox Church, and Rev. Jovan "John" Marcetich (right) of the St. George Serbian Orthodox Church preside over the June 5, 1949, wedding of George and Dorothy (Milanovich) Peyovich—held at St. Archangel Michael when it was located in South Chicago. (Courtesy of St. Sava Serbian Orthodox Church, Merrillville, Indiana.)

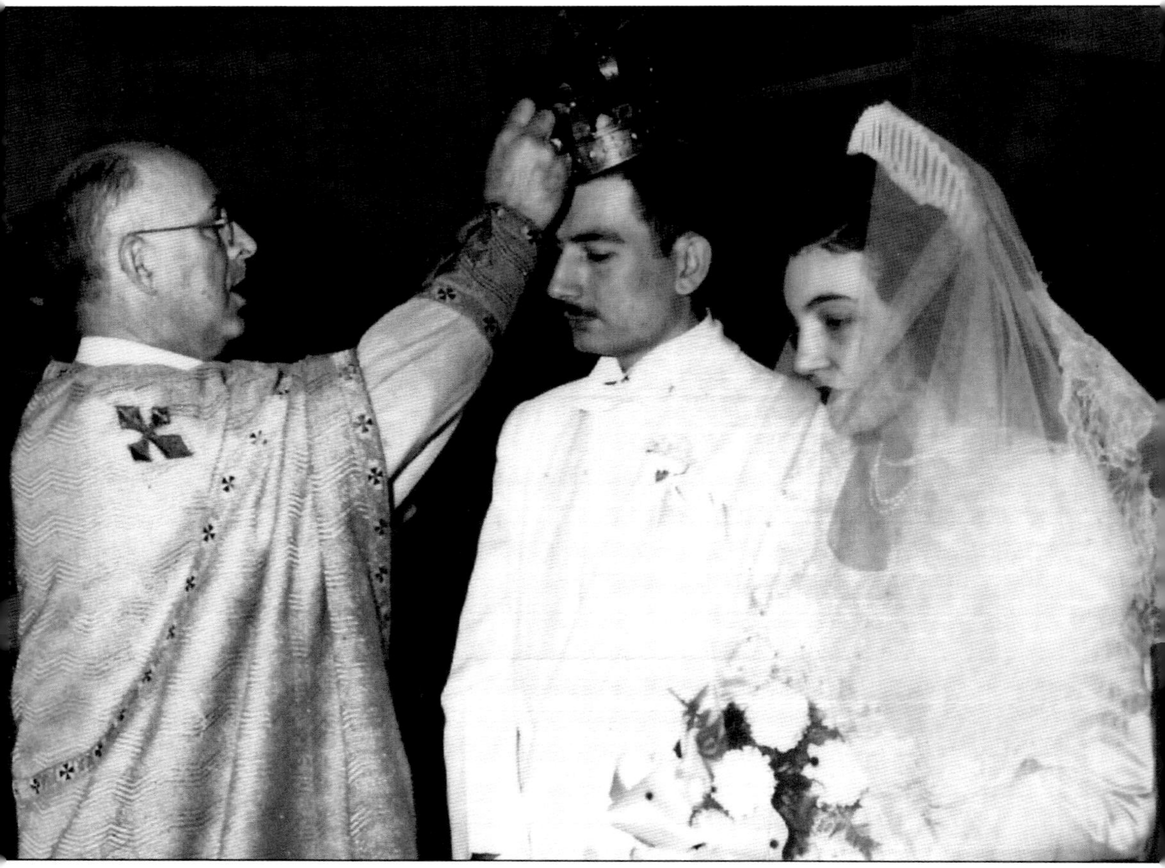

Rev. Andrija Popovich of the St. Archangel Michael Serbian Orthodox Church, places the crown on George Peyovich at his June 5, 1949, wedding to Dorothy Milanovich. In Serbian Orthodox wedding ceremonies, the priest makes the sign of the cross with the crown three times over the couple. The groom kisses the crown before it is placed on his head. The same is done for the bride. The crowns are then exchanged between the heads of the couple three times. (Courtesy of St. Sava Serbian Orthodox Church, Merrillville, Indiana.)

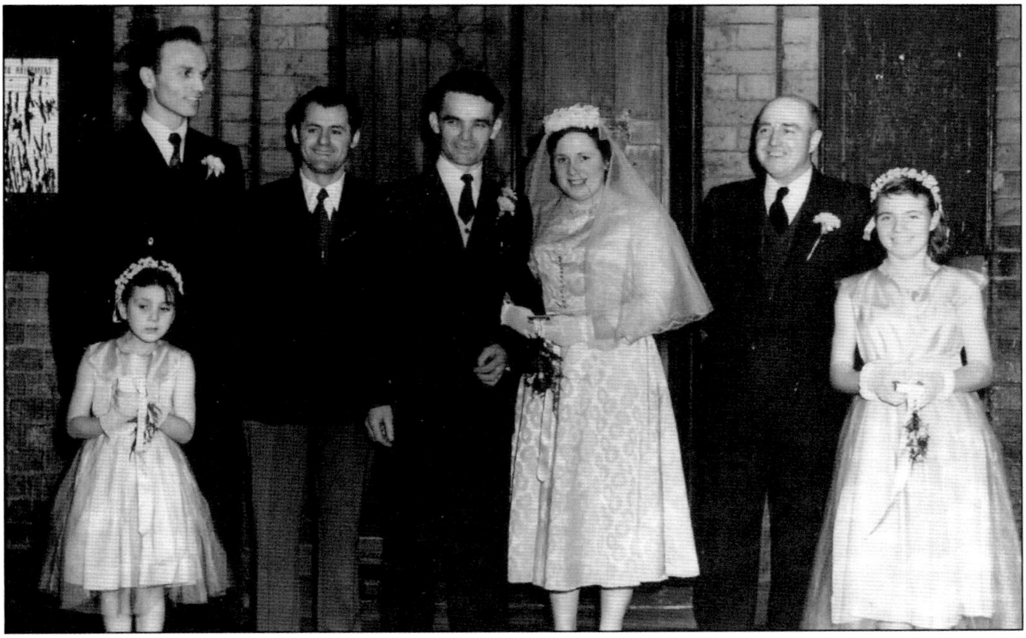

Reverend Nedanovich married Vlade and Sheila Ilić in 1954 at St. Ann's Church—a borrowed church in England where many displaced Serbs married. Vlade met Sheila while she worked as a nurse's aid in the same hospital where Vlade was an assistant cook. They ultimately moved to the Chicagoland area. (Courtesy of St. Sava Serbian Orthodox Church, Merrillville, Indiana.)

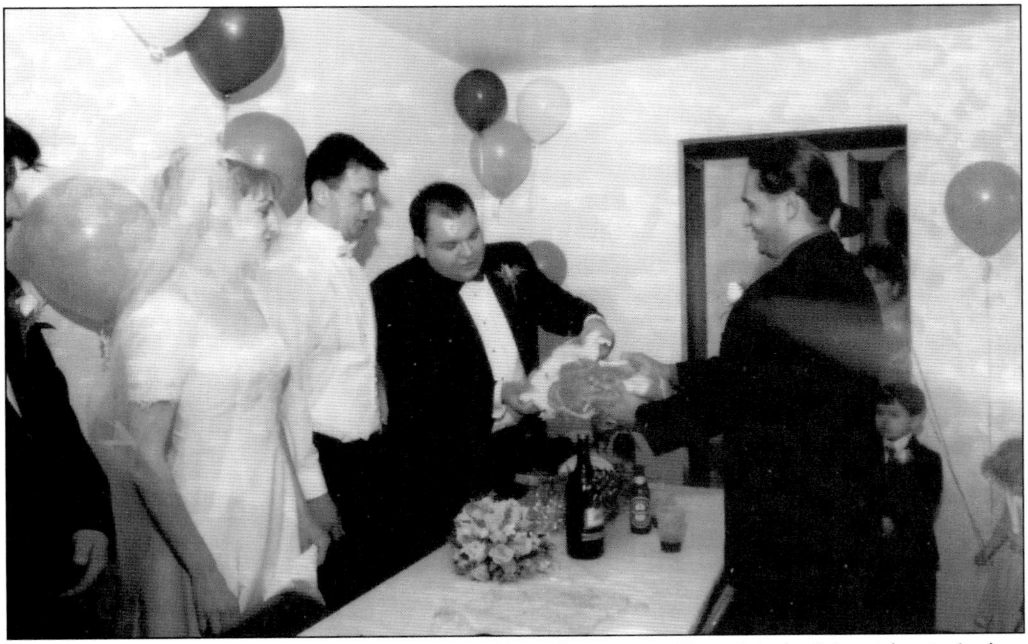

In the Eastern Orthodox religion, priests are allowed to marry. Here, Marko Matić (no jacket)—currently the priest at the St. Sava Serbian Orthodox Church in Merrillville, Indiana—participates in the breaking of the bread during the skup svatova held at his house before his 1999 wedding. (Courtesy of St. Sava Serbian Orthodox Church, Merrillville, Indiana.)

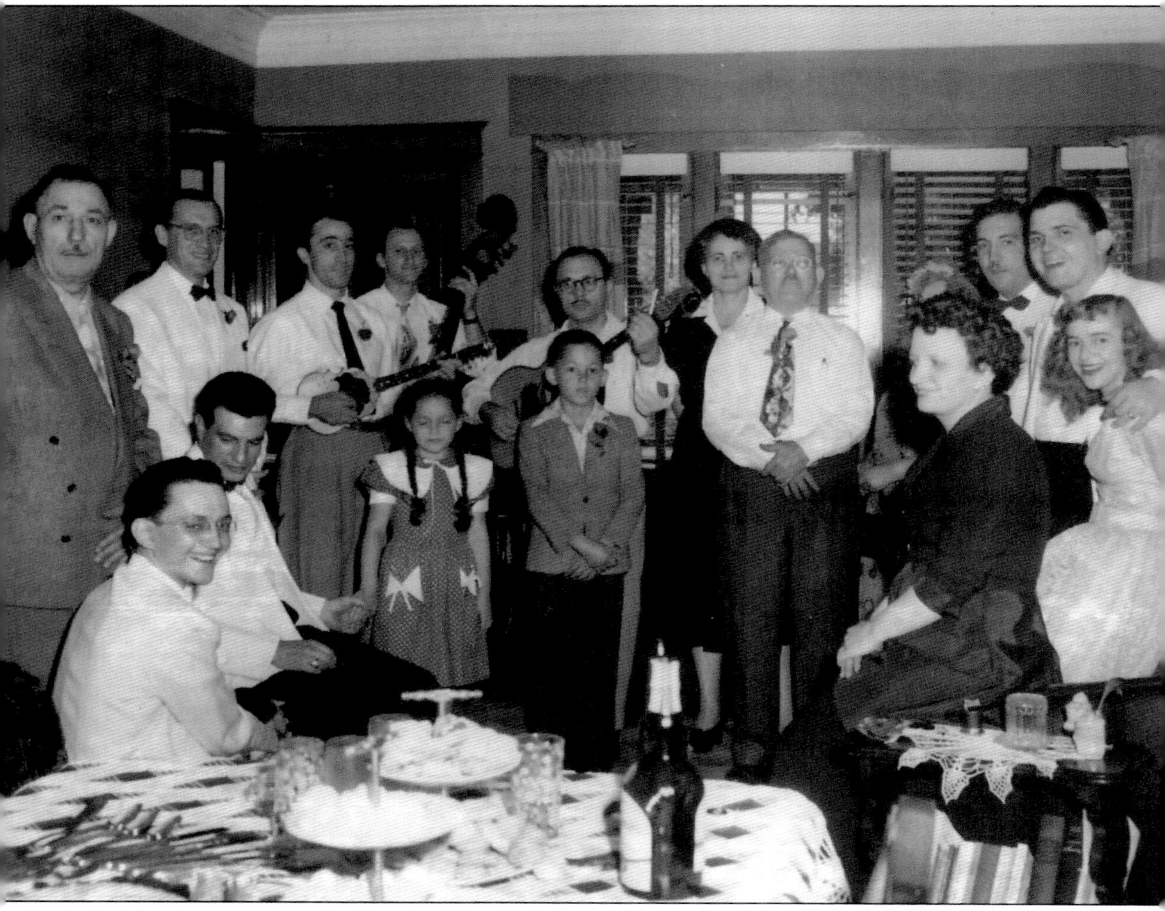

At the skup svatova for George Versal's 1951 wedding, tambura player Horace Mamula (left) entertains guests, including the groom, George Versal (seated in the foreground). (Courtesy of St. Sava Serbian Orthodox Church, Merrillville, Indiana.)

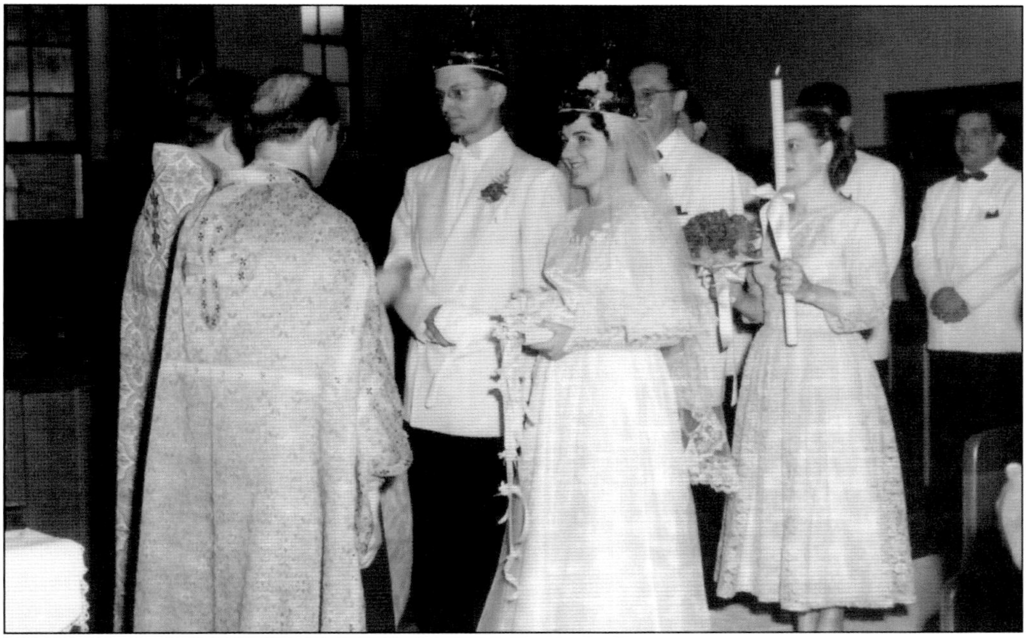

Here, Ann Milovanovich marries George Versal on July 14, 1951, at the St. Sava Serbian Orthodox Church's location on Thirteenth and Connecticut Streets. Peter Mandich, who was mayor of Gary, Indiana, from 1952 to 1958, served as stari svat and is standing behind the groom. (Courtesy of St. Sava Serbian Orthodox Church, Merrillville, Indiana.)

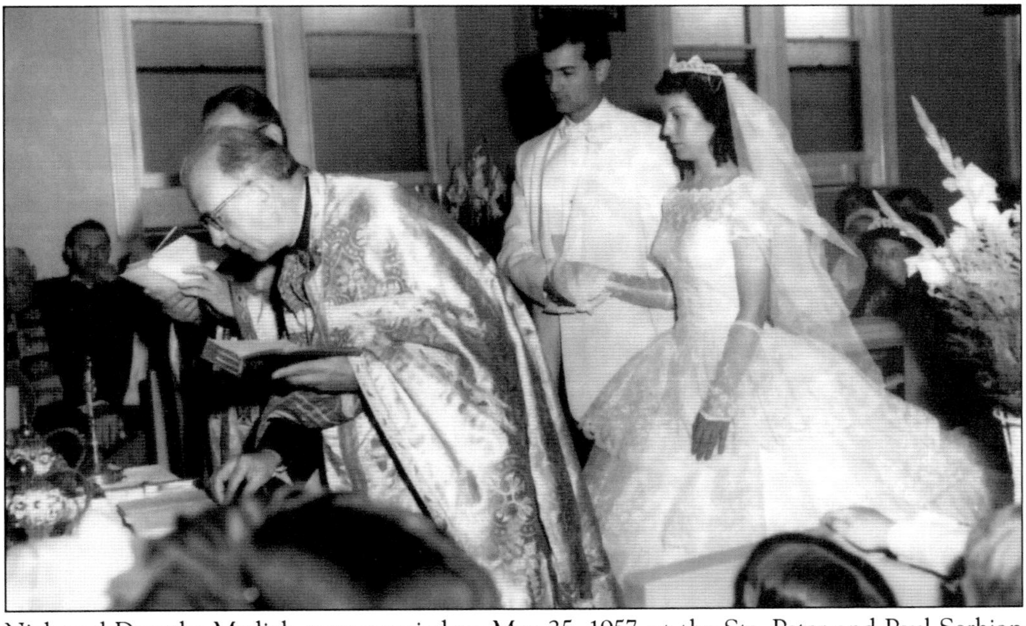

Nick and Dorothy Medich were married on May 25, 1957, at the Sts. Peter and Paul Serbian Orthodox Church in South Bend, Indiana. Dorothy's priest, Rev. Dušan Shoukletovich (left), of the St. Sava Serbian Orthodox Church in Gary, traveled to South Bend to co-officiate the service with Father George Vuckovich. (Courtesy of St. Sava Serbian Orthodox Church, Merrillville, Indiana.)

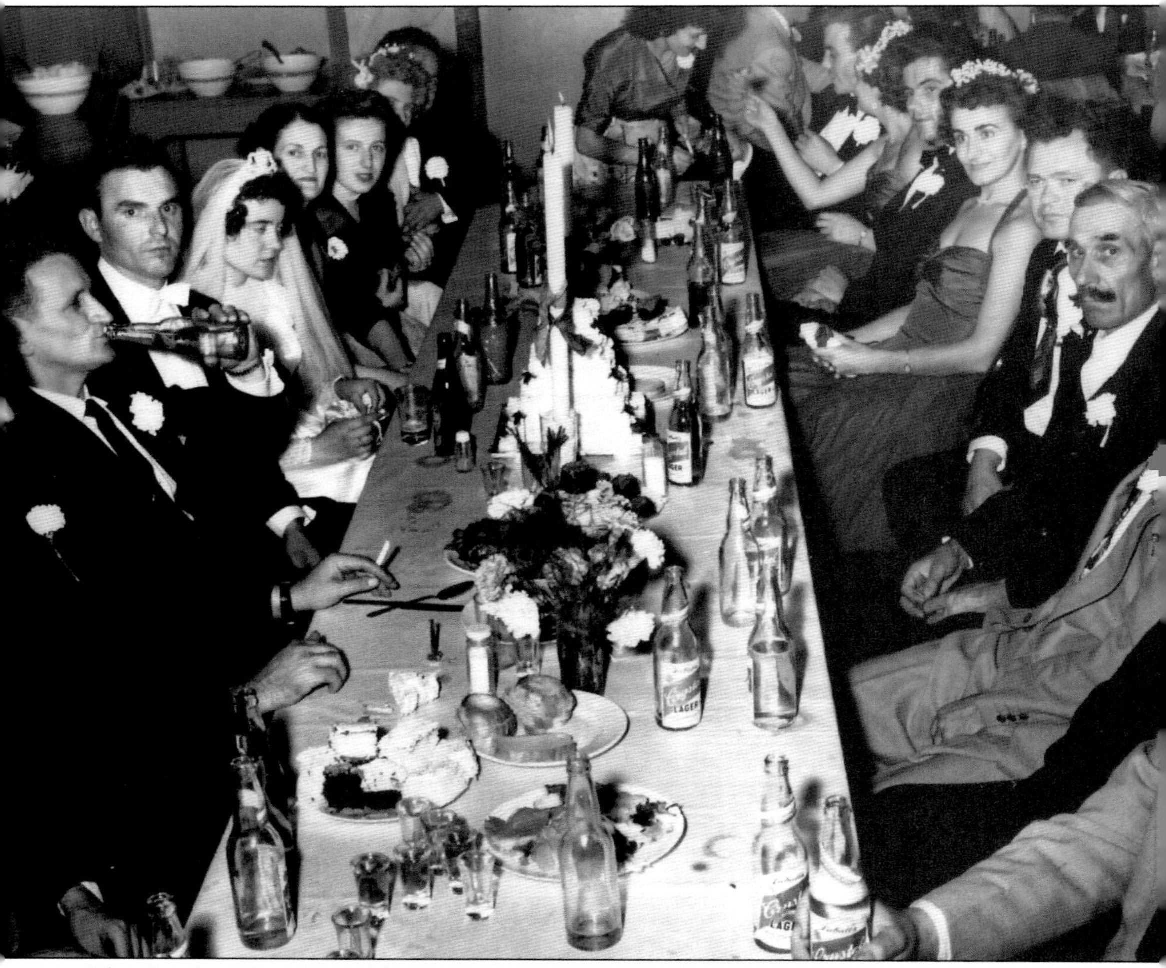

The October 17, 1953, wedding reception of Vaso and Ana Katić was typical of the era. Guests enjoyed food and drink while toasting the couple. Vaso was a displaced person, who met and married Ana in Canada before moving to East Chicago in the mid-1960s to work in the steel mills. It was very common for Serbs who left their villages to first travel to other European countries or Canada before settling in the United States. (Courtesy of St. Sava Serbian Orthodox Church, Merrillville, Indiana.)

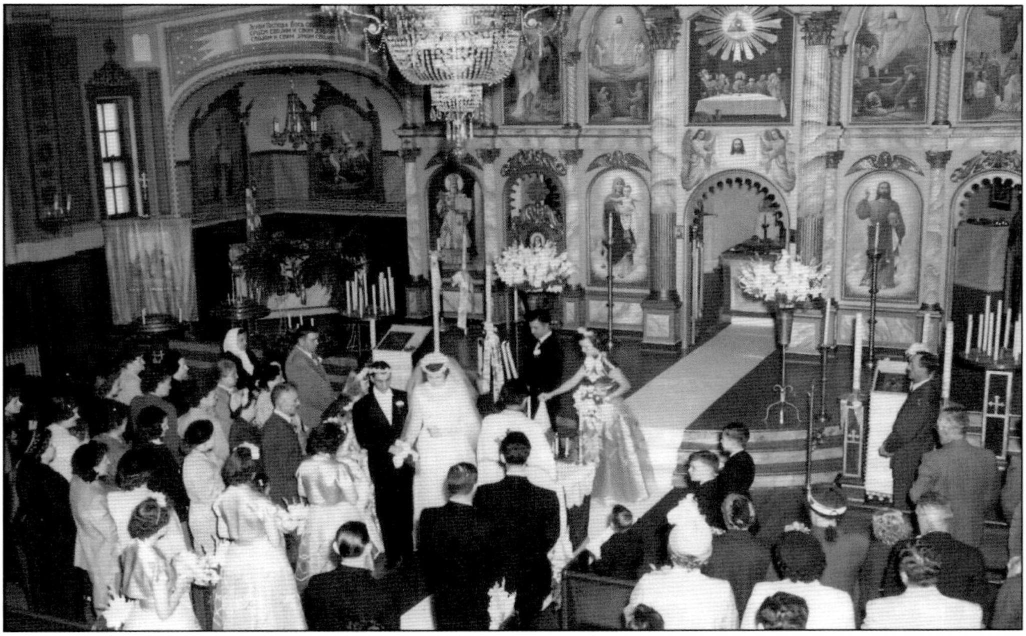

Milan Skrivan and Anne Bires were married on September 22, 1951. Rev. Svetozar Radovanovich led Milan and Anne around the table three times while their kum, Milan Bundalo, and kuma, Violette Panayotovich, watched the couple taking their first steps as husband and wife. (Courtesy of St. Sava Serbian Orthodox Church, Merrillville, Indiana.)

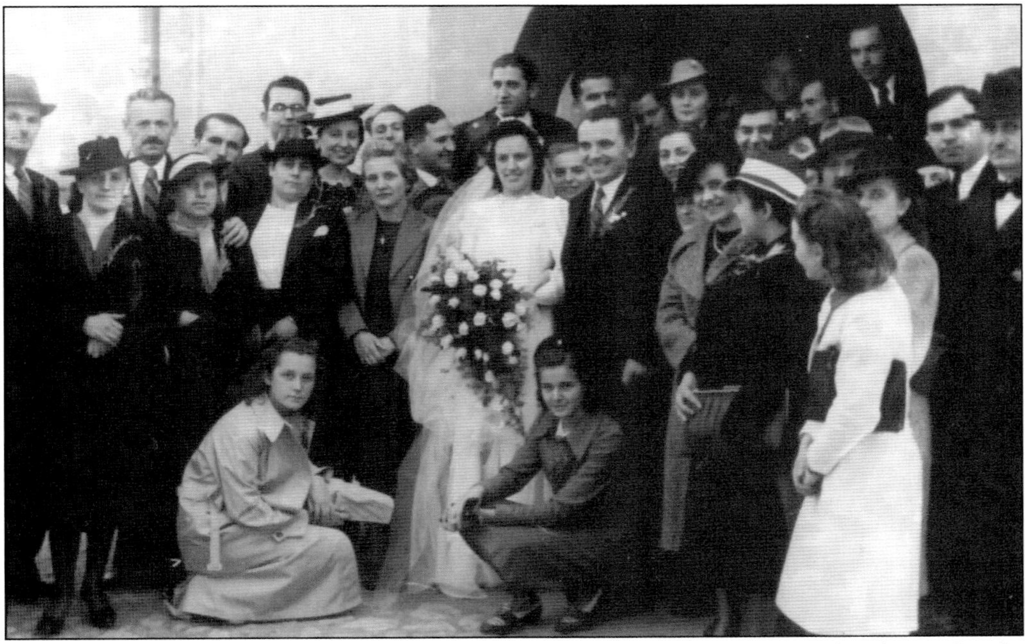

Prior to World War II, Angelina and Andreja Mulin were married at St. Mark's Church in Belgrade, Serbia. Andreja became a prisoner of war and was separated from Angelina for 11 years. They reunited in the Chicagoland area in the mid-1950s. (Courtesy of St. Sava Serbian Orthodox Church, Merrillville, Indiana.)

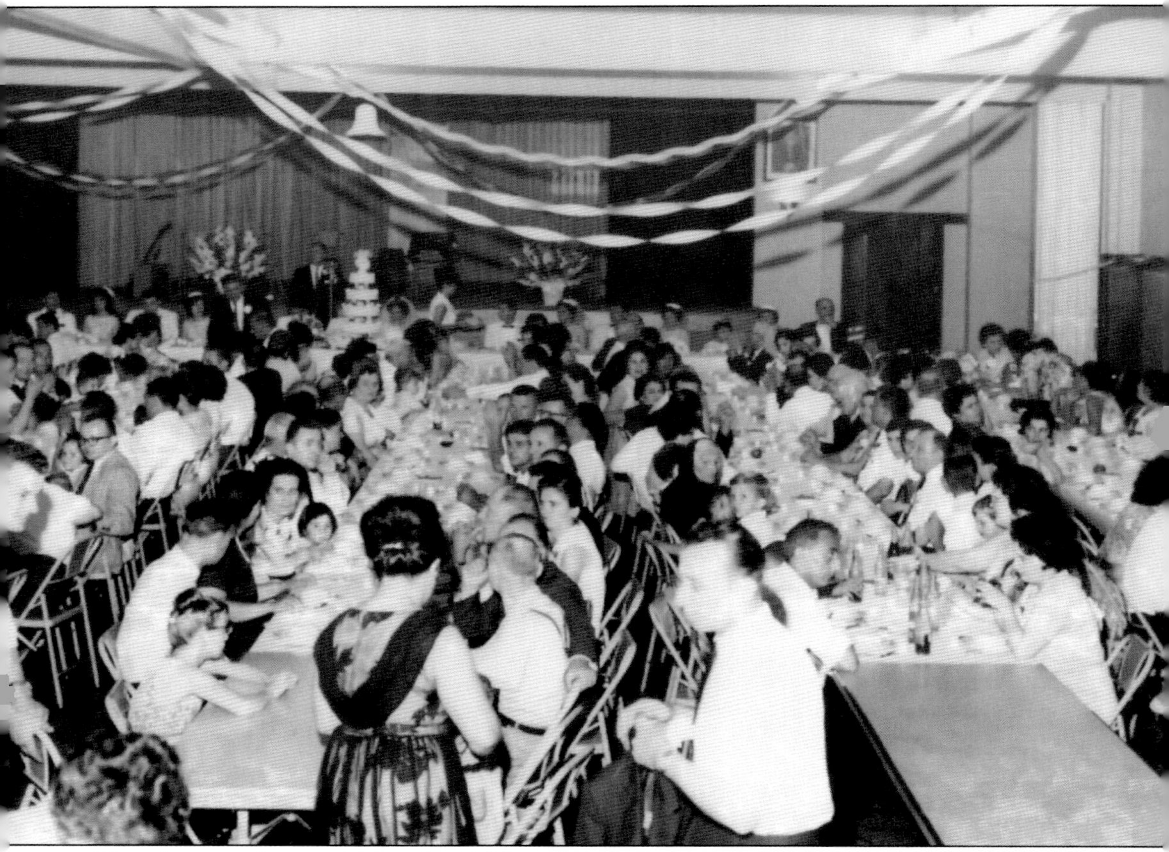

This photograph was taken at the 1964 wedding reception of Mijo and Mara (Rajkovich) Dukić, who wed at the St. Sava Serbian Orthodox Church when it was located in Gary, Indiana. Like many Serbian weddings, many guests were invited and the receptions tended to be held in large church hall basements. The halls were generously sized and adequately arranged to accommodate both large numbers of guests and traditional kolo dancing. (Courtesy of St. Sava Serbian Orthodox Church, Merrillville, Indiana.)

Rev. Peter Bankerovich, of the St. Sava Serbian Orthodox Church, helps bride Mara Rajkovich take a sip of wine from the common cup during her wedding to Mijo Dukić. During a Serbian Orthodox wedding ceremony, couples take three sips of wine from a shared cup. The cup represents life and symbolizes the mutual sharing of joy and sorrow. (Courtesy of St. Sava Serbian Orthodox Church, Merrillville, Indiana.)

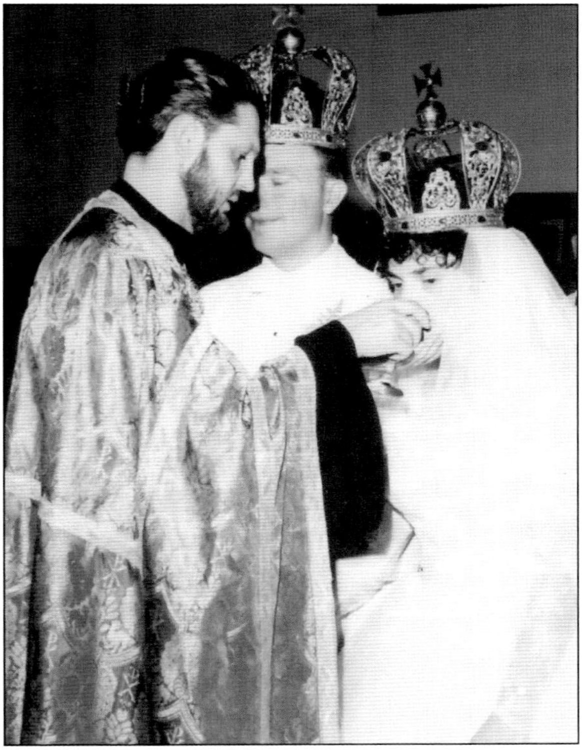

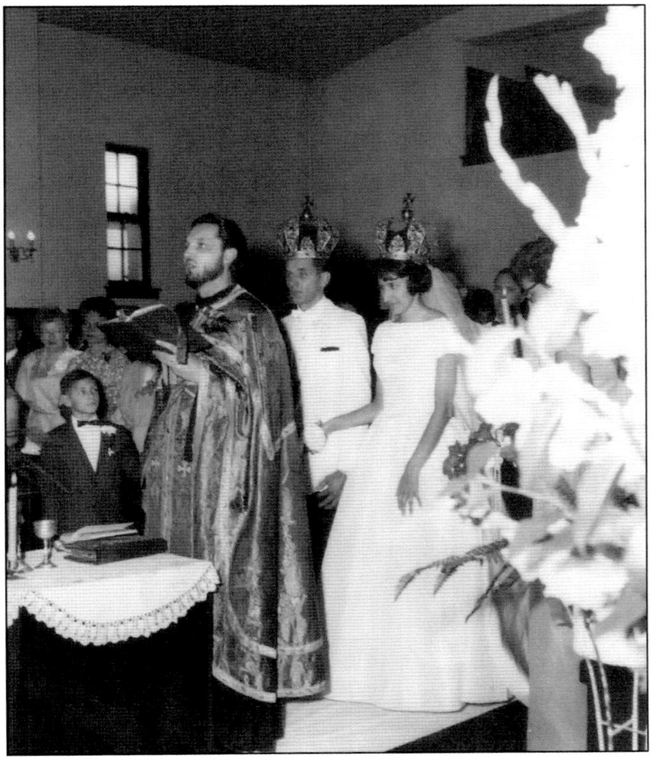

Rev. Peter Bankerovich reads from a liturgical book at the wedding of George Nicolich and Donna Orlich on September 14, 1963, at the St. Sava Serbian Orthodox Church. Bankerovich ultimately became a bishop. (Courtesy of St. Sava Serbian Orthodox Church, Merrillville, Indiana.)

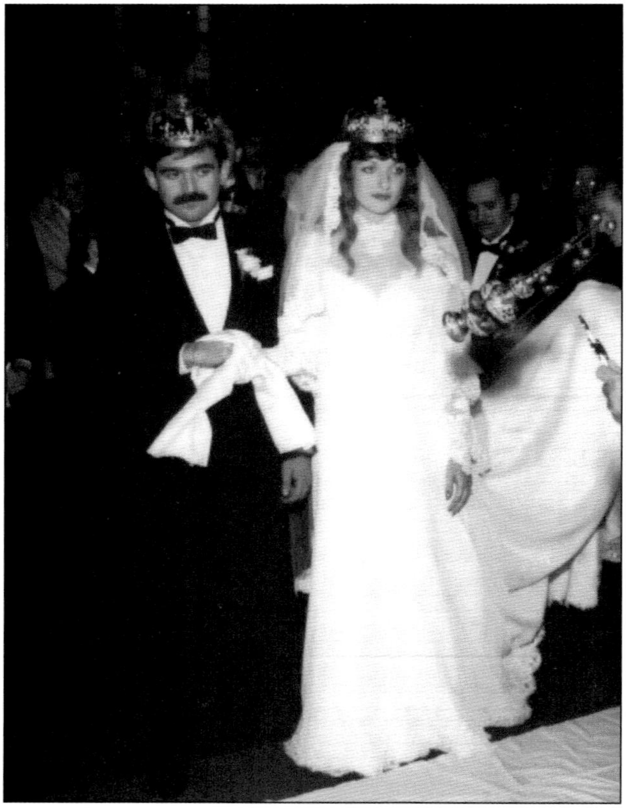

Nadine Roknich and Dragan Djordjević were married on November 12, 1983, at the St. John Baptist Serbian Orthodox Church in Bellwood, Illinois. Regardless of a couple's church, Serbian wedding customs have remained virtually unchanged throughout the centuries. (Courtesy of St. Sava Serbian Orthodox Church, Merrillville, Indiana.)

Traditional Serbian Orthodox weddings include kolo dancing at the bride's or groom's house before the church ceremony. This tradition dates back centuries and is part of the skup svatova. Pictured during a 1991 wedding are, from left to right, Pavle Vukanić, brother-in-law of the bride; bride Nena Dobrosavljević; and Nada Stijović, cousin of the bride's mother-in-law. (Courtesy of Nena Vukanić.)

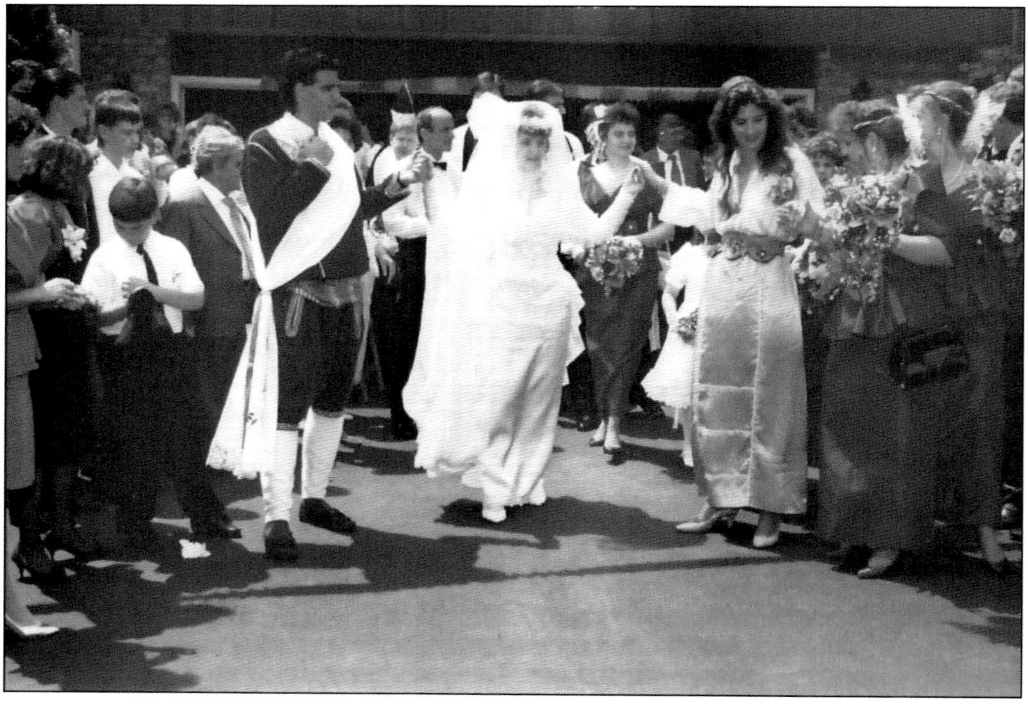

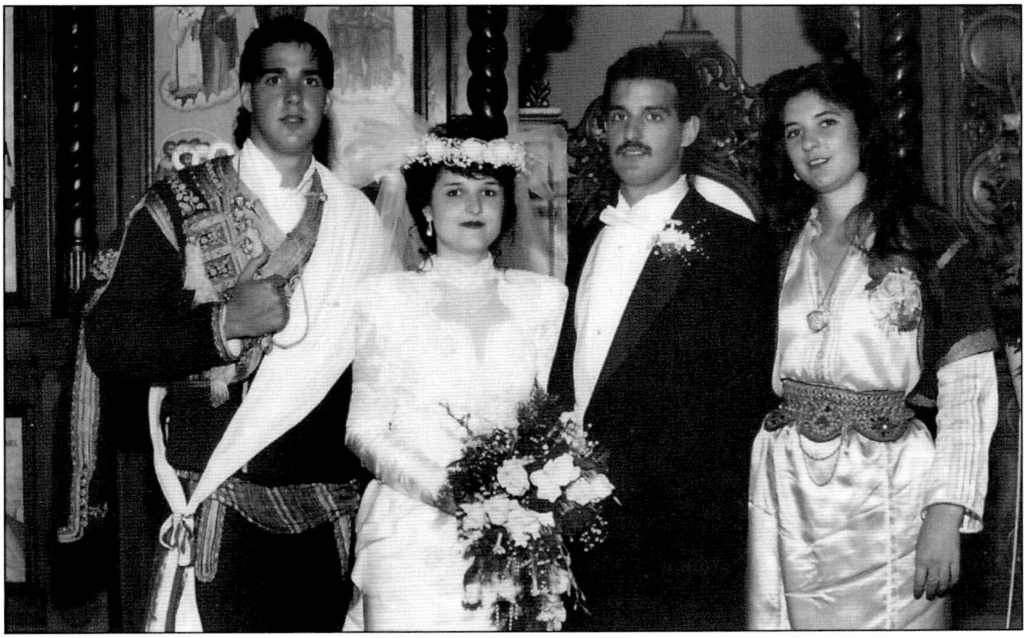

One way Serbs in the Chicagoland area have been able to honor customs and traditions is by wearing traditional folk costumes, called nošnje. Here, Pavle Vukanić (left) and Nada Stijović (right) wear folk costumes associated with Montenegro for a Serbian Orthodox wedding in 1991. (Courtesy of Nena Vukanić.)

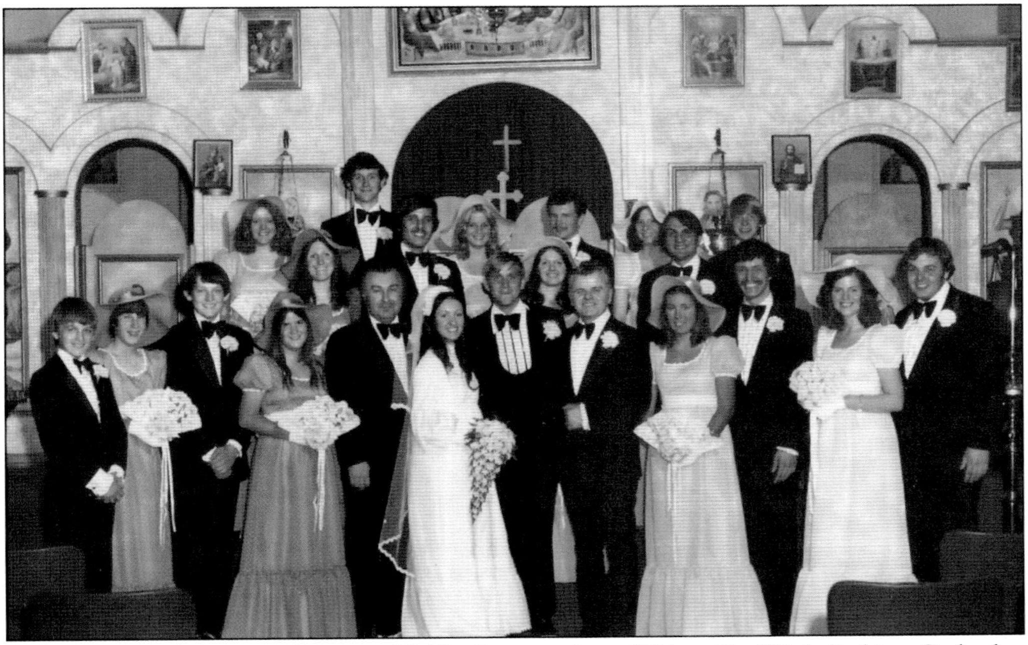

Dorothy (Mulin) Paunovich married Mike Paunovich in 1974, at St. Elijah Serbian Orthodox Church when it was located at Forty-first and Adams Streets in Gary, Indiana. Even though wedding attire has changed over the years, the traditions have remained the same in Serbian Orthodox ceremonies. (Courtesy of St. Sava Serbian Orthodox Church, Merrillville, Indiana.)

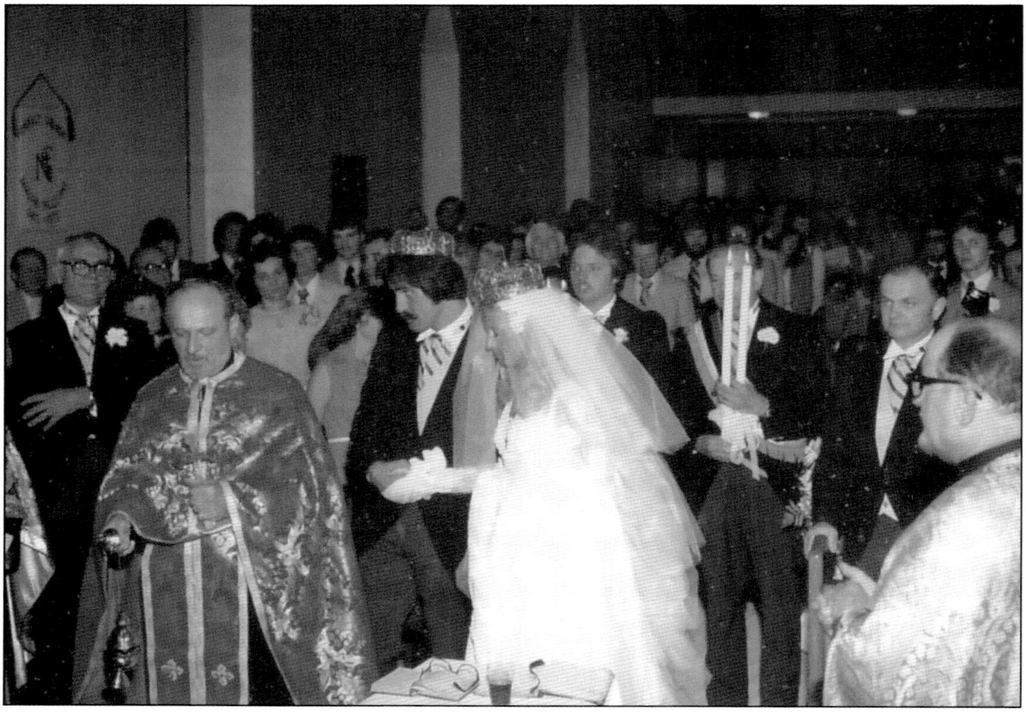

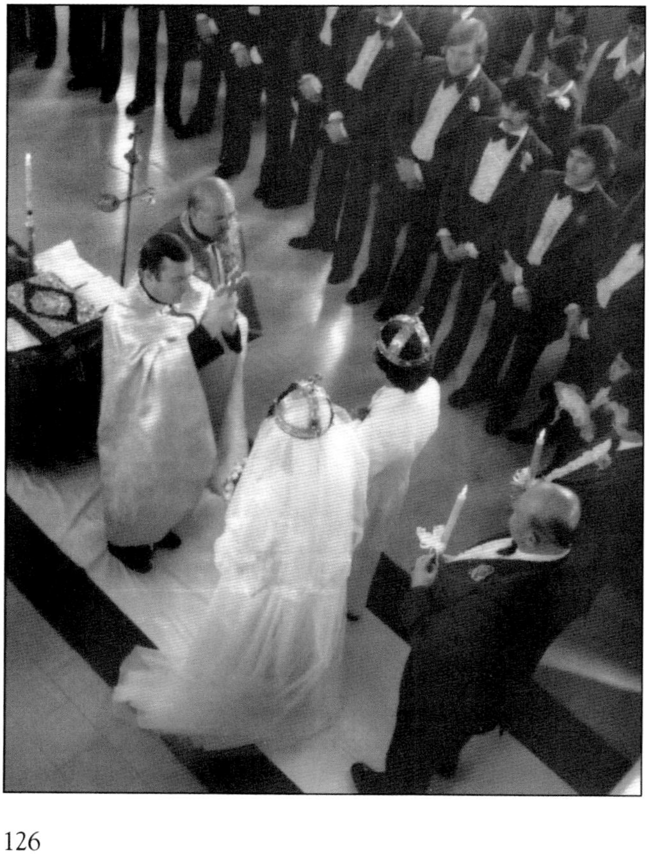

Nick and Melanie (Gruyich) Sever were married in Niagara Falls, Canada, on June 16, 1979, and eventually moved to the Chicagoland area. Each church has its own style of jeweled crown, but the traditions and customs remain the same for any Serbian Orthodox wedding ceremony. (Courtesy of St. Sava Serbian Orthodox Church, Merrillville, Indiana.)

Father Jovan Todorovich (left), from the St. Sava Serbian Orthodox Church, joined Father Jovan "John" Marcetich, from the St. George Serbian Orthodox Church, for the wedding of Vinko and Sonja Mancich on March 5, 1978, at St. George. (Courtesy of St. Sava Serbian Orthodox Church, Merrillville, Indiana.)

Michael Andrew Paunovich and Rada Ferzanovich served as ring bearer and flower girl at the November 20, 1982, wedding of Peter and Jelena Mulin. Despite their young age, both children wear a wedding trobojka in observance of Serbian wedding tradition. (Courtesy of St. Sava Serbian Orthodox Church, Merrillville, Indiana.)

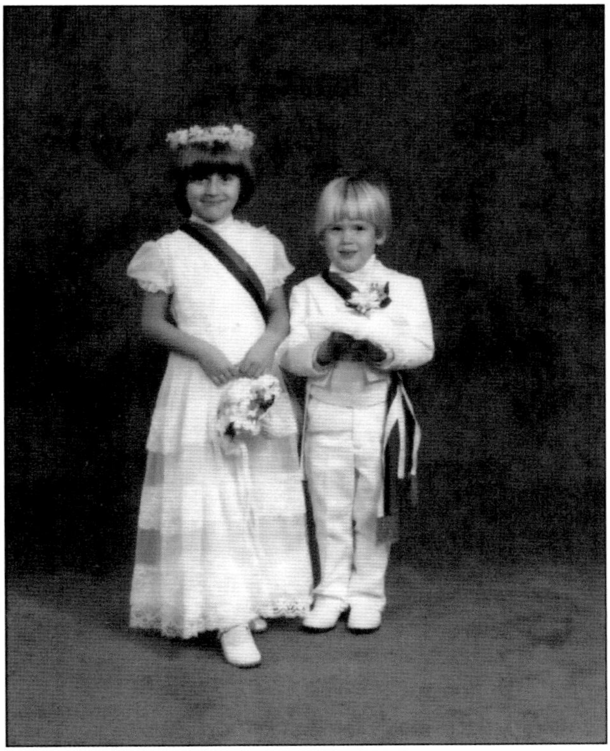

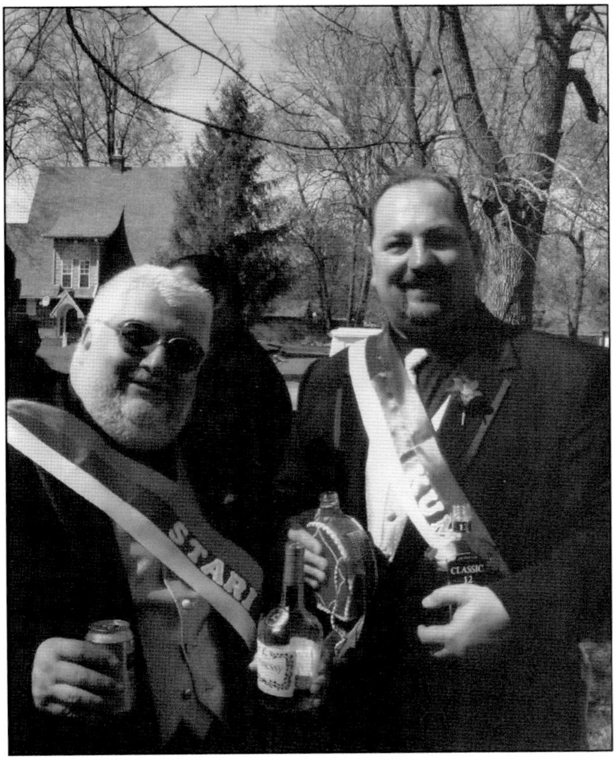

The custom of the male relative or stari svat and kum wearing wedding sashes continues in today's Serbian weddings. Pictured are Gojko Kasich (left), from the St. Elijah Serbian Orthodox Church, and Jovan Djokich, from St. Sava Serbian Orthodox Church, at the 2009 wedding of Hilary Buha and Tobias "Toby" Baldwin in Indianapolis. (Courtesy of St. Sava Serbian Orthodox Church, Merrillville, Indiana.)

Discover Thousands of Local History Books Featuring Millions of Vintage Images

Arcadia Publishing, the leading local history publisher in the United States, is committed to making history accessible and meaningful through publishing books that celebrate and preserve the heritage of America's people and places.

Find more books like this at
www.arcadiapublishing.com

Search for your hometown history, your old stomping grounds, and even your favorite sports team.

Consistent with our mission to preserve history on a local level, this book was printed in South Carolina on American-made paper and manufactured entirely in the United States. Products carrying the accredited Forest Stewardship Council (FSC) label are printed on 100 percent FSC-certified paper.

MADE IN THE USA